THE ESSENCE OF OBJECT-ORIENTED PROGRAMMING WITH JAVA™ AND UML

THE ESSENCE OF OBJECT-ORIENTED PROGRAMMING WITH JAVA™ AND UML

Bruce E. Wampler

✦ Addison-Wesley

Boston • San Francisco • New York • Toronto • Montreal
London • Munich • Paris • Madrid
Capetown • Sydney • Tokyo • Singapore • Mexico City

The publisher offers discounts on this book when ordered in quantity for special sales. For more information, please contact:

Pearson Education Corporate Sales Division
201 W. 103rd Street
Indianapolis, IN 46290
(800) 428-5531
corpsales@pearsoned.com

Visit AW on the Web: www.aw.com/cseng/

Library of Congress Cataloging-in-Publication Data

Wampler, Bruce E.
 The essence of object-oriented programming with Java and UML / Bruce E. Wampler.
  p. cm.
 Includes bibliographical references and index.
 ISBN 0-201-73410-9 (alk. paper)
  1. Object-oriented programming (Computer science) 2. UML (Computer science) 3. Java (Computer program language) I. Title.

 QA76.64 .W359 2002
 005.13'3--dc21   2001053651

ISBN: 0-201-73410-9
Text printed on recycled paper
1 2 3 4 5 6 7 8 9 10—CRS—0504030201
First printing, December 2001

To Trina, Van, and Risa—my family.

"Our house is a very, very, very fine house. . ."

CONTENTS

PREFACE

Why This Book?

The goal of this book is to cover what you need to know to develop object-oriented (OO) software using Java and the Unified Modeling Language (UML). When you are through with this book, you should understand object-oriented software development well enough to answer the following questions.

- What is object orientation?
- What is the UML?
- What is object-oriented analysis and design (OOAD)?
- How do you do OOAD?
- What are object-oriented development methodologies?
- How do you use Java to write truly object-oriented programs?
- What is Swing, and how can you use it to write object-oriented graphical user interfaces?
- What are design patterns?
- What is refactoring?
- What tools do you use to write object-oriented programs?

- What are some guidelines for writing good code?

- What do you need to read next to learn even more about object orientation?

Who Is This Book For?

This book is intended for programmers who know the basics of programming with Java and now want to understand the fundamentals of object-oriented software development. If you're fairly new to programming and have had a class or two in Java, you're probably starting to feel comfortable with Java. Now you're ready to reap the benefits of true object-oriented programming in Java, and this book will help you.

If you're an experienced programmer who wants to move from using an old-style procedural programming language to developing object-oriented systems in Java, this book is also for you. This book will take you well down the path to real object-oriented software development. If you have a Java manual available for quick reference, you will likely be able to learn the most important aspects of Java from the examples included in this book.

However, this book should not be the last one you read on object orientation, the UML, or Java. Instead, it should give you an essential understanding of objects so that you can read additional advanced and detailed books on the topic with greater purpose.

Overview of Chapters

Chapter 1 is a brief introduction to objects and the benefits of object-oriented software development.

Chapter 2 covers the fundamental concepts of object orientation. Object orientation has many important concepts, and of course, its own vocabulary. It is important for you to understand the main concepts and to be familiar with the specialized vocabulary. Even if you are familiar with some object-oriented concepts, you should review them in this chapter. Basic UML is also introduced.

Chapter 3 covers how to use Java to write object-oriented programs. It is not really a Java tutorial, but rather concentrates on using Java to implement object-oriented concepts. The first part of the chapter covers basic Java concepts. The later parts of the chapter cover more-advanced topics, such as object lifetime, copies of objects, and other concepts that are crucial when working with classes and objects.

Chapter 4 covers object-oriented analysis and design (OOAD). Rather than focus on any specific OOAD methodology, this chapter covers basics that are important for any methodology.

The first four chapters cover the essence of object orientation. Chapter 5 takes a look at graphical user interfaces (GUIs) and the Java Swing library, using the object-oriented perspective developed in the previous chapters. This object-oriented introduction to Swing is a somewhat different approach than is typically found in Swing tutorials.

Chapter 6 ties everything together with a case study of a small Java application. The fundamental OOAD concepts covered in Chapter 4 are used to design the application, and the Java and Swing concepts covered in Chapters 3 and 5 are used for the implementation.

The goal of the remainder of the book is to give you a good overview of the practical aspects of object-oriented programming. Chapter 7 introduces design patterns, a recent development that uses previously developed software design patterns to make designing new software easier. Chapter 8 covers refactoring, which is a disciplined object-oriented approach to revising and enhancing existing software. Chapter 9 gives brief overviews of some of the current software development methodologies for large- and small-scale object-oriented software projects. Chapter 10 covers some of the current software tools available for developing object-oriented software. Finally, Chapter 11 gives some of my personal guidelines for developing better software.

About the Author

I wrote my first program more than 30 years ago, and I have been developing software ever since. Most of that software has been for the PC marketplace, which means that my code has had to do a useful job, do it with as few bugs as possible, and be passed on to others for continued development. It has meant that I've had to be efficient and practical. For a long time, I've wanted to share my practical experience with other programmers.

So, what is all this experience I've had? Right after I finished my PhD in computer science at the University of Utah, in 1979, I worked on security software at the Sandia National Laboratory. However, I found the emerging personal computer world much more exciting. I left Sandia Labs, started a small software company, and wrote one of the first spelling checkers that ran on a PC. My next step was to write the first PC-based grammar and writing style checker.

I sold my company and began teaching computer science at the University of New Mexico, a relationship that lasted, at least on a part-time basis, until 1997. But I just couldn't stay out of the PC business. I continued my work on grammar checking, and in 1985 started a new PC software company with some partners in San Francisco. That company, Reference Software International, developed and marketed the Grammatik grammar checker. I was chief scientist there, and built a fairly large software development group to improve Grammatik and build other reference software products. WordPerfect bought Reference Software in 1992, and I went back to teaching at the University of New Mexico. It was there that I first thought of writing a book about object-oriented programming.

In the mean time, I designed and wrote an open source C++ GUI framework, called V. It is an easy-to-use framework for building simple GUI applications on Windows and X, and is in widespread use today. I also wrote the VIDE freeware editor and integrated development environment, which is also widely used.

Of all the advancements in software development I've witnessed over the years, object-oriented programming in Java and C++ has seemed the most significant in terms of how much easier it makes the programming task. While object orientation doesn't solve all the problems of software development, it makes development and long-term maintenance much easier. The result is a real gain in programming productivity. So it is well worth the effort to learn object-oriented software development.

The goal of this book is to introduce you to the essence of object orientation without overwhelming you with all the details of a specific object-oriented development methodology or every nuance of a programming language. After years of teaching programming and software engineering, I've found that learning to use Java or any other object-oriented programming language comes more easily if you first get a good understanding of objects and of designing systems using objects.

I have found that just because programmers are using an object-oriented programming language doesn't mean they are writing good object-oriented programs. Without a good understanding of object orientation, it is impossible to realize its full benefits, including the most important—software that is easier to write and maintain.

ACKNOWLEDGMENTS

First, I must thank my family for putting up with me for the past year while I've been holed up in my office working on this book. I know they would have liked to have me around more, but writing this book has been something I've needed to do for many years. And special thanks to my son, Van, who created the great Kokopelli programmer drawing for the cover.

I also must thank Ross Venables, the editor at Addison-Wesley who discovered an early version of this book on my Web site and encouraged me to turn it into a complete book. And I want to thank Paul Becker, who took on this project and saw it to completion.

I want to thank all the other people who helped make this book better, from the reviewers and editors at Addison-Wesley to all those who sent me suggestions and feedback on the early drafts posted on my Web site.

Bruce E. Wampler
Glenwood Springs, Colorado

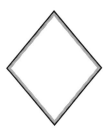

CHAPTER I

Objects, UML, and Java

This book is about object-oriented (OO) software development. Writing real object-oriented programs that are used by real people is more than slapping down a few lines of code in Java (or C++, Eiffel, or any other object-oriented programming language). Ultimately, object-oriented software development includes the complete process—analysis of the problem, design of a solution, coding, and long-term maintenance. Object-oriented development can make any program better, from a small Web-based application to a full-blown business-critical software system.

Object orientation has the potential for building great software, but only if it is used as part of a complete process. Today, there are small, agile development methodologies suitable for teams of two to ten or so programmers, as well as large-scale methodologies for huge projects. Most of these development methodologies use or can benefit from the UML (Unified Modeling Language), a modeling tool that aids the design of any OO system. But before you can understand and use any of these methodologies, you need to move beyond merely getting a program to work to changing your thinking to be object-oriented.

It has been said that any programming language can be used to write object-oriented programs (and it has been done with C), but a true OO programming language makes it a lot easier. Just because you use an OO programming language, your programs are not necessarily object-oriented.

Object-oriented programming works much better when it is used together with an object-oriented analysis and design (OOAD) process. Trying to write an

OO program without first going through the analysis and design steps is like try-ing to build a house without first analyzing the requirements of the house, designing it, and producing a set of blueprints. You might end up with a roof over your head, but the rooms would likely be scattered all over the place, some rooms might be missing, and the whole thing would probably come tumbling down on your head during the first storm (see Figure 1.1). An OO program in any programming language written without at least some OOAD might seem to work, but it is much more likely to be full of bugs and break when you make the first modification.

Object Orientation

Objects are the heart of object orientation. An object is a representation of almost anything you need to model in a program. An object can be a model of an employee, a representation of a sensor, a window in a user interface, a data struc-ture, such as a list—virtually anything. One way to think of an object is as a black box with some buttons and lights (see Figure 1.2). This could be a TV, a car, whatever. To use the object, you need to know what the buttons do, which

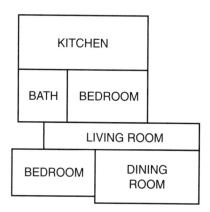

Figure 1.1   A randomly planned house

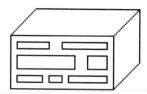

Figure 1.2   A black box

ones you need to press to get the object to do what you need, and what the lights mean about the status of the object. The details of how the box is put together inside are irrelevant while you are using the box. What is important is that the object carries out its functions and responsibilities correctly. A software object is not much different. It has well-defined methods for interacting with the outside world, and it can provide information about its current state. The internal representation, algorithms, and data structures are hidden from the outside world.

In the simplest terms, designing an OO system consists of identifying which objects the system contains, the behaviors and responsibilities of those objects, and how the objects interact with each other. OO can produce elegant, easy-to-understand designs, which in turn lead to elegant and easy-to-understand programs. Individual objects can often be implemented and debugged independently. Libraries of existing objects can be easily reused and adapted to new designs. Most important, a good OO program is easy to modify and resistant to the introduction of bugs during program modification and maintenance.

Object-oriented development is a major advance for software development. Although it may not be a magic bullet that solves all the problems associated with producing software, it is better than other methodologies. While development methodologies, such as structured design and programming, have many valid points, many which carry over and are used for OO development, object-oriented designs are inherently easier to design and maintain over time.

Object-Oriented Languages

There are several object-oriented programming languages, including Smalltalk, Eiffel, C++, Objective C, Objective Pascal, Java, Ada, and even a version of Lisp. There are two clear marketplace winners, C++ and Java.

Today, Java is the emerging object-oriented language of choice for many programmers and software projects. One of the reasons for Java's popularity is the World Wide Web and Java's ability to run Web applets directly on any computer or operating system with a Web browser. Another reason is that Java is an excellent programming language. It is a small, well-designed language that can be used not just for Web applets, but for full-blown programs on almost any computer today. Java was somewhat hampered in its early days because of its performance, but this is really no longer an issue. Because it is such a good language, Java has been widely adopted as the main language used to teach computer science at colleges and universities all over the world. In the whole history of computer science and programming, this is the first time the same programming language has been popular as both a teaching language and a language used for real-world programs.

C++ is also a widely used programming language. It is still the principal language used for the core applications (such as spreadsheets and word processors) used on most computers today. C++ was derived from C, and thus has a heritage of being able to do real things on real systems, and there is compatibility with existing C code. One problem with C++, however, is that it has grown into a large and complicated language, and it is difficult to achieve competence in the full language.

This book is mostly about object-oriented programming. That means it will focus on general principles of object-oriented programming that apply to any programming language. But the book will also show how to translate object-oriented designs to real programs using Java. The focus will be on how to use the capabilities of the Java language to implement OO designs. It is not a tutorial on Java. We assume that you've already learned the Java basics. Now you are ready to learn about objects and how to use Java to write better programs.

Object-Oriented Design and the UML

There are several different object-oriented development methodologies in use today, each with its strengths and weaknesses. The older, more traditional methodologies are often called "heavyweight" methodologies, and are most useful for large software projects involving tens or even hundreds of programmers over years of development effort. The newer methodologies, called "lightweight" or "agile" methodologies, are more appropriate for smaller projects. Many of these are quite new and are still being standardized.

Design and development methodologies have always needed a graphical notation to express the designs. In the past, a major problem has been that each major methodology has had its own graphical notation. This all changed with the emergence of the UML as the standard notation. Any current design methodology, heavyweight or agile, uses or can benefit from the UML.

The UML originated in the mid-1990s from the efforts of James Rumbaugh, Ivar Jacobson, and Grady Booch (The Three Amigos). There is a standard specification of the UML coordinated by the Object Management Group (www.omg.org). OMG is an industry-sponsored organization devoted to supporting vendor-neutral standards for the object-oriented development community. The UML has become the de facto standard object-oriented notation.

The UML is designed for discussing object-oriented design. Its ability to show objects and object relationships is especially useful, and it will be used in examples throughout this book. The various features of the UML will be introduced as needed.

The Payoff of Objects

Object orientation can lead to big payoffs in the software development game. An object-oriented design is likely to be simple and easy to understand. Once designed, you can often implement and test the individual objects separately. Once finished, each object tends to be robust and bug-free. As you make changes to the system, existing objects continue to work. And as you improve existing objects, their interface to the world stays the same, so the whole system continues to work. It is this ease of change and robustness that really make OO development different and well worth the effort.

Chapter Summary

- Object orientation is a way to develop software that leads to well-designed systems that are robust and easy to maintain.
- The UML is a graphical representation useful for designing and understanding object-oriented systems.
- Java is an excellent object-oriented programming language useful for both Web applets and non-Web applications.

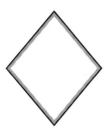

CHAPTER 2

The Essence of Objects

What exactly is object orientation? It is a problem-solving technique used to develop software systems. Object orientation is the culmination of years of experience in finding an effective way to develop software, and it is certainly the dominant method used to develop major software systems today. Object orientation is a technique of modeling a real-world system in software based on **objects**. The object is the core concept. An object is a software model of a real-world entity or concept.

object The basic unit of object orientation. An object is an entity that has attributes, behavior, and identity. Objects are members of a class, and the attributes and behavior of an object are defined by the class definition.

Almost anything can be modeled as an object in software. For example, you could model a temperature sensor as an object. Or, in a more abstract system, you could model color as an object. Even something as basic as a number can be considered an object that has a value and a type. Typically, each object has an associated set of attributes, such as value, state, or whatever else is needed to model the object. Sensor attributes might include a state such as active or inactive, an attribute indicating its current value, and information about its physical location. Objects usually provide the ability to modify their state, as well. In addition to keeping track of the current temperature, for example, a temperature sensor object might provide a way to turn the sensor on or off.

The attributes, or data, used inside an object are really only a tiny part of what an object is and does. An object also has a set of responsibilities that it carries out by providing services to other objects. It is often more useful to think of an object in terms of its responsibilities rather than its attributes. For example, it is the responsibility of a sensor object to keep track of the state of the sensor. A sensor object might respond to requests from other objects that use sensors to check the status of a sensor, to turn a sensor on or off, or to report on the sensor's values. A sensor object could also maintain a history of its values as part of its responsibilities. The outside objects really don't care how a sensor object implements its attributes internally, but rather which services the sensor object can provide—its responsibilities.

While a program is running, individual objects usually don't stand alone. They belong to a collection of other similar objects that are all members of the same group, or **class**. A program is made up of many different classes, with each class made up of similar objects.

> **class**   A class is a description of a set of objects. The set of objects share common attributes and common behavior. Class is similar in concept to abstract data types found in non-OO programming languages, but it is more comprehensive in that it includes both structure and behavior. A class definition describes all the attributes of member objects of that class, as well as the class methods that implement the behavior of member objects.

Classes and objects are closely related, but they are not the same thing. A class is a description or definition of the characteristics of objects that belong to that class. An object is a single instance or member of a class that is created and exists while the program is running. A class may have just a single object or any number of member objects existing at any given time. All members of a class have similar behavior.

For example, consider a software system used to monitor various sensors in a factory. One obvious kind of object present in such a system is a sensor. A class called Sensor would be defined and used to model physical sensors. The class would define the basic characteristics of any Sensor, such as its location, value, and identification number, as well as a set of services used to carry out its responsibilities. Each individual physical sensor in the system would be represented as an object belonging to the class Sensor, and have specific values for the attributes described by the class definition.

The class description includes the means of accessing and changing the state of individual object members of that class. A common representation of color is called RGB, where the color is specified by the values of its red, green, and blue components. One possible design of a class called Color could provide the means of manipulating the color by both retrieving and setting the RGB values of a Color object.

In an object-oriented system, it is typical to describe one class based on a preexisting class, either by extending the description of a higher-level class, or by including the description of another class within the current class. For example, you could create one class that describes the general characteristics of all sensors and then more-specialized classes that describe specific sensors, such as temperature or pressure sensors, each based on the original general Sensor class.

Placing attributes and responsibilities in a top-level, general class can provide many benefits. For example, if the responsibilities of the general Sensor class included keeping track of a history of readings from a sensor, programming that capability could get somewhat complex. By placing the history code in the top-level class, that code need be defined only once and won't be repeated in new classes. Each of the specialized sensors can then use the history capabilities of the top-level Sensor class.

Objects and classes are really the heart of object orientation. OO software systems consist of objects of different classes that interact with each other using well-defined methods or services specified by the class definitions. When used properly and consistently, object-oriented software development leads to programs that are robust and easy to debug, modify, and maintain.

To produce successful OO programs, it is important to always "think objects." Just because a program is written in Java or C++ does not mean it is an object-oriented program! If you have a programming background that is not OO based, or even if you've just learned Java, one of the great challenges is to switch the way you think about programming to use the object-oriented programming paradigm.

What Is an Object-Oriented System?

Just what is an **object-oriented** system? What makes an OO system different from other software systems? One way to define an object-oriented system is to use a list of properties that characterize object-oriented systems. A non-object-oriented system might share some properties, such as using abstraction or encapsulation, but will not be built using objects or classes. It is also possible to use an object-oriented language to implement a system using classes or objects, but the system must have all the following properties to be considered a true object-oriented system.

object orientation   A method of developing software that uses abstraction with objects, encapsulated classes, communication via messages, object lifetime, class hierarchies, and polymorphism.

Any object-oriented software system will have the following six properties.[1]

1. Abstraction with objects

2. Encapsulated classes

3. Communication via messages

4. Object lifetime

5. Class hierarchies

6. Polymorphism

Fundamental Properties of an Object-Oriented System

This section gives a brief overview of each of these properties; the following sections give more-detailed explanations of each.

Abstraction with Objects
An **abstraction** is a mechanism that allows a complex, real-world situation to be represented using a simplified model. Object orientation abstracts the real world based on objects and their interactions with other objects. For example, one possible abstraction of a color is the RGB model.

[1.] You can find different definitions of what makes a system object-oriented, but you would have trouble finding two OO developers who agree to any one definition. We will use this definition of object orientation.

> **abstraction**   A model of a real-world object or concept.

Encapsulated Classes

The abstractions of related ideas are **encapsulated** into a single unit. The states and behaviors of the abstraction are incorporated into an encapsulated whole, called a class. The actual internal implementation of the states and behaviors is hidden from the rest of the system. While this not a new programming technique, in OO the encapsulation is an inherent and integral part of the system and design. Earlier, we described a Color class that provides a way to change its red, green, or blue values. In fact, as long as the outside world continues to see and use a Color object in a consistent way, it wouldn't matter just how color is represented internally by the Color object. It could use either the HSV (hue, saturation, value) color model or the RGB model internally, and the outside world would be unaffected. The state and behavior of objects are controlled by well-defined and restricted interfaces to the object. Encapsulation ensures that the internal details of an object are hidden from the rest of the world, that each object maintains its own unique identity and state, and that the state can be changed only by well-defined messages.

> **encapsulation**   The process of hiding all the internal details of an object from the outside world. In Java, encapsulation is enforced by having the definitions for attributes and methods inside a class definition.

Interaction via Messages

In order to accomplish useful tasks, objects need to interact with other objects. The interaction can be between objects of the same class or between objects of different classes. This interaction is handled by sending messages (in Java, this is done by calling methods) to other objects to pass information or request action. For example, when a user selects a command button in a dialog box on the screen by clicking the mouse, a message is sent to the dialog object notifying it that the command button was pressed. Messages can be used to change the state of an object or to request an action by the object.

Object Lifetime

All objects have a lifetime. They are created and initialized as they are needed during program execution, exist and carry out their functions, and are eventually destroyed. While objects exist, they maintain their own identity and state. Many objects that are instances of the same class can exist at any given time. Each object has a unique identity and will have attributes that are different from other instances of objects in the same class.

Class Hierarchies

In an OO design, classes of objects are arranged into hierarchies that model and describe relationships among the classes. The simplest relationship is an *association*.[2] For example, there could be an employment association between a person and a company. These simple associations exist between different classes.

Hierarchies can also be used to build the definitions of individual classes. One way is to include other classes as part of one class. For example, consider a dialog graphical user interface class. Such a dialog would contain control objects such as buttons, lists, or value sliders. Thus, all the different control objects would be parts of the whole dialog class. This kind of hierarchy is called *aggregation* or *composition*.[3]

A second way to use a hierarchy is to define additional specialized classes based on an existing generalized class. For example, a dialog class can be considered a specialized case of a more general window class. The more specialized class will automatically share the attributes of the more general class (for example, size and screen position), and will probably add new attributes and behaviors to the generalized class (for example, associated control objects). This kind of hierarchy is called *inheritance*.

Polymorphism

Polymorphism is the final fundamental characteristic of object-oriented systems. When inheritance is used to extend a generalized class to a more specialized class, it will usually include extending some of the behaviors of the generalized class. The specialized class will often implement a behavior that is somewhat different from the generalized class, but the name used to define the behavior will be the same. It is important that a given instance of an object use the correct behavior, and the property of polymorphism allows this to happen automatically and seamlessly. Polymorphism is actually easier to use than it is to explain. We will discuss polymorphism in more detail later.

[2.] An association is not a hierarchy in its strictest sense, but a relationship between peer objects. However, it can simplify your thinking to include associations in the grand scheme of object hierarchies.

[3.] Aggregation and composition are similar. We will cover the differences later.

If you read about OO in other sources, you will no doubt find slightly different terminology than we use here, but abstraction, encapsulation, messages, lifetime, hierarchies, and polymorphism are really the heart of the matter. The presence of all these properties is required for a software system to be considered object-oriented. *If a system doesn't include abstraction, encapsulation, messages, lifetime, hierarchies, and polymorphism, then it isn't object-oriented, even if it is written using Java, C++, or some other OO language.*

Abstraction with Objects

Abstraction is one of the basic tools of all programming, not just OO programming. When trying to write a program to solve some real-world problem, abstraction serves as a way to model the real-world problem. For example, if you are trying to write an address book program, you might use abstractions such as names, addresses, phone numbers, alphabetical order, and other concepts associated with an address book. You would also define operations for manipulating the attributes, such as adding a new name or changing an address. Abstraction is modeling the real world in terms that can be implemented as a computer program.

Abstraction and OO fit together well. It is natural to model using objects. With an OO language such as Java, you can define objects with all the attributes and responsibilities needed to implement the model. The OO features of Java make it easy to map your abstractions to objects once you know what your objects are. Designing with objects can be challenging, and it is not always easy to find the right objects for your model, but once you learn to think in objects, the process becomes almost second nature.

Almost anything you need to model in software can be considered an object—a temperature sensor in a control system, a person in a subscription system, a room of a building, a word in a sentence. Each of these objects has attributes and responsibilities. In the context of an abstraction, an object is a thing or concept. It can be a real-world thing or concept, or it can be an abstraction of a thing or concept expressed as a software representation.

Encapsulated Classes

Encapsulation is one of the most important aspects of OO. It is what allows each object to be independent. The exact implementation of attributes and of object behavior is hidden from the rest of the world through encapsulation.

The class definition is the main programming tool that is used to implement encapsulation. A class is a description of a collection of objects with common **attributes, behavior,** and responsibilities. The definition or specification of a class includes the definitions of the attributes comprising the **state,** the **methods** that carry out the responsibilities of the class by implementing the behavior, and how to set the initial attribute state of an object. A class is identified by a name.

attribute   Used to hold state information of an object. An attribute might be as simple as an on or off boolean variable, or it might be a complex structure, such as another object. A class definition describes the attributes and operations (methods) of a class.

behavior   The activity of an object that is visible to the outside world. Includes how an object responds to messages by changing its internal state or returning state information to other objects.

method   An operation or service performed upon an object, defined as part of the declaration of a class. Methods are used to implement object behavior. Synonyms for *method* include *member function*, *operation*, and *service*.

state   State reflects the current values of all the attributes of a given object and is the result of the behavior of an object over time.

A class should never allow direct access to state information by the outside world. Instead, it should change the state as part of its responsibilities, or sometimes provide methods for accessing and changing the state. As long as you maintain a well-defined interface to the rest of the world, you can easily modify your class definition without breaking the rest of the system.

Java programs are defined as collections of classes. Normally, each Java class is defined in a separate file. The attributes of a class are defined by the declaration of variables of various types, such as `int` or `boolean`. A Java class includes the definitions of the methods used to implement the behaviors of the class. The method definitions are integral parts of the class definition.

Communication via Messages

Messages are how objects communicate with each other. Any object may send a message to other objects, and it may receive messages from other objects. In practical programming terms, sending a message is accomplished by invoking or calling some class method; receiving a message is accomplished by having a class method called by a different object.

Usually, a message is sent by a method call as a normal part of the execution of the program logic of an object. However, messages may also originate from the operating system interface or language runtime system. Consider an object that implements a dialog interface with a user. When the user clicks on a button, a message is sent to the dialog object or button handler telling it that a specific button has been pressed (the implementation specifics aren't important). In this case, however, the user program usually doesn't monitor the mouse itself to determine which button was pressed. Instead, the underlying system monitors the mouse and sends the message to the appropriate user program object. The Java runtime system and libraries provide many other support classes that can send and receive messages for user programs. This message to an object approach is easier to program than the technique usually known as callbacks, which is used by non-OO programming languages. Instead of defining a separate callback procedure and then registering it with the system, a Java program creates an object based on a standard Java system library, and appropriate messages (such as a button press) automatically are sent by the system to the appropriate object method.

There is another important aspect of the concept of messages. Messages drive program execution flow. The fact that messages can originate from the system, as well as from the program itself, means that OO programs often do not have the traditional linear program execution typical of non-OO programs (although they can, of course). Consider an interactive program with a graphical user interface (GUI). The parts of a GUI program required to execute in response to some command are controlled by the user interactively. Depending on which menu item the user selects, or what the user does with the mouse, different parts of the program are executed. The messages corresponding to a menu pick or mouse gesture originate with the GUI system, and are sent to the appropriate program objects, which then have the responsibility of responding with some action. The order and timing of these messages is determined by the actions of the user, not by the control flow of the program.

Object orientation is a natural for this kind of programming. In an OO program, what you often end up with is a set of objects that can respond to a set of messages originating from a variety of sources, such as a mouse click, a sensor value change, or a database transaction. Individual encapsulated objects can respond to messages and send their own messages to other objects in response. Objects in the system interact via well-defined messages with other objects in the system.

Object Lifetime

Objects are dynamic entities. They are created on an as-needed basis during program execution. When an object is created, it is **instantiated**, or bound to the class definition. An instantiated member of a class is called an object, or equivalently, an **instance**. When a new object first comes into existence, a special method called the **constructor** is automatically invoked by the runtime system. The constructor is responsible for giving an instance its initial state. Once an object has been created, it can receive and send messages.

instantiation   Creating an instance of an object of a given class. Instantiating an instance brings it into existence.

instance   A specific object that is an instantiation of a class. An instance has specific attributes and behaviors, and it has a unique identity. Instance and object are often used interchangeably.

constructor   An operation that creates an object and defines its initial state. For complex objects, construction can be a significant activity and cause the constructors of other objects to be invoked as well.

object lifetime   The time an object exists—from its instantiation in its constructor until the object no longer exists and has been finalized by the Java garbage collector. The creation point of an object is under program control, but the exact moment when an object ceases to exist cannot be determined because of the way the Java garbage collector works.

While it exists, an object has state and behavior. State is expressed by attributes; behavior is expressed by the methods associated with the object. State usually reflects changeable attributes of an object. Objects can also have nonstate attributes (for example, a serial number). Individual objects have **identity** and are distinct things and can be distinguished from other objects. Using any object requires the use of its identity. Java uses **references** to keep track of individual objects. Java references are variables declared using the class name or type of the object. It is possible to have more than one reference to the same object. Messages are sent to an object by using its reference with the appropriate method name.

Once an object is no longer needed, it can be destroyed. Objects routinely go out of existence as a normal part of program execution. Perhaps the most common case of this is when temporary objects created by some method are no longer needed when the method is done and returns to its caller. Some programming languages (for example, C++) allow for the explicit destruction of objects. However, in Java an object ceases to exist whenever it no longer has any references to it from other objects, at which point it may be **garbage collected** by the Java runtime system.

identity The characteristics or state of an object that allows it to be distinguished from other objects.

reference A data element whose value is an address. In Java, all objects are accessed by reference. Any object variable is a reference to an actual object, not the object itself.

garbage collection The automatic detection and freeing of memory that is no longer in use. An object becomes available for garbage collection when it is no longer referred to by any other object. Java uses garbage collection rather than explicit destructors found in other OO languages, such as C++.

To get an idea of object lifetime, consider graphical user interface classes, such as those in the Swing library provided with Java. One type of object included in a GUI is a dialog interface. Upon some action by the user, say selecting a menu item, a dialog object is created. As part of the creation process, its constructor is called. The constructor sets up the initial state of the dialog, which would likely include its size, the buttons and controls it has, and its position on the screen.

While the dialog object exists, it is able to respond to messages and to send messages to other objects. For example, the dialog could respond to a message from the system that a particular button was clicked by sending a new message to some other object in the program to take some action described by the button press.

When the user closes the dialog, the dialog object is no longer needed. Once it no longer has any references to it, it can be garbage collected by the Java runtime.

Basic UML Class Notation

The basic UML notation for a class is a rectangle with three horizontal parts. The top part is used to hold the name of the class. The middle part shows attributes, and the bottom is used to hold the class operations (methods). Depending on the level of detail needed, the middle attribute and bottom method parts may not be included.

Associations are shown by lines between classes and are usually labeled with the name of the association.

Continues

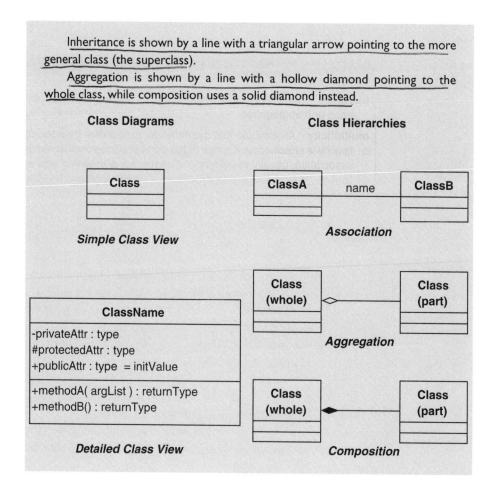

Inheritance is shown by a line with a triangular arrow pointing to the more general class (the superclass).

Aggregation is shown by a line with a hollow diamond pointing to the whole class, while composition uses a solid diamond instead.

Class Diagrams   **Class Hierarchies**

Simple Class View   *Association*

Detailed Class View   *Aggregation*

                                                  Composition

Class Hierarchies

One of the most important aspects of creating object-oriented programs is the arrangement of classes into **hierarchies**. The simplest hierarchy is called an **association**.[4] Two classes are associated by a named relationship. For example, consider a software system that tracks books that readers check out from a library. Two classes present in this system could include a LibraryBook and a Reader. There is an association between LibraryBook and Reader that could be called either borrowing (readers borrow books from a library) or lending (a library lends books to readers).

---

4. Again, note that a simple peer-to-peer association is not strictly a hierarchy, but a relationship.

association   An association is a relationship between two classes. The association will indicate how objects of the classes relate to each other.

hierarchy   An ordering of classes. The most common OO hierarchies are inheritance and aggregation.

multiplicity   An attribute that quantifies an association between objects. The multiplicity is specified as a range of the number of objects that can participate in the
association, usually in the form *n..m*, where *n* is the lower limit and *m* the upper
limit. A *** means an unlimited number, although a single value can also be used.
Common multiplicities include *1, 0..*, 1..*,* and ***.

Depending on what makes the association clearer, it can be labeled as a big-
picture, class-level association (for example, `borrowing` as in Figure 2.1), or as a
specific name for each class in the association (for example, using `borrowedBook`
and `borrower` by each class instead of `borrowing`). Figure 2.2 shows the alternate way to name the association.

Classes in an association usually occupy equal places within a hierarchy. In
our example, `Readers` and `LibraryBooks` are independent classes of equal
standing. Associations are used to show the relationship between different, independent classes in the overall object-oriented design.

Associations also can have a **multiplicity** attribute. In the borrowing example, note the 0..* and 0..1 values right next to each class diagram. The 0..* by the
`LibraryBook` diagram means that a `Reader` can borrow an unlimited number of

Figure 2.1   A borrowing association

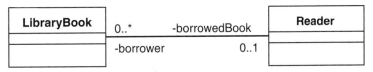

Figure 2.2   Alternate names for the association

books, from 0 to an unspecified number. The 0..1 by the Reader diagram means that a specific book will be borrowed by at most one reader. The multiplicity values can specify explicit values if needed (for example, 0..4 would mean a Reader could borrow at most four books). If a multiplicity is not specified, 1 is assumed.

Plain associations involve classes that are independent of each other. Hierarchies with classes that aren't independent are also an important part of OO systems. There are two ways commonly used to organize such class hierarchies.

The first is to include one class as part of another. This is called a **whole/part** hierarchy, and it is characterized by a **has-a** relationship. For example, a library is made up of a collection of books, which are themselves composed of pages, and so on. A library has some books, which have some pages. You can look at this as a **part-of** relationship. A page is a part of a book, which is part of a library.

> **whole/part**   A relationship between classes in which one class is made up of or contains objects of another class.
>
> **has-a**   A way to state a whole/part relationship. The whole object *has-a* part.
>
> **part-of**   The opposite of *has-a*. The component is a *part-of* the whole.

Parts of a class can be essential to its existence, or they can be parts that come and go. For example, a car has wheels but would not be a car without the wheels. A library has books, but the books can come and go. A library without books is simply an empty library. A book without pages is not a book (see Figure 2.3). Note that the borrowing association between a reader and a library book is independent of the whole/part relationship of a library and its books.

The common OO term for a whole/part hierarchy is **aggregation**. Objects that are in an aggregation association can come and go. If the object is an integral part of the whole, then the hierarchy is called **composition**. Most OO programming languages, including Java, haven't defined special language support

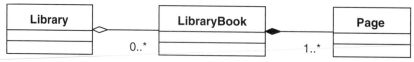

Figure 2.3   A book whole/part hierarchy

for whole/parts. Nevertheless, whole/part hierarchies are critical to most OO programs.

It is not difficult to define aggregation and composition in terms of existing programming language features. There are two ways to implement a whole/part relationship. In practice, the most common way to implement aggregation and composition is to include an instance of the aggregate object as an attribute of the containing class. For example, the definition of a book class could include a reference to the page class (or more likely, a list or vector of pages). Java also allows nested class declarations. Implementing aggregation and composition is discussed more fully in the Java chapter.

aggregation   A whole/part hierarchy. An aggregate object includes (*has-a*) other objects, each of which is considered to be a part of (*part-of*) the aggregate object.

composition   A composition is a form of aggregation in which the whole cannot exist without having the parts.

The second kind of class relationship is the **generalization/specialization** hierarchy. Generalization/specialization (or gen/spec for short) is characterized by an **is-a** relationship. For example, if you were designing a class hierarchy to model animals, you might have a class for Dog, which *is a* specialization of the class Carnivore, which *is a* specialization of the class Mammal, and so on (see Figure 2.4). Key to this concept is the fact that a Dog is a Carnivore, which is a Mammal, which is an Animal.[5]

generalization/specialization   An inheritance hierarchy. Each subclass is a specialization of a more generalized superclass.

is-a   A term used in inheritance hierarchies. In general, a subclass *is-a* specialized kind of a more general superclass.

[5.] These may not be exactly taxonomically correct, but they serve our purposes for this example.

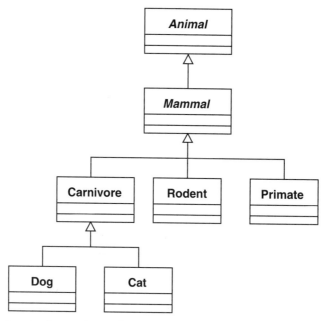

Figure 2.4   An animal generalization/specialization hierarchy

The main mechanism for implementing a gen/spec hierarchy is called **inheritance**. With inheritance, a new **subclass** is **derived** from an existing parent **superclass**. The topmost class of the hierarchy is called the **root class**. Not only does the derived subclass inherit the properties of the superclass, but it can extend and modify its behaviors and attributes. Defining inheritance in code is not as simple as using a reference to an object, so all major OO programming languages, including Java, provide direct language support for generalization/specialization inheritance.

Note that the UML uses an open arrowhead pointing to the more general class to show inheritance. Thus, in Figure 2.4 of the animal hierarchy, a `Mammal` inherits from `Animal`, and so on.

You can show more or less detail in UML diagrams, depending on the information on which you want to concentrate. For example, since Figure 2.4 is focused on the inheritance relationships, it doesn't show the attribute or operation boxes. We use this same diagram in Figure 2.5, but show more detail, including some selected operations.

inheritance A mechanism that allows one class (subclass) to share the attributes and behaviors of another class (superclass). Inheritance defines an *is-a* relationship between classes. The subclass, or derived class, inherits the attributes and behaviors of the superclass and usually extends or modifies those attributes and behaviors.

subclass In an inheritance hierarchy, a subclass is derived from an associated superclass. A subclass is a specialization of the generalized superclass.

derived In an inheritance hierarchy, a subclass is derived from a superclass. The derived subclass inherits the attributes and methods of the parent superclass.

superclass In an inheritance hierarchy, a superclass is a more generalized class. A subclass will be derived from a superclass. (A superclass is also known as a parent class or a base class.)

root class The topmost or most generalized user class of an inheritance hierarchy. In Java, all classes are at least implicitly derived from the Java `Object` class, which makes it the most primitive root class. Most applications have many hierarchies, with different non-`Object` root classes.

A superclass is extended without altering its definition or source code. A subclass can be selective about which properties of the superclass it inherits. The subclass can extend the superclass by adding new properties and by selectively **overriding** existing properties of the superclass.

Inheritance is an especially important and powerful concept. It means that an existing class can be used as-is by a new class, with its properties modified and extended through the inheritance mechanism. Classes can be designed to provide useful **default behaviors** and attributes that can be extended and modified only if the derived subclasses need to implement different behavior.

overriding When a subclass specifies an alternative definition for an attribute or method of its superclass, it is overriding the definition in the superclass. This is also called overloading. Java can only overload methods.

default behaviors In an inheritance hierarchy, the class behaviors defined by superclasses that will be used by default unless they are overridden by some subclass.

Consider the mammal hierarchy. All mammals share a number of character-istics. These can be captured once in a generalized `Mammal` class. The general mammal characteristics are then available by inheritance to additional special-ized subclasses, such as `Carnivore` or `Rodent`. The class `Carnivore` inherits all the general characteristics of `Mammal`, such as having hair and bearing live young that are fed milk, while extending the attributes to having certain kinds of teeth, and the behavior to eating meat. The `Rodent` subclass of `Mammal` extends the `Mammal` superclass with different attributes than a `Carnivore`. The `Mammal` class itself could be derived from an even more general `Animal` class.

This really represents an economy of expression. We can describe the general characteristics in a superclass while expressing the specializations in a subclass. We don't need to repeat all the general characteristics for each instance of a mammal, just those specific to the subclass. And when the behaviors of different subclasses vary, such as in the eating habits of specific mammals, these too can be specialized in a subclass.

In Java, a subclass can inherit from only one superclass. This is called **single inheritance**. Other OO programming languages, such as C++, allow classes to be defined that inherit from more than one superclass. This is called **multiple inheritance**. Compared to single inheritance, multiple inheritance is used infrequently and can lead to some confusion in the program design. Java does not support multiple inheritance. Instead, Java supports what is called an **interface**, with an actual class definition supplied to **implement** the interface. This facility is often used in cases that would otherwise require multiple inheritance. In practical terms, implementing an interface allows a class to be used in well-defined ways by other classes.

single inheritance   When a subclass is derived from a single superclass, it is said to have single inheritance.

multiple inheritance   When a subclass is derived from multiple superclasses, it is said to have multiple inheritance. Java does not allow multiple inheritance, but provides interfaces as an alternative.

interface   In Java, an interface is a specification of methods that a class using the interface must implement. An interface is a specification and does not define any code. It provides an alternative to multiple inheritance.

implements   In Java, a specification that the class will implement the code required by an interface.

Note that the *is-a* relationship is critical to proper design of a class. If a subclass cannot be defined with an *is-a* relationship to its superclass, then the design is likely to be faulty and there is not an inheritance relationship. A Dog is a Mammal, but it is not a Rodent or a Color. You should always apply the **is-a test** when defining classes with inheritance hierarchies.

> **is-a test**   A simple test to check for proper inheritance design. If you cannot say a subclass *is-a* kind of the superclass, then inheritance is probably not appropriate.

Many discussions of object orientation give special emphasis to programming with inheritance. In fact, both aggregation and inheritance are important parts of object-oriented programming. Both kinds of hierarchies are used to design programs that reflect the characteristics of the problem being modeled. Any class can be defined using a combination of both forms of hierarchy.

Polymorphism

For a given class hierarchy, it is possible for different subclasses to be derived from a common superclass. Each of the subclasses can override and extend the default properties of the superclass differently. **Polymorphism** is a characteristic of inheritance that ensures that instances of such subclasses behave correctly.

When a subclass overrides a default method, it uses the same name defined in the superclass. If the behavior of the default method is adequate, a given subclass does not need to override the method, even if other subclasses do. The derived method can implement completely new behavior, or use the default method while extending it with additional behaviors.

> **polymorphism**   Polymorphism is what allows the appropriate method for any specific object to be used automatically. Polymorphism goes hand in hand with inheritance and classes derived from a common superclass. It is supported by dynamic binding of an object to the appropriate method.

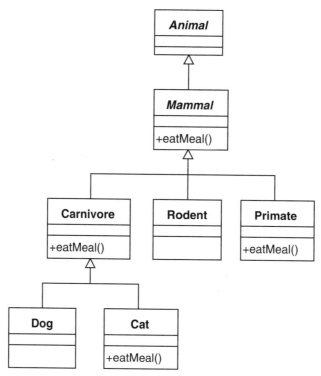

Figure 2.5   Polymorphism means a Cat uses its own eatMeal, a Dog uses the Carnivore eatMeal, and a Rodent the Mammal eatMeal.

Figure 2.5 shows an Animal hierarchy. Since all mammals need to eat, there would likely be a general method defined by the Mammal class to handle eating, called eatMeal, for example. While all Mammal objects might share some eating behaviors that are defined in the general Mammal eatMeal method, some would require specialized eating behaviors different from other Mammal objects. The eating habits of a Dog are different from those of a Cat, which are different from those of a Rodent, which are different than those of a Primate. Thus, each subclass definition can include an eatMeal method that implements the specialized eating for that subclass. Not all subclasses need implement a specialized method if the superclass method is satisfactory. In the figure, the Dog uses the more general Carnivore eatMeal while the Cat has its own specialized eatMeal, which might add the behavior "play with food first." The Rodent uses the general Mammal eatMeal. Because all animals may not need an eatMeal (some may absorb their nutrition from the environment), there is no eatMeal method defined by the Animal class. Note that all these methods have the *same* name, eatMeal, even though they implement different behaviors.

If the system were to process a mixed list of different `Mammal` objects, then it would need to use the appropriate `eatMeal` method for each `Mammal`. For example, if the `Mammal` instance were a `Dog`, then the `eatMeal` method defined for the class `Carnivore` would need to be used, not the `eatMeal` for a `Rodent`.

Polymorphism is what allows the appropriate method for any specific object to be used automatically. Polymorphism goes hand in hand with inheritance and classes derived from a common superclass. The mechanism that allows polymorphism to work is **dynamic binding**. The actual binding of a call to a specific method is delayed until runtime. Only then can the class that a particular object instance belongs to be determined and the correct method from that class be called.

dynamic binding   Definition bound at runtime.

Polymorphism almost seems like magic. It is difficult to believe that the proper `eatMeal` is used for each object. Fortunately, polymorphism is easier to use than it is to understand, and you won't have to think about it explicitly most of the time. Using it comes automatically, and it becomes a natural part of using objects with inheritance.

An Example: Putting It All Together

In this section, you will find a small example design that uses all the major OO relationships: association, aggregation, composition, and inheritance. This small example could be considered a starting point for designing a full application for a library system. The example will also show the relationships between a library customer and the library. Figure 2.6 shows the UML for this design.

This example has two generalized superclasses, `Book` and `Person`. Each describes a generic object. Presumably, each would contain attributes common to all `Books` and to all `Persons`, such as a name. Note that a `Book` is composed of `Pages`. The composition relationship indicates that a `Book` has from one to any number of pages. Any methods a `Book` requires to manipulate `Pages` would be implemented in the `Book` class, and would be available for subclasses of `Book`. A `LibraryBook` is derived from `Book`, and is a specialized kind of `Book`. It might have additional attributes, such as an acquisition date, borrowing status, and an identification number.

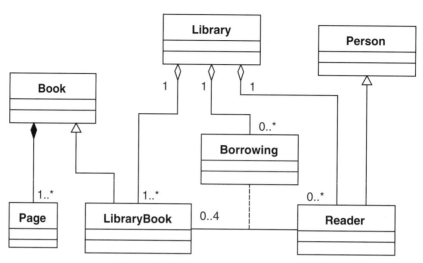

Figure 2.6   Relationships between a library and its customers

A Reader is a special case of a Person who uses the Library. A Reader object contains specialized attributes such as a list of checked-out books.

The Borrowing class in this example is used to implement the same borrowing association between a reader and a library book as we used in Figure 2.1. Now, however, a Borrowing is also a part of a library—a list of all books borrowed. We could use the same simple direct association as we used before, but then the library would still need some other object to track books that have been borrowed. In addition, the Borrowing class can now have the added responsibility of tracking down when a Reader borrows a LibraryBook, for example, or could track overdue books. The dashed line from Borrowing is the UML notation to show this relationship. In our earlier example, the borrowing association could be implemented as a simple double link between a LibraryBook and a Reader. Using a class to implement this association means the links between the LibraryBook and the Reader are managed by the Borrowing class. Note the 0..4 multiplicity for a Reader borrowing LibraryBooks. This would indicate that a reader can borrow from none to four books.

Figure 2.6 shows an aggregation relationship between a Library and LibraryBooks. One might think that a library is not a library without any books, and that the relationship should be a composition. Perhaps. But one of the differences between aggregation and composition is that when an object is destroyed, so are all its components, while the parts of an aggregation remain. So if you destroy a Book, the Pages are gone, too. On the other hand, if you close a Library, all the Books still exist.

And finally, note that both LibraryBook and Reader pass the *is-a* test for inheritance. A LibraryBook is a Book, and a Reader is a Person.

Other OO Concepts

The six basic principles we've just discussed—abstraction with objects, encapsulated classes, communication via messages, object lifetime, class hierarchies, and polymorphism—represent the pure essence of object orientation. While these six principles are the core of object orientation, there are other essential concepts of real object-oriented programming languages and designs. This section covers some of these other concepts.

Abstract Classes

When building a class hierarchy, it is common to design some classes that will never have any instances and are intended to be used only by subclasses. For example, the Animal class in the animal hierarchy is such a class. There will never be an instance of an Animal. Instead, there are additional specialized subclasses of Animal, such as Horse or Snake, that would have instances. Classes that have no instances are called **abstract classes.**[6] Abstract classes usually define a common interface for subclasses by specifying methods that all subclasses must override and define. For example, the Animal class might define a method called reproduce. Since all animals reproduce, each subclass would have to define a reproduce method. But the definition of reproduce for the Animal class would be empty because it is an abstract class and serves as a guideline or specification for derived subclasses.

> **abstract class**   A class that has no instances. It is usually defined with the assumption that concrete subclasses will be derived from it and extend its basic attributes and behavior. In Java, an abstract class is one that includes an abstract method.

[6.] Note the names Animal and Mammal are shown in italics in the UML diagram (Figure 2.5). UML uses italics to designate abstract classes.

A **concrete class**, on the other hand, is one that can have actual objects or instances. Dog and Cat are examples of concrete classes because there can be instances of Dog or Cat. In Java, interface definitions can be considered as a type of abstract class that has only methods and no attributes.

concrete class   A class that is completely specified and can have instances. A Java class derived from an abstract class defines all the abstract methods from the abstract class.

A related concept is the root class we discussed earlier. In any hierarchy, the root class is at the top of the hierarchy and does not have a superclass. The root class in the hierarchy we've been using is Animal, but the root class could even be more general (for example, Life) if necessary. A root class may or may not be an abstract class. It is more common that an abstract class is also a root class, although it isn't required.

An OO system can have many root classes for different object hierarchies. This can be visualized (Figure 2.7) as a forest of class trees. In some OO programming languages, including Java, all classes are actually derived from a single system-defined root class.[7] There are various advantages, as well as disadvantages, to this requirement. The master root class in Java is the Object class. Although all Java classes are derived from the Object class, this is most commonly done implicitly—that is, you don't have to explicitly include the Object class in your class definitions. The class forest in the figure does not include a topmost-level root class.

Visibility of Methods

Recall that encapsulation is one of the most important characteristics of object-oriented programming. One aspect of encapsulation is the hiding of all the implementation details of an object inside the class definition while presenting a well-defined interface to the outside world via the class's methods. Object-oriented programming languages such as Java provide direct language support to control the **visibility** of a class's attributes and methods.

[7.] The root system class is not usually shown in UML diagrams.

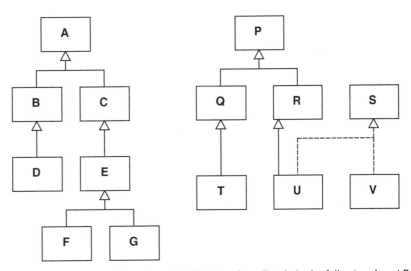

Figure 2.7 Some relationships shown by this "class forest" include the following: A and P are root classes. P is a superclass of Q, R, T, and U. A, C, and E are all superclasses of F and G. B is a subclass of A, and D is a subclass of B. B and C are both derived from the common superclass A, using single inheritance. U is derived from R and implements the interface S. D, F, G, T, U, and V will certainly be concrete classes, since they are at the bottom of the hierarchy. Higher-level classes could be either abstract or concrete. Note that in Java, A and P would be derived (probably implicitly) from the Java Object class.

visibility The ability of one class to see and use the resources of another class. Visibility is controlled by various programming language features such as Java's public, protected, and private specifiers.

Object-oriented languages usually provide four levels of visibility for classes. These levels of visibility are usually directly supported by language keywords. Normally, the levels of visibility apply to both the attributes and operations of the class. The four levels are

1. **Public visibility.** Public attributes and operations are visible to the whole world. Any other class can access the public items of a class.

2. **Private visibility.** Private attributes and operations are visible only to members of the given class.

3. **Protected visibility.** Protected attributes and operations are visible to the class and its subclasses.

4. **Friend visibility.** Friend attributes and operations are visible to a specified set of other classes. In Java, the `package` is used to define friend visibility. In C++, the `friend` specifier is used.

Encapsulation is enforced by limiting the number of public items. Normally, attributes are never defined to be public. Instead, a class should provide only public operations, which can provide services, and allow other classes to interact with its attributes via a well-defined public interface.

When a class needs to provide information about its state, the convention is to use what are known as **setters** and **getters**, also known as accessors and mutators. In general, however, it is best to minimize the number of setters and getters defined by a class. Classes that are more data oriented (such as a Color or Coordinate class) are more likely to require setters and getters. Other classes should modify their internal attributes as a result of the operations they perform, and not by direct requests.

setter   A method that allows the outside world to modify an attribute of a class. Setter methods are also known as mutators. Setter methods by convention have names such as `setLimit` or `setWidth`.

getter   A method that returns the value of a class attribute. Getters are also known as accessors or selectors. By convention, getter methods have names such as `getLimit` or `getWidth`.

Class Versus Instance

When a class is defined, it can have two different kinds of attributes and methods. The difference between these two is defined by whether they apply to the class as a whole, or if they relate to specific instances of the class. **Class attributes** and **class methods** apply to the class as a whole. For example, it might be useful to know how many instances of a specific class have been created. In that case, a class attribute called `instances` could be defined to track this information for the class as a whole.

Instance attributes and **instance methods,** on the other hand, relate to specific instances of a class. Commonly, any instance of a class needs its own copies of attributes. It also needs methods that use those instance-specific attributes.

class attribute   Attributes of a class that are shared by all instances of the class. There is only one copy of each class attribute, and it is possible to access these class attributes without creating any instances of the class. These are sometimes called static attributes in Java.

class method   A method defined by a class that operates only on class attributes. Class methods can be used without creating any instances of the class. These are sometimes called static methods in Java.

instance attribute   An attribute of a class that is associated with a particular instance of the class. Each instance will have its own copies of instance attributes.

instance method   Methods defined by a class that operate on instance attributes. This is the most common type of method defined by a class. An instance method is used only with its associated instance of the class.

Accessing Objects

Object-oriented languages provide the basic mechanisms needed to access the various parts of an object. But just as convention calls for setters and getters, other special cases for accessing the attributes and methods of an object have their own terminology. The following definitions cover the terms used for different kinds of object access.

container   A class whose instances are collections of other objects. These collections may be objects all of the same type or of mixed types, although they usually have a common superclass. Containers include lists, stacks, queues, bags, and others. They usually provide a method to iterate over each object in the container.

iterator   An iterator is a method (or methods) used to access or visit each part of an object. This allows the outside world controlled access to all important parts of an object, without the need to know the internal implementation details of a specific object. Iterators are often used with container classes and typically work by accessing the first item in a container, then each subsequent object, until all objects have been accessed.

mix-in   A class (or usually an interface in Java) that is used to define a single behavior. Mix-ins are usually not stand-alone classes, but are used to provide a standard for implementing the designed behavior.

callback   A method that is called when an event has taken place. Usually used in association with a listener. When a listener detects an event, it invokes the callback of objects that need to know the event has occurred.

listener   A method that responds to events. These are usually system events such as mouse clicks or timer events. The listener typically invokes callbacks of objects that need to respond to the event.

link   A reference to another class. Used to build associations between classes.

this   Also called *self*. A reference to the current object. Within a class definition, references to the attributes and methods of the class are implicit. The *this* reference can be used for clarity to make a reference explicit. Most commonly, however, *this* is used to pass a reference to the current instance to another object. It can also be used to set a class variable to refer to a specific instance of the class.

A Low-Level View of Objects

At some point while a program is running, class instances must have some low-level implementation in the memory of a computer. Having an understanding of how objects can be implemented at this low level can help you understand what is going on.

The UML representation of an object with the separate attribute and operation fields is, in fact, a reasonable model of how objects are represented in memory. There are really two main components of any object: the data, or attributes; and the code that implements the methods. We will discuss the code part first.

A class definition includes the code for all methods of a class. The compiler translates the high-level Java code into low-level Java Virtual Machine code. This is the code that runs on each computer. Because every instance of a class uses the same methods, there really needs to be only one copy of each method defined by a class. There does not need to be a separate copy for each object instance. This is true for instance methods and for class methods and attributes. So, for each class, there is a single copy of all the code for the methods, as well as the storage for any class attributes.

On the other hand, the instance data associated with each object is unique to each instance of a class. Each object exists as a separate entity with its own identity. Thus, when an object is first created with a new operator, Java dynamically creates the storage space required for the instance attributes. Because this dynamic storage must be initialized, most object-oriented languages, including Java, invoke a special class method, called the constructor, whenever an object is first created.

Java creates new objects only by explicit use of the new operator. It never automatically creates new objects. Since only class methods (static methods) can be invoked without creating an instance of a class, your program's main entry point is the class method `static void main`.

Java automatically creates temporary storage for primitive items such as `ints`, as well as for object references. This storage is created to hold the parameters passed when a method is called.

Most implementations of Java use four different areas of memory to store these items. First, there are two areas of memory to hold the method code and the class or static data. This memory is allocated only once, when a program or object is first loaded. The parameter and dynamic object data storage is usually implemented using two dynamic areas of memory. The first is called the stack and is used to hold the temporary copies of parameters and copies of variables local to a method. When a method is called, enough stack is used to hold the parameters and local method variables needed for that call. This is done on a last in, first out basis, so that when a method returns to its caller, the temporary parameter values and method locals are simply removed, or popped, from the stack. The memory required for instance variables when an object is first created is allocated to a dynamic area of memory called the heap. Unlike parameters and locals, instance variables are needed as long as an object still exists. The heap usually consists of most of the free memory available.

When the memory for an object is allocated, it consists of the space required to hold all the attributes of the object. It also contains a reference to the methods defined by the class. It is this dynamic allocation of method references that allows polymorphism to be implemented efficiently. Depending on the actual type of the object, the proper method is bound to the object at runtime.

Just as objects have memory allocated for them when they are created, it is necessary to free that memory when objects are no longer needed. Various object-oriented languages use different techniques to control the freeing of this unused storage. We will discuss Java's technique, garbage collection, more in the next chapter.

What does all this have to do with object-oriented programming? It is part of the nature of objects that they each have their own existence, their own identity, and their own lifetime. As a consequence, each object has a representation in memory. The difference between instance and class attributes and methods affects just how a particular object works. The fact that an object must be created and initialized, and that objects can go out of existence, means you must be aware of these consequences when you program.

Chapter Summary

- Object orientation is a significantly different way of thinking about solving problems and developing software solutions.

- An object-oriented system is one that has been designed using abstraction with objects, encapsulated classes, communication via messages, object lifetime, class hierarchies, and polymorphism.

- An object represents an instance of a real or abstract thing.

- A class is the definition of the attributes and methods needed to model a related group of objects.

- Classes can be organized into hierarchies. Association is a relationship between classes. Aggregation and composition represent whole/part relationships. Inheritance represents generalization/specialization.

- Inheritance allows subclasses to selectively derive the properties of a superclass.

- Polymorphism goes hand in hand with inheritance and means the right methods are used for individual objects in a derived class.

- An understanding of how objects are created and implemented can make it easier to write good OO programs.

- Just as any other specialized discipline, object orientation has its own vocabulary.

Resources

Object Orientation

Fundamentals of Object-Oriented Design in UML, Meilir Page-Jones, Addison-Wesley, 2000, ISBN 0-201-69946-X.

UML

UML Distilled, *Second Edition*, Martin Fowler and Kendall Scott, Addison-Wesley, 2000, ISBN 0-201-65783-X.

CHAPTER 3

Objects in Java

In Chapter 2, we covered the essence of object-oriented programming. The terms we used there really apply to any object-oriented programming language: C++, Smalltalk, and of course, Java. In this chapter, we will focus on Java and how it supports object-oriented programming.

This chapter is not an introduction to Java. We assume you've already had some introduction to programming in Java. You have probably even used some basic object-oriented properties of Java, such as defining objects and using inheritance. The approach of this chapter will be to take a concept from object-oriented programming, such as a class, and describe how Java supports that concept. It will not be the usual "here's the next language feature of Java" approach.

Since you are probably somewhat familiar with Java, some of the material covered in this chapter may seem very basic. Even though you may already know some of these Java features, you may still find it useful to review them from the object-oriented perspective.

To keep the focus on objects, most of the examples will be first shown as a UML object diagram, then mapped to the equivalent Java code. As we said earlier, just because a program is written in Java does not mean it is object-oriented. The goal is to keep your thinking object-oriented, not Java-oriented. Starting with UML objects will help keep the focus on objects.[1]

---

[1] Of course, even using UML doesn't guarantee object-oriented programs.

Defining Classes in Java

The class is the fundamental unit of Java programs. A Java program is made up of a collection of class definitions. Each Java class is defined in a single file with the exact name of the class, but with a .java file extension.[2]

For many of the examples in this chapter, let's assume we are working with a program that draws and manipulates various geometric shapes. In some cases, for clarity we will give names to our classes that conflict with names of classes that are part of the standard Java class library (such as Point and Color). In any event, these examples are designed to illustrate how to use Java to implement classes and class relationships, and would likely be somewhat different in a real-world application.

Our model of shapes assumes that each shape has an *x,y* origin, expressed as a floating-point value. The shape would eventually be drawn on the screen at some physical location that represents the shape's real origin. Because each shape needs to specify at least one *x,y* coordinate, we will start by defining a Point class. A general Point class is likely to be useful for other aspects of drawing shapes.

The following UML class diagram (Figure 3.1) shows a possible implementation of a Point class.

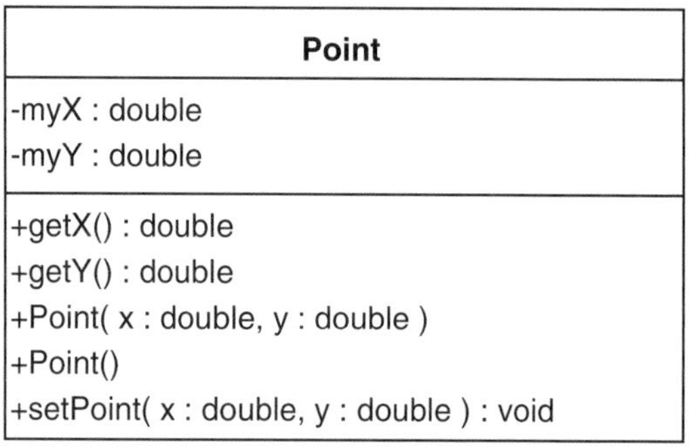

Point
-myX : double
-myY : double
+getX() : double
+getY() : double
+Point(x : double, y : double)
+Point()
+setPoint(x : double, y : double) : void

Figure 3.1 UML diagram of Point class

Listing 3.1 is the equivalent Java code for the Point class and must be saved in a file called Point.java.

---

[2] Actually, you can build Java source files that define more than one class, but there can be only one public class in each file. Any other classes within a file serve as utility classes for the main public class in that file.

Listing 3.1   `Point.java`
Point Class

```java
/**
 * Point - a double x,y coordinate
 */
public class Point
{
    // Attributes

    private double myX;
    private double myY;

    // Constructors

    public Point(double x, double y)
      {
        myX = x; myY = y;
      }

    public Point()
      {
        myX = 0.; myY = 0.;
      }

    // Methods

    public double getX()
    {
        return myX;
    }

    public double getY()
    {
        return myY;
    }

    public void setPoint(double x, double y)
    {
        myX = x; myY = y;
    }
}
```

Notice the exact mapping from the UML class diagram to the equivalent Java code. With good UML design tools, such as those discussed in a later chapter, it is possible to have much of the code associated with your program generated automatically. Initially, a design tool generates the code that represents all the attributes and methods provided by your class. You fill in the lines of code that actually implement the actions supported by the class methods. As you work with and modify your class, a good UML design tool automatically incorporates the changes you make into the UML class diagrams.

In this example, the Point class is defined as public class Point. The first part of the class definition includes the private attributes of the class. The public methods associated with the class (getX, getY, setPoint, and so forth) are defined next. While Point is a simple class, it still hides the real internal implementation of *x* and *y* from the outside world and provides public setters and getters. This class is so simple that you might be tempted to rename myX and myY to x and y and make them publicly available. In fact, you will find many classes in the standard Java library that do give direct access to the attributes. However, the standard Java libraries represent a compromise between practical and efficiency considerations and truly good object-oriented design. Thus, the standard Java libraries are unfortunately not always great examples of object-oriented software design and should not necessarily be taken as examples of good OO programming.

In general, it is hardly ever a good idea to allow direct access to the attributes of a class. Even providing getters and setters can expose implementation details that might better be left hidden. In practice, however, especially for simple objects, it is sometimes acceptable to expose the underlying model. In this case, we've chosen to expose that we are keeping the *x* and *y* of a point as doubles. Using setters and getters helps protect the integrity of the model. For example, we could easily add validity checks for a range of valid points if necessary, and the programs using the Point class would not need to change.

If we wanted to change our representation of a Point from double to int values, for example, we would have some difficulties. We would need to change any places in the rest of our code where doubles are used to ints. Depending on the stage of the development, even small changes like that can affect many lines of code. Fortunately, the strong type checking of the Java compiler would flag places where doubles need to be ints.

Figure 3.2 and Listing 3.2 (opposite) illustrate a slightly more complicated example. It is a Circle class that uses the Point class we just defined. Even though this is a simple definition of a Circle class, it has some problems. Because we already had a Point class, we used a Point to define the Circle's origin. However, we represented the color of the Circle directly. Our design should undoubtedly define a Color class, too. And if we were designing a program to represent different shapes, it would make sense to define a Shape class for items that are common to all shapes (such as origin and color) and to derive specific shapes like Circle or Rectangle from that Shape class. We will do that later in this chapter.

Note that a Point is merely a simple attribute of a Circle. A Point is really similar to a fundamental type such as a double or an int. There is no higher-level association relationship between a Circle and a Point. We will examine higher-level associations later.

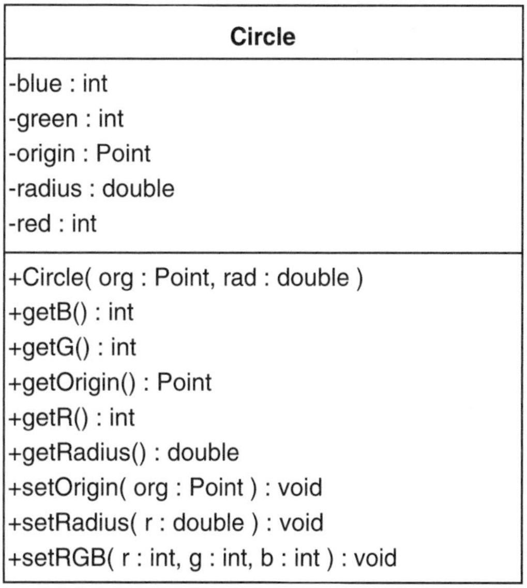

Circle
-blue : int
-green : int
-origin : Point
-radius : double
-red : int
+Circle(org : Point, rad : double)
+getB() : int
+getG() : int
+getOrigin() : Point
+getR() : int
+getRadius() : double
+setOrigin(org : Point) : void
+setRadius(r : double) : void
+setRGB(r : int, g : int, b : int) : void

Figure 3.2   UML diagram of Circle class

Listing 3.2   `Circle.java`
First version of Circle

```
/**
 * Circle.java - a simple Circle class
 */
public class Circle
{
    private int red;        // color of circle
    private int green;
    private int blue;
    private Point origin; // origin of circle
    private double radius; // radius

    public Circle(final Point org, final double rad)
    {
        red = 0; green = 0; blue = 0;   // black
        origin = new Point(org.getX(), org.getY());
        radius = rad;
    }

    public int getB()
    {
        return blue;
    }
```

```java
public int getG()
{
    return green;
}

public int getR()
{
    return red;
}

public void setRGB(int r, int g, int b)
{
    // Simplification: doesn't check for valid values
    red = r; green = g; blue = b;
}

public double getRadius()
{
    return radius;
}

public void setRadius(double r)
{
    radius = r;
}

public Point getOrigin()
{
    return origin;
}

public void setOrigin(Point org)
{
    origin.setPoint(org.getX(), org.getY());
}
}
```

Visibility

When viewed in the overall context of object-oriented programming and encapsulation, it is easier to understand all the visibility features of Java. For a class to be useful, it must provide some services to be used by objects of other classes, while keeping the internal details hidden.

Java uses the `public` specifier to define which attributes and methods are available to the entire outside world. Any variable or method in the top level of a class definition with a `public` specifier is available for use by any other class. Note the various public methods provided by the definition of the Point example: `getX`, `getY`, `setPoint`, and the `Point` constructor. It is best to give public access only to class methods, not to class attributes.

The remainder, nonpublic parts of a class, must be hidden from the outside world. This includes both attributes (remember that attribute is the object-oriented term for a data structure and other variables used in a class definition) and any methods needed to support the internal class implementation. Java provides three ways to control the nonpublic visibility of attributes and methods.

Java Naming Conventions

Choosing names for Java classes, variables, and methods is not a random process. Since its inception, there has been a set of standards for choosing Java names. These standards were originally proposed by Sun and have been widely adopted by the Java programming community. You should follow the generally accepted guidelines for naming Java items in your own programs. The conventions presented here are adapted directly from Sun's own standards, posted on Sun's Java Web pages.

Packages

The prefix of a unique package name is always written in all-lowercase ASCII letters and should be one of the top-level domain names, such as `.com`, `.edu`, or one of the other official top-level names.

Subsequent components of the package name vary according to an organization's own internal naming conventions. Use dots to separate the parts.

Examples: `com.sun.eng`, `com.objectcentral.javatools`

Classes

Class (and interface) names should be nouns descriptive of the purpose of the class. Names are in mixed case, beginning with a capital and with the first letter of each internal word capitalized. Use complete words and avoid abbreviations.

Examples: `Point`, `Shape`, `MovieEditor`, `ClientList`

Methods

Methods should be verbs descriptive of the purpose of the method. Method names are in mixed case, with the first letter lowercase and the first letter of each internal word capitalized. There are prefix conventions for general types of methods, such as using `get` and `set` for getters and setters.

Examples: `getOrigin`, `findSmallest`, `drawGraph`, `saveModel`

Continues

Variables

Except when used as constants, all variables are named using mixed case with a lowercase first letter, and with internal words starting with capital letters. Variable names should be meaningful enough to convey their use to someone reading the code. Avoid abbreviations. Use one-letter variable names only for temporary variables. Using meaningful variable names is one of the most important things you can do to make your code easy to read and maintain.

Examples: `myMovie`, `editedMovie`, `backgroundColor`, `lastItem`

Constants

The names of variables used as constants should be all uppercase, with words separated by underscores ("_").

Examples: `MAX_SIZE`, `R_PG13`, `TERM_LIMIT`

For simple class attributes and operations that are used only by the class itself and won't be used by any derived subclasses, the `private` specifier means that a variable or method is visible only within the given class. Neither the outside world nor classes derived from the class can see or use `private` attributes and methods. In the `Point` example, the attributes `myX` and `myY` are private.

When a class is designed to serve as a parent class and have derived subclasses, the `protected` specifier allows the given class and its subclasses to see those attributes or methods. Classes not related to that class by inheritance cannot see protected attributes or methods.

Finally, Java provides what is called package visibility for attributes and methods. Any attribute or method defined without using any visibility specifier (`public`, `private`, `protected`) has package visibility. A package is a collection of related classes tied together by the Java `package` statement, which must be the first statement in each file that is a part of the package. Package visibility is much like public visibility except that it is limited to other classes included in the same Java package.

Package visibility is usually not a good thing. Using package visibility breaks class encapsulation. It couples the definitions of the classes in the package, and can lead to problems later as the package is maintained over time. When classes work closely together, as they often do in a library, using package visibility can avoid making some attributes or methods public, so it can be useful.

There are a couple of other complicating factors with package visibility. First, *all* nonprivate attributes and methods are visible to other classes in the same package. This means `public`, `protected`, and unlabeled attributes and methods. Second, if you don't put a class into a package, it automatically is placed into the default package, which usually consists of all classes in the current file directory. The small example classes shown in Listing 3.3 demonstrate this. The example consists of two files, `PackageVisibility.java` and `Foo.java`, contained in the same file directory. Because neither file has been explicitly placed in a package, the default package visibility makes `Foo.protectedInt` visible to the `PackageVisibility` class. Beware.

Listing 3.3 `PackageVisibility.java`, `Foo.java`
Example showing default package visibility.

```
/* This example demonstrates "default package visibility."
 * Foo is defined in the same directory as PackageVisibility.
 * Thus, only the Foo private attribute privateInt is really
 * private. PackageVisibility sees all three other variables.
 */

public class PackageVisibility
{
    public static void main(String args[])
    {
        Foo foo = new Foo();
        int fooPublic = foo.publicInt;      // public
        int fooPackage = foo.packageInt;    // package
        int fooProtected = foo.protectedInt; // default package
        // Following is not visible, would cause compiler error
//      int fooPrivate = foo.privateInt;
    }
}

public class Foo
{
    // Simple class to demonstrate visibility
    public int publicInt;
    protected int protectedInt;
    int packageInt;
    private int privateInt;
}
```

As a rule, always use a `public`, `private`, or `protected` specifier in the definition of each attribute and method in a class definition. The only exception is when you require package visibility for a library or other Java `package`, then the class definition must use a Java `package` specification.

The UML provides a notation for specifying visibility of attributes and methods. Note in the UML class diagram of `Point` that the private `myX` and `myY` attributes have a "-" at the beginning, which means private visibility, while the methods `getY`, `getX`, and `setPoint` have a "+" to indicate public visibility. The UML uses a "#" to indicate protected (and Java package) visibility.

Inheritance

Inheritance is a fundamental feature of object-oriented design and programming. While the use of class association, aggregation, and composition is just as important as inheritance when developing real programs, inheritance differs in that implementation support for it must be provided by the object-oriented programming language. It is in the language support for inheritance that C++ most differs from C, and Java differs from earlier languages such as Pascal.

In the earlier Point and Circle example, we noted that having a Color class might be useful, and that it would make sense to generalize the concept of a shape. To demonstrate inheritance in Java, we will develop a simple example that uses a Point class, a Color class, and a Shape class that are used to define Circle and Rectangle classes. (We could define other shapes, but two are enough to illustrate how to use the UML and Java to implement inheritance.)

First, let's design a general Shape class. What is common to a Circle and a Rectangle? Both have an origin and a color. Furthermore, all shapes have some other common geometric attributes, such as area and perimeter. Thus, we will design a parent Shape class that accounts for these common factors by including objects of the Point and Color classes as attributes of Shape. Area and perimeter will be handled by defining methods. The calculation of area and perimeter will be defined by the subclasses of Shape.

In our example, we can reuse the Point class from earlier, but we need to add a new Color class. We also need a base Shape class that can be used to derive other specialized shapes. For our example, we will design new Circle and Rectangle classes that are derived from a Shape class.

First, Figure 3.3 shows UML class diagrams for the new Color class and again for Point.

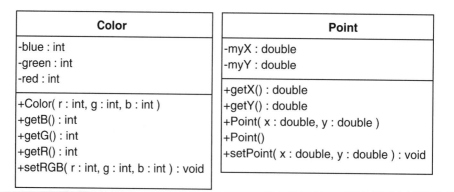

Figure 3.3   Point and Color UML

The corresponding code for `Color` (see Listing 3.1 for `Point`) is as follows.

Listing 3.4 `Color.java`
RGB Color class

```java
/**
 * Color - a simple RGB color representation
 */
public class Color
{
    // Attributes
    private int blue;
    private int green;
    private int red;

    // Constructors
    public Color(int r, int g, int b)
    {
        red = r; green = g; blue = b;
    }

    // Methods
    public int getB()
    {
        return blue;
    }

    public int getG()
    {
        return green;
    }

    public int getR()
    {
        return red;
    }

    public void setRGB(int r, int g, int b)
    {
        red = r; green = g; blue = b;
    }
}
```

Now we will show the UML diagrams for our new shapes. Recall that to show inheritance (or generalization/specialization), the UML uses a line from the class diagram of the specialized class connected to the diagram of the more general class with an open-headed arrow pointing to the parent class.

In this design, it would never make sense to have a Shape object—there would just be instances of Circles or Rectangles. Thus, the Shape class should be an abstract class. This is shown in the UML by using *italic type* for the class name. In addition, we specify that all specific Shapes must provide methods for area and perimeter. Because each shape uses a different formula to calculate its area and perimeter, the area and perimeter methods of the Shape class are declared abstract, and the specific implementations are defined in the derived subclasses.

Figure 3.4 shows the UML diagram for Circle and Rectangle classes derived from the abstract Shape class.

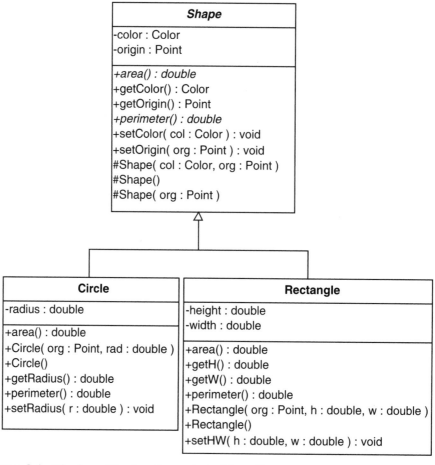

Figure 3.4   Circle and Rectangle are derived from Shape

Here is the corresponding code.

Listing 3.5   Shape.java
Abstract base class for shapes

```java
/*
 * Shape - an abstract base class for other shapes
 * Defines color and origin of shape, getter/setters for them
 * Defines abstract methods area and perimeter for actual shapes
 */
public abstract class Shape
{
    // Attributes
    private Color color;
    private Point origin;

    // Constructors
    protected Shape(Color col, Point org)
    {
        origin = new Point(org.getX(), org.getY());
        color = new Color(col.getR(), col.getG(), col.getB());
    }

    protected Shape(Point org)
    {
        origin = new Point(org.getX(), org.getY());
        color = new Color(0,0,0);      // black by default
    }

    protected Shape()
    {
        origin = new Point(0.0, 0.0);  // 0.,0. origin
        color = new Color(0,0,0);      // black by default
    }

    // Methods
    public abstract double area();       // real shape defines

    public abstract double perimeter(); // real shape defines

    public Color getColor()
    {
        return color;
    }

    public void setColor(Color col)
    {
        color.setRGB(col.getR(), col.getG(), col.getB());
    }
```

```
    public Point getOrigin()
    {
        return origin;
    }

    public void setOrigin(Point org)
    {
        origin.setPoint(org.getX(), org.getY());
    }
}
```

Listing 3.6 Circle.java
Circle derived from Shape

```
/*
 * Circle - a Shape representing a circle
 */
import java.lang.Math;          // for PI

public class Circle extends Shape
{
    // Attributes
    private double radius;

    // Constructors
    public Circle()
    {
        super();
        radius = 0.0;
    }

    public Circle(final Point org, final double rad)
    {
        super(org);
        radius = rad;
    }

    // Methods
    public double area()
    {
        return Math.PI * radius * radius;  // Pi r Squared
    }

    public double getRadius()
    {
        return radius;
    }

    public double perimeter()
    {
        return 2 * Math.PI * radius;     // 2 PI r
    }
}
```

```
        public void setRadius(double r)
        {
            radius = r;
        }
}
```

Listing 3.7 `Rectangle.java`
Rectangle derived from Shape

```
/*
 * Rectangle - defines height and width to specify rectangle
 */
public class Rectangle extends Shape
{
    // Attributes
    private double height;
    private double width;

    // Constructors
    public Rectangle()
    {
        super();
        height = 0.0; width = 0.0;
    }

    public Rectangle(Point org, double h, double w)
    {
        super(org);
        height = h; width = w;
    }

    // Methods
    public double area()
    {
        return height * width;
    }

    public double perimeter()
    {
        return 2 * (height + width);
    }

    public double getH()
    {
        return height;
    }

    public double getW()
    {
        return width;
    }
```

```
public void setHW(double h, double w)
{
    height = h; width = w;
}
}
```

The Java extends specifier is used by the definitions of Circle and Rectangle to specify that they inherit from the Shape class. The Java abstract specifier is used by the definition of Shape to indicate that it is an abstract class, and that area and perimeter are abstract and do not have implementations in Shape.

The base class can provide implementations of the attributes and methods common to all subclasses. Thus, Shape provides the declarations for the color and origin attributes, and the implementations of the getColor, getOrigin, setColor, and setOrigin methods. It is up to the definitions of the subclasses Circle and Rectangle to provide appropriate implementations for area and perimeter.

This simple example illustrates how a simple UML diagram can be mapped to Java code. In these examples, we've used all three of the public, private, and protected Java specifiers. All are examples of specific features of Java used to support inheritance.

Notice that Java uses the dot (.) operator to provide access to individual attributes or methods of a class. For example, the line

```
color = new Color(col.getR(), col.getG(), col.getB());
```

from the Shape class constructor used col.getR() to access the red value of the color passed into the constructor. In Circle.java, we find the line

```
return 2 * Math.PI * radius;
```

which references the constant value for PI from the Java core math package.

Most of the variables used in the rest of the code don't use the dot operator. These are references to attributes of the given instance of the class. Each of these references has an implicit "this." associated with it, and sometimes it adds clarity to the meaning of a program to explicitly specify this.

Association, Aggregation, and Composition

While the UML has special symbols to represent association, aggregation, and composition, Java (like other OO languages) does not provide special programming language constructs to support them. Fortunately, implementing these designs in code is not very difficult. Usually, association, aggregation, and composition are all implemented in the same way—using links. When there is only one object involved (a multiplicity of 1), then a simple object reference variable will do. When more than one object can be involved in the relationship, then a list or Java Vector can be used.

The links are attributes of the classes involved in the relationship. There can be either a one-way link or a link in both directions, depending on the requirements of the design. This directional connection is called navigability. If the navigability is one way, that direction is shown in UML by an arrow on the association connection line. No arrow implies two-way navigability.

There are conventions that can be used to choose the name of the link variable. Associations are usually named and often have specific names for each end of the association. If the ends are named, then that name should be used for the link variable. If there is no name on the end, then simply use a lowercase version of the class name. Thus, for aggregation and composition, which usually don't have an association name, use the lowercase name of the class at the other end. This is usually the name of the part class in the whole/part relationship.

Just to demonstrate how these links can be implemented, let's revisit the simple Library hierarchy we discussed in Chapter 2. Figure 3.5 shows the hierarchy again. Note that in the code that implements the UML hierarchy, you can't really tell the difference between any of these associations from the link declarations in the code. The different behaviors required for association, aggregation, or composition are properties of how the code works.

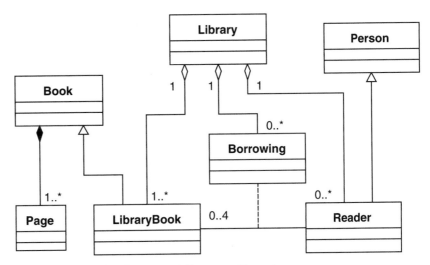

Figure 3.5 Relationships between a Library and its customers

The following Java code shows how the links between the different objects can be implemented in Java. Note that this code just shows the links. It does not show constructors or any other methods that would be required to actually use these objects.

Listing 3.8 Library.java
Links to parts

```
/*
 * Library.java - Outline only. Code not complete.
 */
public class Library
{
    private Vector libraryBook;   // List of all LibraryBooks
    private Vector borrowing;     // List of Borrowings
    private Vector reader;        // List of Readers

    // ...
}
```

A vector is a container class.

Listing 3.9 Book.java
Vector page implements composition links

```
/*
 * Book.java - Outline only. Code not complete.
 */
public class Book
{
    private Vector page;    // list of Pages
}
```

Listing 3.10 Page.java
No links

```
/*
 * Page.java - Outline only. Code not complete.
 */
public class Page
{
    // ...
}
```

Listing 3.11 LibraryBook.java
Borrowing borrowed implements association

```
/*
 * LibraryBook.java - Outline only. Code not complete.
 */
public class LibraryBook extends Book
```

```
{
    private Borrowing borrowed;      // link to Borrowing object

    // ...
}
```

Listing 3.12 Person.java
Root class

```
/*
 * Person.java - Outline only. Code not complete.
 */
public class Person
{
    // ...
}
```

Listing 3.13 Reader.java
Extends Person, Vector borrowing implements association

```
/*
 * Reader.java - Outline only. Code not complete.
 */
public class Reader extends Person
{
    private Vector borrowing; // Borrowings of LibraryBooks

    // ...
}
```

Listing 3.14 Borrowing.java
Reader reader and LibraryBook libraryBook implement association

```
/*
 * Borrowing.java - Outline only. Code not complete.
 * This code would implement a Borrowing; it will link a
 * specific LibraryBook to the corresponding Reader.
 */
public class Borrowing
{
    private Reader reader;              // Link to the Reader
    private LibraryBook libraryBook;   // Link to the book

    // ...
}
```

Java Interfaces

Java does not support multiple inheritance. In practice, multiple inheritance is infrequently used. Java does provide a language feature called interfaces. Java interfaces support the most common use of multiple inheritance—mix-in classes. A mix-in allows a class to implement a specific behavior defined by the mix-in class. When multiple inheritance is available, the mix-in can be a true class, with methods and behavior of its own. A Java interface just allows a specification of methods, without providing any code implementation of those methods. It is up to the class using a Java interface to provide the actual implementation of the methods described by the interface specification.[3]

An examination of a real Java utility class that uses an interface for its functionality will help demonstrate just how useful a mix-in interface can be. The core Java utility package provides a class called `Observable` that implements the Observer design pattern.[4] It is a common programming problem to have one object that is of special interest to several other objects that need to know when that one object changes its state. Consider a single sensor that monitors the status of a door, for example. When that sensor triggers because someone opens the door, several other objects may be affected by that event. There could be an object that controls lighting and needs to turn on lights automatically if the door opens. Another object might notify a guard station or alarm system, and another simply count how many times the door has been opened. So whenever the door sensor detects that the door has opened, it would need to notify all objects interested in that event. The Observer design is ideal for this purpose.

The sensor is the `Observable` object and would be designed by inheriting from the Java `Observable` utility class. Any other object (light controller, guard station) interested in being notified whenever the `Observable` object (the door sensor) changes state would register itself with the `Observable` object. Then, when that object (door sensor) changes state, it would send a message to all registered `Observers` using the `notifyObservers` method provided by the Java `Observable` class. The `notifyObservers` would then call the `update` method implemented by each `Observer` object that registered. The UML for this is shown in the "Interfaces in UML" sidebar.

In this case, the `Observable` class provides some real functionality. It has a method (`addObserver`) that builds a list of all `Observers`. When its `notify-Observers` method is called, it uses that list to call the `update` method of each `Observer`. On the other hand, the only function of the `Observer` definition is to specify that there is an `update` method provided for the `Observable` to call. Since the behavior of each `Observer` is likely to be quite different, there is no

---

[3.] While the Java keywords *interface* and *implements* describe the language features quite well, the terms are also commonly used to describe a user interface and code that implements a program feature. Usually, context will tell the true meaning.

[4.] Design patterns are design solutions for a large number of problems commonly found in object-oriented programs. They are discussed in more detail in Chapter 7.

Interfaces in UML

Interfaces are specified slightly differently in the UML from the way classes are specified. The main diagram is like a class box, but includes <<interface>> or a circle to indicate it is an interface and not a class. And because interfaces don't have attributes, the attribute section is usually not included. Classes that implement an interface use a dashed *realizes* connection rather than the solid *generalization* connection.

The following UML illustrates the Observer interface discussed in this section. Note the association between Observable and Observer with the triangle direction indicator.

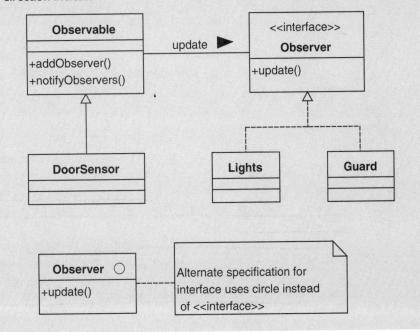

need for any functionality in the Observer specification. Thus, Observer is defined as a Java interface that specifies a single method, update. Furthermore, it is likely that some of the classes that implement Observer objects will be derived from other classes. Thus, the fact that Observer is an interface means it serves as a simple mix-in to the actual classes that define Observers, without the need for multiple inheritance.

While multiple inheritance can be useful for some programming problems, it does in fact lead to some significant problems for the language compiler and runtime implementation (These issues are beyond the scope of this book, but are real, although solvable at some cost). The Java interface provides a similar functionality to multiple inheritance, but avoids the big complications that multiple inheritance brings to a language implementation. Thus, it gives most of the benefits, without the added cost of true multiple inheritance.

Object Lifetime in Java

As we discussed in Chapter 2, all objects have a lifetime. They are created, carry out their responsibilities, and usually go away, either when the program is finished using an object or when the program terminates. (It is possible to have persistent objects that "live" from one invocation of the program to another, but such persistent objects are a different matter.)

No Java object exists until it has been created with the Java new operator. Because a program has to start by creating new objects, a Java program requires a static component—for example, public static main(String args[]). The main method exists statically, and creates new objects to get the program running.

Constructors

When a Java object is created with the new operator, it begins its lifetime by having its constructor automatically called by the runtime system. The constructor is really a special-purpose method. The constructor has the same name as the class, with no other type attribute. The constructor can be declared to be public, private, or protected.

The goal of a constructor is to initialize the class. It should set all class attributes to a known state. It can create other subobjects that are a part of the class. When the constructor is done, the newly created object should be ready to use. A constructor does not return a value, but it can throw an exception. The new operator returns a reference to the newly created object.

Java allows you to define multiple constructors for a class. Each constructor has a different signature determined by the order and type of the constructor's arguments. The default constructor has no arguments. It is often useful to define several constructors to initialize objects to different values.

If a class is derived from another class, the constructor of the parent should be called. This is done with the Java super() statement. Java automatically calls the default constructor of the parent class if you don't explicitly use a super() statement. If you want to use a parent constructor other than the default one, you can use super() with an appropriate set of arguments.

Almost every Java example shown in this book has constructors you can study to learn the different ways constructors can be used.

Garbage Collection

After an object has carried out its purpose, it is often not needed by the program any longer. All objects consume at least some system resources, and it is important to free these resources when an object is no longer needed. Whenever an object no longer has any references to it, the Java runtime system considers the object unused, and therefore available for garbage collection.

Automatic garbage collection is a great simplification for the programmer. Unlike the case in other object-oriented languages, such as C++, the Java programmer is not responsible for explicitly freeing resources used by an object. The garbage collector handles all this. (Usually. See the next section, "Memory Leaks.")

However, having garbage collection is not a free ride. First, you never can predict when the garbage collector will be invoked, and thus won't know when an object has its resources freed. Java provides a special method for each class, called `finalize()`. The finalizer is called when the garbage collector frees the resources of the object. In theory, this should allow the object to free other resources it might have used, such as file handles. In practice, this is not something to rely on, and `finalize()` is in fact relatively worthless for all but a few specialized cases that most programmers never see. If you have an object that uses system resources such as file handles or network connections or whatever, you should be sure that the object frees them when you know you are done with the object and before you release the last reference to it. Do *not* count on `finalize`.

There is another problem with garbage collection. When the garbage collector does run, it can more or less freeze a program for a few moments while garbage collection takes place. As processors get faster, this issue becomes less important, but it is still possible to see a Java program momentarily pause for no apparent reason. This is the garbage collector running.

Memory Leaks

Releasing the memory used by an object is easy in Java because Java uses garbage collection. When an object no longer has any references to it, it becomes available for garbage collection. All you need to do is let go of all references to the object. You never have to worry about corrupting memory or causing a runtime error by freeing an object more than once, as you would in other languages, such as C++.

You do, however, have to worry about getting rid of all references to an object when you are finished with it. If you leave a dangling reference to an object, it will never be garbage collected, and you can still end up with a memory leak, just as in C++.

It isn't always easy to generate unused references to an object, but it does happen. One way is to add objects to a list, then use only one item in the list and never empty the rest of the list. You can create dangling references using some core Java library routines that use listeners. Failing to unregister listeners is a common error that can create memory leaks. On the other hand, if you eliminate all references to an object that, in turn, references other objects, the garbage collector also reclaims the memory from those indirectly freed objects.

Most of the time, just reassigning a Java object variable to a different object lets go of the reference to the original object. It is good programming practice to explicitly assign `null` to an object reference variable when you are done with the object, if you aren't reassigning it to a different object. This practice helps to ensure that objects don't have unused references to them and allows them to be garbage collected.

Class Versus Instance Methods and Attributes

Recall that class methods and attributes go with an entire class. They exist even if no instances of a class have been created. They are available for use by any instance of the class, and are sometimes used by objects outside the class. There is only one copy of any class attribute, and its value is independent of how many instances of the class are created.

Instance methods and attributes exist and are useful only after an instance of the class has been created. Each instance of the class gets its own copy of instance attributes, and these attributes can have different values, depending on the state of the specific object. Instance methods can use both instance attributes and methods and class attributes and methods.

Java uses the keyword `static` to indicate class variables and methods. Class or static methods and attributes can be accessed without having any instances of the class. To access static methods and attributes, you can simply use the name of the class, rather than a class reference variable. A class method must not access instance variables or methods of the class.

Before instance methods and attributes can be used, you must first create an instance of the class with the `new` operator. You must then use the object reference variable to access the instance methods or attributes for a specific instance of the class.

Class attributes can be declared as `public static final` and given an initial value. This is the typical Java idiom for defining constants for use within a class and by other classes. For example, the `Circle` class discussed earlier used the Java math package's constant `Math.PI`, which is the value of pi. Using constants like this is one case in which it is acceptable to use a class attribute directly rather than through a getter. The `Card` example used in the next section demonstrates using class attributes to represent playing cards.

Copies of Objects

When programming with an object-oriented programming language such as Java, it is important to understand what is going on when you assign the value of one variable to another. With variables of standard primitive types, such as `int`, it is easy. Take, for example the following.

```
int a, b;
a = 1;
b = a;
```

It is clear that the value of b is 1, just like a. When the variable is an object reference, however, the situation is not so clear. For example, look at the following.

```
Circle c1, c2;
c1 = new Circle(0.5);
c2 = c1;
```

In this case, c1 is a reference to a `Circle` object with a radius of 0.5. The important thing to note is that c1 is a *reference* to a `Circle`, not a `Circle` object. Thus, the assignment c2 = c1 makes c2 a reference to the same `Circle` object to which c1 refers. Thus, c2 is a **reference copy** of c1. While you are programming, it is easy to think of c1 as a particular `Circle` object, but as soon as you start assigning one object variable to another, you must remember you are really using references to objects.

Consider the following code fragment.

```
Circle c1, c2;
c1 = new Circle(0.5);
c2 = c1;
c1.setRadius(1.0); // Change the radius of c1
int r1 = c1.getRadius();
int r2 = c2.getRadius();
```

What are the values of r1 and r2? Both are 1.0, because both c1 and c2 are references to the same object. If the goal of having the c2 variable was to keep a copy of the original value of the circle, then this code did not accomplish that task. There are plenty of times when you want and need a copy of an object reference, but there are also times when you want and need a copy of an entire object, not just its reference.

Java provides a mechanism for creating copies of objects, called cloning. However, just to confuse matters even more, there are two different ways to make a copy of an object—**shallow copy** and **deep copy**. Depending on just how you are using a copy of an object, sometimes shallow copy will be all you need. At other times, you will have to use deep copy.

reference copy A reference copy of an object is simply another reference variable that is a duplicate reference to the same object.

shallow copy A bit-wise copy of an object. A new object is created that has an exact copy of the values in the original object. If any fields of the object are references to other objects, only the references are copied.

deep copy A complete duplicate copy of an object. If an object has references to other objects, complete new copies of those objects are also made.

A shallow copy makes a bit-by-bit copy of your object, including references to other objects. Thus, if the object you are copying contains references to yet other objects, a shallow copy refers to the same subobjects. Sometimes this is fine, especially if the values of the subobjects aren't going to change.

A deep copy generates a copy not only of the primitive values of the original object, but copies of all subobjects as well, all the way to the bottom. If you need a true, complete copy of the original object, then you need to implement a full deep copy for the object.

Java supports shallow and deep copy with the Cloneable[5] interface to create copies of objects. To make a clone of a Java object, you declare that an object implements Cloneable and then provide an override of the clone method of the standard Java Object base class. When making a clone of an object, the assignment statement looks like the following example:

```
MyObject copy = (MyObject)original.clone();
```

(Note: clone always returns an Object, thus the need for the cast.)

[5.] Cloneable is Java's (mis)spelling.

Implementing `Cloneable` simply tells the Java compiler that your object is `Cloneable`. The cloning is actually done by the `clone` method. The default behavior of the `clone` method provided by the standard Java `Object` class is to make a shallow copy of the object. To build a deep copy, you override `clone` with a version that calls the standard `clone` method to first create a shallow copy, and then explicitly create the copies of the subobjects used by the class. If all the subobjects are `Cloneable`, you can simply clone each subobject. It is good programming practice to make all subobjects of a class `Cloneable` if you need to implement deep copy. The examples presented in Listing 3.15 should help clarify the whole issue.

Whether you need a reference copy, a shallow copy, or a deep copy of an object is usually clear from the context of your program. Many Java programs never need to use anything other than a reference copy of an object. But it is important to understand what it means to use a reference to an object rather than either a shallow or deep copy (clone) of the object.

The following examples should make the differences among the three types of object copies clear. We will use a small console-based Java program to demonstrate this.

There are two classes in this example program. It requires two classes to demonstrate the difference between shallow and deep copy.

Listing 3.15 CardHand.java
Demonstrates reference, shallow, and deep copy

```
/* CardHand.java - an example to show the differences among
 * reference copy, shallow copy, and deep copy.
 * Copyright (c) 2001, Bruce E. Wampler
 */
public class CardHand implements Cloneable
{
    private Card c1;                   // A CardHand has 2 cards
    private Card c2;

    public CardHand(Card cd1, Card cd2)
    {
        c1 = cd1; c2 = cd2;
    }

    public String toString()
    {
        return "c1:" + c1 + ","+" c2:" + c2;
    }

// **** UNCOMMENT the clone method for SHALLOW and DEEP COPY
//       // override Object.clone()
//       public Object clone() throws CloneNotSupportedException
```

```
//      {
//              // To clone, first shallow clone whole object.
//              CardHand c = (CardHand) super.clone();
// // **** UNCOMMENT next THREE line for DEEP COPY ONLY
// //          // now clone the deep parts
// //          c.c1 = (Card) c1.clone();
// //          c.c2 = (Card) c2.clone();
//              return c;
//      }

    static void main(String args[])
                throws CloneNotSupportedException
    {
        Card newCard = new Card(Card.HEART,7);
        CardHand origHand =
            new CardHand(new Card(Card.SPADE, 1),
                         new Card(Card.SPADE, 13));

// **** UNCOMMENT next 3 lines for copy by reference ****
        CardHand saveHand = origHand;
        System.out.println("\n**** REFERENCE COPY ****\n\n"
            + "BEFORE: saveHand = origHand; :\n"

// **** UNCOMMENT next 3 lines for SHALLOW COPY ****
//        CardHand saveHand = (CardHand) origHand.clone();
//        System.out.println("\n**** SHALLOW COPY ****\n\n"
//            + "BEFORE: saveHand = origHand.clone(); :\n"

// **** UNCOMMENT next 3 lines for DEEP COPY version ****
//        CardHand saveHand = (CardHand) origHand.clone();
//        System.out.println("\n**** DEEP COPY ****\n\n"
//            + "BEFORE: saveHand = origHand.clone(); :\n"

            + "\n          origHand is " + origHand
            + "\n          saveHand is " + saveHand
            + "\n          newCard  is " + newCard + "\n");

        origHand.c1 = newCard;
        origHand.c2.setCard(Card.DIAMOND,4);
        newCard.setCard(Card.CLUB, 2);

        System.out.println(
            "AFTER: origHand.c1 = newCard;\n"
          + "       origHand.c2.setCard(DIAMOND,4);\n"
          + "       newCard.setCard(CLUB,2); :\n"
          + "\n          origHand is " + origHand
          + "\n          saveHand is " + saveHand
          + "\n          newCard  is " + newCard + "\n");
    }
}
```

This example, `CardHand.java`, simply defines a hand containing two `Cards` as defined in the class shown in Listing 3.16. All three cases, reference copy, shallow copy, and deep copy, can be demonstrated by adding and removing appropriate comments. We've chosen to use comments this way to help you to see how similar the program is for all three ways, all in one place. The program, as shown in Listing 3.15, is commented to build the reference copy version. The program creates an original card hand, makes a copy of the original, and then changes the values of the original. Depending on the kind of copy used, the results are completely different.

Listing 3.16 is the code for the `Card` object. `Card` has been made `Cloneable` so that it can easily be used by other classes that implement deep copy. Just because it is `Cloneable` does not mean that objects that use a `Card` need to make clones. And because a `Card` has only `ints` for attributes, a shallow copy and a deep copy of a `Card` would produce identical copy objects.

Listing 3.16 `Card.java`
Needed to distinguish shallow and deep copy

```
/* Card.java - a simple class for cards - part of clone demo
 * Copyright (c) 2001, Bruce E. Wampler
 */
public class Card implements Cloneable
{
    public static final int CLUB = 1;     // constants for suits
    public static final int DIAMOND = 2;
    public static final int HEART = 3;
    public static final int SPADE = 4;

    private int suit;
    private int value;

    public Card(int s, int v)
    {
        suit = s; value = v;
    }

    public Object clone() throws CloneNotSupportedException
    {
        return super.clone();    // all ints, so just use super
    }

    public void setCard(int s, int v)
    {
        suit = s; value = v;
    }

    public int getSuit() { return suit; }
    public int getValue() { return value; }
```

```
public String toString()
{
    String str;

    if (value == 1)
        str = "A/";
    else if (value == 11)
        str = "J/";
    else if (value == 12)
        str = "Q/";
    else if (value == 13)
        str = "K/";
    else
        str = Integer.toString(value) + "/";
    switch (suit)
    {
        case CLUB:
            str += "Clubs";
            break;
        case DIAMOND:
            str += "Diamonds";
            break;
        case HEART:
            str += "Hearts";
            break;
        default:
            str += "Spades";
            break;
    }
    return str;
}
}
```

Reference copy is the easiest. The statement

```
CardHand saveHand = origHand;
```

is the place where the reference copy is made. Note that even though the Card object is Cloneable, this statement does not make any clones, because clone() is not used. Figure 3.6 shows the output for the reference copy version.

Because saveHand is simply a reference to origHand, any changes to orig-Hand simply show up when we reference the same object using saveHand instead. This is also true when we assign newCard to origHand.c1. We are making a reference copy, so any changes to newCard show up when origHand.c1 is used; it is a reference to the same object.

```
**** REFERENCE COPY ****

BEFORE: saveHand = origHand; :

            origHand is c1:A/Spades, c2:K/Spades
            saveHand is c1:A/Spades, c2:K/Spades
            newCard  is 7/Hearts

AFTER: origHand.c1 = newCard;
       origHand.c2.setCard(DIAMOND,4);
       newCard.setCard(CLUB,2); :

            origHand is c1:2/Clubs, c2:4/Diamonds
            saveHand is c1:2/Clubs, c2:4/Diamonds
```

Figure 3.6   Output showing results of reference copy

To implement shallow copy, we simply change the statement in which the copy is made to use clone instead:

```
CardHand saveHand = (CardHand) origHand.clone();
```

This makes a shallow copy (see output in Figure 3.7). Because we haven't yet uncommented the clone method override, the code uses the default protected clone method of the Object class. (Note that we had to explicitly override clone in the Card class to change clone to public.) Thus, the only difference between the code for the reference copy version and the shallow copy version is the use of origHand.clone().

After the clone, saveHand is no longer a reference to the same object as origHand. Instead, it now contains copies of the references to the two Cards, c1 and c2. It does not have new copies of the Cards, however. Thus, when orig-Hand.c1 is set to refer to newCard, saveHand.c1 is not changed. However, when the Card that origHand.c2 refers to is changed by the setCard call, it is the same Card object that both origHand.c2 and saveHand.c2 refer to that is changed.

Finally, we show the results of a deep copy (see Figure 3.8). To do this, we uncomment the clone override in CardHand. Now the statement

```
CardHand saveHand = (CardHand) origHand.clone();
```

creates not only copies of the references to the Cards as in a shallow copy, but copies of those Card objects, as well. This now means that the setCard call changes the origHand.c2 Card, but not the saveHand.c2 Card copy. And orig-Hand.c1 and newCard still refer to the same Card object, while saveHand.c1 refers to the original "A/Spades" Card object.

```
**** SHALLOW COPY ****

BEFORE: saveHand = origHand.clone(); :

            origHand is c1:A/Spades, c2:K/Spades
            saveHand is c1:A/Spades, c2:K/Spades
            newCard  is 7/Hearts

AFTER: origHand.c1 = newCard;
       origHand.c2.setCard(DIAMOND,4);
       newCard.setCard(CLUB,2); :

            origHand is c1:2/Clubs, c2:4/Diamonds
            saveHand is c1:A/Spades, c2:4/Diamonds
            newCard  is 2/Clubs
```

Figure 3.7   Output showing results of shallow copy

```
**** DEEP COPY ****

BEFORE: saveHand = origHand.clone(); :

            origHand is c1:A/Spades, c2:K/Spades
            saveHand is c1:A/Spades, c2:K/Spades
            newCard  is 7/Hearts

AFTER: origHand.c1 = newCard;
       origHand.c2.setCard(DIAMOND,4);
       newCard.setCard(CLUB,2); :

            origHand is c1:2/Clubs, c2:4/Diamonds
            saveHand is c1:A/Spades, c2:K/Spades
            newCard  is 2/Clubs
```

Figure 3.8   Output showing results of deep copy

Messages

When thinking in object-oriented terms, one says that an object passes a message to another. Most messages in a Java program are really calls to some method of a class, which can then respond to the message by returning a value. While you can say that you are calling or invoking a class method, it is better to think in terms of passing messages and to say Class A passes a message to Class B.

Asynchronous messages, such as those caused by events, are somewhat different. In these cases, the idea of really sending a message is close to what is going on. This kind of message can be handled by a Java listener and callback. We looked at callbacks earlier. The Java interface construct is useful for building this kind of message handling. You define a Java interface that describes the name of the callback method, then you implement the callback in the class that needs to receive a message. Then some other class can send a message by calling the callback method described in the interface.

Chapter Summary

- Java is a truly object-oriented language.
- Java has direct support for defining the attributes and methods of a class.
- There are standard conventions for naming things in Java.
- Java provides public, protected, private, and package visibility.
- Java supports single inheritance directly in the language.
- Association, aggregation, and composition are usually implemented with reference variables.
- The Java interface provides a mechanism to support mix-ins, and substitutes for multiple inheritance in many cases.
- All Java objects are built with the new operator and have constructors for initialization.
- Java uses garbage collection to recover the resources of unused objects.
- The static keyword is used to define class attributes and methods. Others (non-static) are instance methods and attributes.
- A simple assignment to an object variable creates a reference to an object. Java provides the Cloneable interface and clone method to support shallow and deep copy.
- Messages are usually implemented as calls to the methods of a class.

Resources

Java

The Java Tutorial, from Sun: java.sun.com/docs/books/tutorial/

Code Conventions for Java, from Sun: java.sun.com/docs/codeconv/

Java Documents, from Sun: java.sun.com/docs/index.html

Thinking in Java, Bruce Eckel, Prentice Hall, 1998, ISBN 0-13-659723-8.

Java in a Nutshell, David Flanagan, O'Reilly, 1999, ISBN 1-56592-487-8.

Practical Java™ *Programming Language Guide*, Peter Haggar, Addison-Wesley, 2000, ISBN 0-201-61646-7.

Object-Oriented Software Development Using Java, Xiaoping Jia, Addison-Wesley, 2000, ISBN 0-201-35084-X.

Java: An Introduction to Computer Science & Programming, Walter Savitch, Prentice Hall, 1999, ISBN 0-13-287426-1.

Java 2 Just Click! Solutions, Tom Swan, Hungry Minds, 2001, ISBN 0-7645-4823-9.

CHAPTER 4

Object-Oriented Analysis and Design

So now you are starting to think in objects. You know what an object is, how objects can be used together in various kinds of organizations, and how you can build objects using Java. Now you are ready to write some great software.

Good software doesn't just happen. Even the world's best programmers can't just sit down in front of a computer and write great software. Developing great software involves knowing what the software is supposed to do, having a plan to build that software, and using good practices to produce a high-quality, working system. Most software projects involve many people and are developed over a period as long as several years. Even simple one-person projects should be developed with some discipline. The process of building an entire software system is often called object-oriented analysis and design (OOAD). In this chapter, we will cover the essential parts of OOAD.

The process of building a software system has many things in common with building a house or building. For a very small building, the process can be informal. But if you need to build a large office building, the process is much longer and more complex. The same is true for a software system.

The first step, of course, is knowing what you want to build. Typically, there is someone who wants a building (customer) and someone who will design and build it (designer). Sometimes, but usually only for small projects, those two are the same person. But there is still that first step—we need a building, it will be this size, more or less, and will serve some purpose, whether it is a storage shed, a home, or a warehouse.

Once the decision has been made to build a building (or a software system), the next step is to develop some specifications. Even if you are building a simple shed as a weekend project, you have to decide where it will go, how big it will be, what material you will use to build it. It is even possible to decide to buy a predesigned kit. This analogy holds for a small software system. You must start with at least some analysis of what the software should do, what its basic features are, and where you will use the software, even if there is an existing system that serves your needs. As with a small building, a small software system doesn't necessarily require a lot of people or super experts to design it successfully.

Now, consider building a house. The process is more complicated. The customer usually starts with an architect or experienced designer. After a month or more of interaction between the designer and the customer, the result is a set of fairly detailed plans, including how big the house will be, how the rooms will be laid out, and perhaps what basic materials will be used. After this design is settled on, the details need to be filled in. What siding will be used? What color will the rooms be? What lighting and plumbing fixtures will be used? Finally, the home will actually be built, usually with a crew of fewer than ten workers, over a few months of construction. Tools required to build a house are usually basic and not expensive. Often, the designer supervises or even participates in the construction of the home.

A small to medium-size software project isn't a whole lot different in approach. There is a period of planning between the customer and the software designer. The customer is the one who specifies what is most important to include in the software system. The designer analyzes the requirements and produces a high-level design for the system, including what it needs to do, how it will be organized, what its parts are. After the customer and designer agree, then a more detailed design is produced to determine such details as what programming language will be used, what the objects in the system are, and what the basic structures of those objects are. Finally, programmers turn the design into a running program. Time frames for this size project typically run about a year or so. The number of programmers varies—usually at least two or three but fewer than ten. And depending on the application, there usually isn't a need for developers with specialized knowledge. For projects of this size, basic software tools are often enough, with perhaps a few specialized tools required.

Finally, consider building a huge office building. Now the situation is much different. The customer likely has put a considerable effort into deciding to build a big building and determining just what that building will do for the business. The customer then needs to work with a large architectural firm with considerable experience in building large office buildings. Different firms would be used if the project were for a highway, airport, or power plant. The analysis and design phase of the project can take many months, even years, before the actual construction begins. The construction company is likely to be completely independent of the design company and use tens or hundreds of workers skilled in constructing office buildings. The company works with a detailed set of plans and specifications produced by the designers. The project will likely need large, expensive equipment that requires specialists to operate. The whole project may require layers of management to keep everyone involved on track.

A large software project is in many ways similar. The up-front analysis and design phase can take years. The design process likely requires input from experts in various fields of the application area, as well as experts in designing large software systems of a specific nature. The result of the analysis and design is a detailed specification that can be passed on to software companies that specialize in building large systems. The whole process may take years and involve tens or hundreds of software designers and programmers. Expensive software tools that require extensive training to use may be needed to make the project work, and outside consultants may be required.

Buildings and software have some other traits in common. First, the result of either effort should be around for a long time. You may think you are writing a quick and dirty software application, but inevitably, it will continue to exist for years and years. Second, after you are finished, there will be bugs. You will have missed getting a nail in the right spot, and your shed roof leaks. Your software will also have bugs. And finally, you will end up wanting to add on—either to your building or to your software. And you will probably need to refurbish to keep up with the latest trends in house interiors—or user interface design.

Of course, the analogy isn't perfect. People have been building structures for a long time. There are standard construction materials and techniques as well as official building codes, and inspectors to make sure the codes are followed. Software isn't quite that mature, and in many ways, software can be more complex. The number of lines of code in a software project can easily exceed the number of parts used in a building. And software doesn't have the equivalent of building codes and building inspectors (and it isn't clear that it ever can, although people are trying). There is another difference. For many software projects, good programmers are likely to participate in all phases of building the system, from start to finish.

Even so, there are some important things to learn from this analogy. First, even the smallest projects really need some level of analysis and design. Smaller projects can be done with fewer people and less formal techniques. As the complexity of a project increases, the more it can benefit from more-formal analysis and design methodologies.

How do you develop a real software system? Where do you start? What do you do next? In the rest of this chapter, we will go over some basic software analysis and design techniques that can be used at some level in almost any software system.

Software Methodologies

Over the years, many of the best software experts have discovered and designed object-oriented design techniques that raise software development above the level of black magic and artistry to something closer to using standard engineering practices. Not all software projects are the same. Some are very big, some small, some involve well-understood problems, and some are risky and explore uncharted territory, and different design techniques apply to different software projects.

A development methodology is a set of practices or guidelines used to develop software. Over the years, there have been many, often competing, software development methodologies. The most current methodologies are designed to work especially well with object-oriented development. Because not all software projects are the same, there are currently several development methodologies that can be applied to various kinds of projects. Some methodologies, such as the Rational Unified Process, seem best used for very large, multi-year projects with large teams of programmers. Other methodologies, such as Extreme Programming (XP), work better with smaller-scale projects with ten or fewer programmers.

Methodologies developed before the widespread use of object orientation are now known as structured methodologies. While object orientation has proven itself to be much more productive than older, structured development and is the dominant development paradigm today, there are still many active software projects that use non-object-oriented languages and structured methodologies. We will focus exclusively on OO methodologies in this book.

Note that the UML is not a development methodology, but a notation. While the design of the UML was influenced heavily by the designers of the Rational Unified Process methodology, it can be used by almost any of the other methodologies, although not all elements of the UML are necessarily used by one methodology.

In this chapter, we will try to cover analysis and design techniques that can be applied to any development technology. We will discuss the specifics of some current methodologies in more detail in Chapter 9.

Even though the different development methodologies vary widely in their detail, there is some commonality. When examined at the fundamental level, almost all of them include in some way or another the following three basic parts:

1. Plan

2. Build

3. Release

Different methodologies or other summaries of OOAD may use different vocabulary and names, have different steps, or more steps; but you can usually map other viewpoints back to these three steps. A slightly expanded view of these steps includes some of the terms often used by other methodologies:

1. **Plan** = analysis, design

2. **Build** = code, debug, unit test

3. **Release** = integration test, learn, maintain

Before the widespread use of object-oriented programming, older development methodologies tended to treat these steps in a strictly sequential order, often known as waterfall development.[1] Each step of the development cycle flowed downstream into the next. Object-oriented methodologies tend to treat development as a more iterative process: plan, build, release a version, and then repeat with refinements. The exact steps used by each methodology vary, but the software system is typically implemented in a series of development iterations. Each iteration usually results in a release of the system with partial functionality. After each iteration, the process is repeated, with lessons learned in previous iterations applied to the next to improve the process. The different object-oriented methodologies vary most in the details of the overall process and in the approaches they take with each of the plan, build, release steps.

One thing that almost all modern methodologies have in common is their ability to use the UML. The fact that different parts of the UML can be used for various phases of software design by almost any methodology accounts for its widespread acceptance.

The Elements of a Software Project

As we noted earlier, software projects come in all sizes. Although a high portion of current software development is maintenance and enhancement of existing systems, new software projects, big and small, are started all the time. Just how does a new project begin?

A software project gets started when some individual or organization, most often after considerable contemplation, decides that a new software system is

---

[1.] The steps of the traditional waterfall development cycle include feasibility study, analysis, design, coding, testing, and maintenance. One of the most important aspects of object-oriented methodologies is the recognition of the need for feedback and allowance for dynamic change in the design.

needed by the organization. At this point, the organization, or **customer**, contacts a software **developer** to discuss creating such a system. The customer and developer may be from the same company, but software development is also commonly done by external organizations.

The customer provides a description of the software system to the developer. This description will be from the perspective of the customer and the **problem domain** of the system. Together, the customer and developer will produce a more detailed **initial specification,** which can then be used by the developer to determine the **feasibility** and costs for the proposed project.

customer   The organization that needs a software system and is paying for the development. The customer should have a clear idea of what the system needs to do and how it can best help the customer's organization.

developer   An organization that develops software for a customer. The developer works with the customer to design a software system that best meets the needs of the customer, given the time and financial constraints imposed by the customer.

problem domain   The field or area for which a software system is being developed. An accounting system would fall into a financial problem domain, and require input from financial experts to its design, for example.

initial specification   An early description of what a software system needs to do. Depending on the overall size of the project, the initial specification may be simple or may consist of extensive documentation.

feasibility   Given an initial specification, the developer will work with the customer to decide if it is feasible to continue with the development of a software project given the technical, time, and financial constraints. This is also known as risk assessment—is it within acceptable risks to proceed with the project?

These steps are the first part of the process. The amount of effort required for this initial planning depends on the size of the project. Just as building a shed might require a simple sketch and a call to the lumberyard to get an idea of what the materials cost, a simple software project might involve a meeting or two between the customer and the developer to determine the feasibility and costs of the project. As the complexity increases, so does the need for more careful initial planning.

Once a project gets at least an initial green light, the planning process moves into a more detailed analysis phase. The scale of the analysis phase again depends on the scale of the project. For large projects, the initial planning usually does not involve any real coding, although some small prototypes or coding experiments might be required for the feasibility study.

There are typically at least two parts to any planning phase. The first part is analysis of the current state of the system. Analysis involves the software developers, project managers, and customers of the system. The second part of planning is design. The results of the analysis planning are used by the development team to produce a software design that can be used for the build phase.

In older, structured methodologies, the analysis and design phases were distinct operations. With object-oriented systems, the difference between analysis and design is somewhat less distinct. The most significant difference is likely to be the participants and the level of detail involved in the process.

In OO, a major goal of both the initial analysis and design is to discover which objects the system requires, what the responsibilities of the objects are, and how they should interact with each other. In analysis, objects are treated at a higher level than in design. The inner details of the objects are ignored, as are the exact interactions and implementations of objects. These details are worked out during design.

The planning process is repeated in subsequent iterations of the development cycle. The results of the previous build and release are used to refine the specifications of the system. This includes refining the features of the system, as well as the objects used by the system.

The overall size of the project determines how distinct the different parts of the planning, building, and release phases of a project are. For some newer, agile development methodologies, such as XP, suitable for small to medium-size projects, the three phases can become quite fuzzy. The larger the project, the more likely it is that a heavyweight methodology will be required, and that the distinctions among the phases will be more apparent.

In this section, we've just given a brief description of the early steps in a software project. A project of any size requires experienced developers to carry out the analysis and design required. Many early issues require significant input from management.

Designing a large software system requires extensive participation from the most experienced analysts, designers, and programmers, and these three roles are often (but not always) quite distinct. As the size of the project shrinks, the more likely it is that all team members will participate in all phases of the project.

Even the smallest project can benefit from a certain amount of up-front analysis and design. In the next section, we will go over some fundamentals of object-oriented analysis any programmer should know and be able to use.

UML Use Cases

Use cases are used to understand interactions among different parts of a system. Each use case is made up of scenarios, which are sequences of steps describing an interaction between a user and the system. The users are called actors.

Consider our example of a reader borrowing a book from a library. In such a case, the Reader will usually interact with a Librarian, who will carry out the transaction. In a library system, the simplest case, or scenario, would consist of the following steps.

1. Reader finds a Book to Borrow, hands to Librarian.
2. Librarian identifies the Reader in Library system.
3. Librarian identifies the Book in Library system.
4. Librarian lends the Book to the Reader, with Library system.
5. Borrowing is registered in Library system.

This is just one scenario; there are others. The Reader might not find the desired book. The book might not be allowed to leave the Library. The Reader might have overdue books, or not be in the system yet. Each of these possibilities should be examined in alternative scenarios. Together, the scenarios make up one use case.

The goal of this is to identify actors, objects, and interactions among them. All this can be a useful part of the analysis and aid in understanding the system. The actors don't need to be people; they can be other objects in the system, for example.

This simple borrowing scenario serves as the basis for a UML use case diagram. A borrowing use case is depicted here as a librarian lending a book to a reader. In the figure, we include not only the use cases with the Reader and the Librarian, but also use cases of the Librarian maintaining the system. This example is greatly simplified, and a real library system would have many more use cases.

In the following UML use case diagram, the stick figures represent the Reader and Librarian actors. The use cases are in the ovals, and the arrows represent actors interacting with a use case.

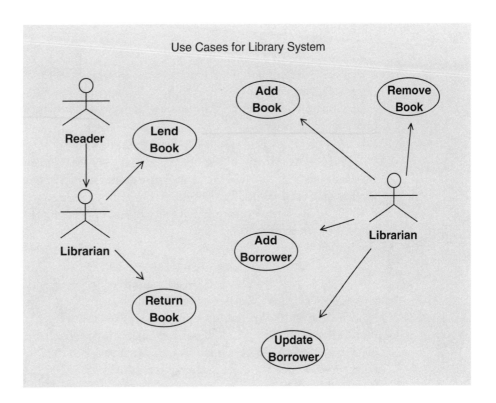

Use Cases for Library System

The Essence of Object-Oriented Analysis

Traditionally, object-oriented analysis (OOA) has been used at the initial stages of a software project. The results of the OOA are then used for the next step of the development process, object-oriented design (OOD). With the advent of more-iterative methodologies, OOA is used to some extent for each development iteration, and the distinction between OOA and OOD can become blurred. OOA should involve both the development team and the customer. It is the customer who best knows the problem domain and what the system needs to do; the development team best knows how to use programming and software resources to design a system that meets the customer's requirements.

In this section, we will cover *some* major aspects of OOA. There can be many different techniques, steps, and strategies used for OOA, some depending on which methodology is used. The goal here is to provide you with an understanding of OOA that will help you to write better software.

Object Discovery

No matter which OO methodology is used, a crucial aspect of the analysis and design is the determination of which objects and classes to include. Objects are at the core of any OO system, and it requires experience and judgement to determine which objects belong in the system. Thus, one of the primary activities of OOA is called object discovery. The goal of object discovery is to find objects that can potentially become a part of the software system.

One of the first steps of the object discovery process is to examine the system specifications that are developed during the initial phases of the analysis. The level of detail of the specification varies, depending on the size of the project. But even the smallest project should have some kind of written specification that can be used by the development team.

In this section, we will cover some general techniques that can be used for object discovery. Two sidebars, CRC Cards (page 85) and UML Use Cases (page 80), cover techniques that can be used alone or in combination with the techniques discussed here to help with object discovery.

The first step of the analysis process is to use the written problem specification to determine likely candidates for objects in the system. Objects are really instances of classes. During analysis, it is often easier to think in terms of specific objects rather than the more general concept of class. As the model of the system is refined, objects found in the analysis phase are carried over directly to the design phase to create the architecture of the system, and most eventually end up implemented as class definitions in real code.

One of the main differences between the analysis and design phases is the level of detail produced about the objects. Objects are treated at a much higher, less detailed level during analysis. The UML is especially effective at showing different levels of detail (see the sidebar on page 92). In the analysis phase, the UML can be used to show just a class or object. During design, the details of specific attributes, operations, and class relationships can be added.

When starting out with object discovery, try to find as many candidate objects as possible. While finding too may objects can be a problem, it is probably better to find too many, because you will be able to shorten and refine the list of candidate objects later. Just because you are using an object-oriented approach doesn't mean the customer knows or understands anything about objects.

Customers may not know exactly what they want or need, and the specification is not likely to be totally accurate or complete. It is common to find flaws in a customer's specification, and thus it is important for the customer and the developer to work together during the early stages of the project.

A good first pass at object discovery is to use the textual problem description to pick out the nouns and verbs. The nouns represent candidate objects, and the verbs represent candidate operations or methods that go with the objects.

Coming up with a definitive candidate list of objects is not a trivial task, and no two analysts or designers are likely to come up with the same list. Picking objects from the nouns and verbs in the description is a simple and direct way to get started. Often, once a few objects have been identified, it is easier to find other candidate objects by additional examination of the problem specification.

The following is a list of things to look for that can help with object discovery.

- Look at the problem space itself, together with any diagrams, pictures, and textual information provided by the customer.

- Look at other systems that communicate or interact with the system being modeled.

- Look at physical devices that will exist in the environment and interact with the system, regardless of the technology used to implement the system itself.

- Look at events that must be recorded and remembered by the system.

- Look at roles played by different people who interact with the system.

- Look at physical or geographical locations and sites that may be relevant to the system.

- Look at organizational units (departments, divisions, and so on) that may be relevant to the system.

As you go through this list, you will find that you discover candidate attributes, as well as candidate objects. In the early stages of analysis, it is not always clear whether an item should be an object or an attribute. It is likely, however, that many items you identify in this process will end up as one or the other in the final model.

Once you have some candidate objects, it is important and useful to examine the responsibilities of each object. What function does an object perform; what are its responsibilities to the rest of the system? One way to look for responsibilities is to concentrate on the verbs in the problem statement. Sometimes, discovering a function can lead to the discovery of several objects required to carry out that function.

After you have some candidate objects, the techniques used with CRC cards can be useful. Not only do you focus on the responsibilities of a class, you also focus on collaborators of a class. Collaborators are other classes that use or are needed by a class.

It can be useful to do some behavioral role playing or personification with a candidate object. Try to personify or imagine yourself as the object. Ask yourself questions. With whom do I interact? How do I respond to a message from some other object? What is my job? What do I do? What do I contribute to the system? What do I need to remember? CRC cards are good for this because you can hold the card in your hand while you ask these questions.

The answers to these questions can provide clues to whether the candidate object is a good object and possibly to other classes needed to support its behavior. They can also lead to the discovery of methods needed to support an object.

Evaluate Candidate Objects

Once you have a list of candidate objects, it is important to evaluate each object. It is easy to get too many objects. Remember inheritance and look for the possibility of generalizing some of your objects into a higher-level class. On the other hand, it is possible to try to group objects using inheritance when aggregation or composition is more appropriate. Use the *is-a* and *has-a* tests. And ask yourself if the objects you have are all necessary. Could they be combined into a common class? In general, smaller is better.

There are some objective criteria that can be applied to objects to evaluate their "goodness." Consider the following points.

- Each object should have some data. You don't have to know all the attributes yet, but you should be sure that at least some attributes exist.

- If the candidate object has only one attribute, perhaps that should be represented as an attribute of another object rather than as a new object. There can be objects with only one, or even no, attributes, but having only one serves as a flag for closer inspection.

- An object must do something to justify its existence, so you should be able to identify one or more methods for the candidate objects. It is unlikely that an object will have no methods.

- In the analysis phase, the function and purpose of a candidate object should be independent of the hardware or software technology used to implement the system. If it is not, then it isn't an essential object, but rather an implementation object that should wait until a later stage of development for more consideration.

- All the attributes of a proposed class should apply to all the objects in that class. If you find exceptions (for example, this attribute applies in all cases except for that special object), then you may have combined subclasses when they should be part of a hierarchy. Although you may want to combine classes as much as you can, it is sometimes necessary to split a class into more-specialized subclasses.

- Many of the "smells" applied to refactoring apply equally well to a design. See Chapter 8.

- Just as all the attributes should apply to every instance, all methods, or operations, should apply to all objects in the class.

CRC Cards

CRC Cards represent a simple yet useful OOA technique. CRC stands for class-responsibility-collaborator. The idea is to generate a set of 3×5 or 4×6 index cards that include the classes that make up a system. Each card lists the name of the class, the responsibilities of the class, and other classes the class uses or collaborates with. These cards are usually generated in interactive work sessions involving the customers, analysts, and developers. While a set of CRC cards might eventually be used to generate UML diagrams, they are really most useful for exploring interactions among classes in an open discussion format.

CRC cards were originally developed in the late 1980s by Kent Beck and Ward Cunningham as a technique to help procedural programmers move to the design perspective needed by object-oriented programming. In many ways, CRC cards are so easy and basic that their original paper still stands as a good reference. CRC cards have been found to be so useful they have become a standard OO design tool.

What Is a CRC Card?

Class Name	
Responsibilities	Collaborators

Continues

The top line of the card specifies the name of the class in large letters. A class, of course, is a collection of objects—the things of most interest in the system being modeled.

The responsibilities of the class are listed on the left side of the card. A responsibility is a high-level description of what the class does. The responsibilities should be short, concise descriptions of what the class knows about, and what it does with that information. One of the points of the small CRC card is to force you to keep these descriptions small and high-level. A class should have no more than two or three responsibilities. Thinking in terms of responsibilities is important; it gets away from a data-centric view of objects.

On the right side is a list of collaborator classes. These are classes that provide information or services for the class at hand. Each collaborator class has its own CRC card. Note that a collaborator is a class that is used by the given class—the collaborator CRC card does not necessarily list the classes that use it. As more CRC cards are added, they can be laid out and physically grouped by classes that are related.

The backs of the CRC cards are often used to give more details of the data and methods needed to implement the class. These details can be used later, when the classes are actually implemented in code.

Note that you are allowed to write only as much as will fit on the card. This keeps your classes from getting too big or complex. The section in Chapter 5 on Model/View/Controller has an example using CRC cards.

Using CRC Cards

CRC cards are quite flexible in how they can be used. They are often used in what is called a *session*. A CRC session can vary from an informal meeting with a couple of programmers to a formal session involving designated roles and scribes to officially record the session. Because it is an interactive process, a CRC session should not have more than five or six active participants (although passive observers are allowed as well).

CRC sessions often focus on a scenario—a sequence of interactions among objects suggested by a particular use case or part of the problem description. Cards can be placed on the table in groups, picked up, and moved around. In using CRC cards to act out a particular scenario, the need for other classes or different responsibilities is often discovered. Many designers using CRC cards find it useful to use role-playing—picking up a card and moving it around, and essentially becoming that object.

As the session starts, one of the first goals is to come up with some objects. The techniques we discussed in the object discovery section can be useful here to come up with some initial CRC cards.

Once the interactions and responsibilities of the different classes represented by the CRC cards have been explored, the information can be transferred to a more formal notation, such as the UML. UML sequence and collaboration diagrams can be developed from the interactions discovered from using the CRC cards. UML class diagrams can be derived from the class information contained on a CRC card. Associations between classes can be used to build association diagrams. However, the main goal of using CRC cards is to gain understanding of the system and how it might work, not to produce UML diagrams. Many projects have used CRC cards as their chief documentation process.

Determine Object Hierarchies

After you have a good list of candidate objects, the next phase of OOA is to organize the basic objects into hierarchies. Object discovery and hierarchy discovery often overlap. While examining a problem for objects, it is often apparent that some objects naturally form a hierarchy. Other hierarchies are not as obvious and must be discovered explicitly.

The main goal of this phase is to identify the hierarchies that can take advantage of the OO paradigm. Remember the two major forms of hierarchies: generalization/specialization, or inheritance; and whole/part, or aggregation/composition.

The concept of inheritance with superclasses and subclasses is natural for many problems. Inheritance implies that a subclass inherits the properties of the superclass, as well as adding new properties of its own.

Whole/part discovery often takes place after the initial object discovery. Sometimes, the whole/part relationship is obvious, but sometimes it is helpful to look for whole/part hierarchies explicitly.

Hierarchies reveal how related or similar objects fit together. Objects also have relationships with other objects that reflect how the objects interact in ways other than inheritance and aggregation. For example, a relationship might indicate that one object uses the services of or generates an instance of another class. A Customer object might generate an Order object.

Objects don't have to fit into a hierarchy. Sometimes, a class, usually a simple one, is simply an attribute of another class. These are sometimes called helper classes.

Discover Object Attributes

So far, we have discussed finding objects and discovering object hierarchies and relationships. OOA must also examine object attributes. An object's attributes describe its meaning—what data it holds, what state it is in, what connections it has to other objects.

At the design level, objects generally have two kinds of attributes—public and private.[2] Public attributes are available to the world, whereas private attributes are used internally. Generally, during OOA, you are concerned primarily with the public attributes.

Imagining yourself to be the object works for attribute identification, just as it does for object identification, as discussed earlier. Become the object in your mind and ask questions such as:

- As an object X, how am I described?

- How am I described in this problem domain?

- What do I need to know to carry out my function?

- What state information do I need to remember over time?

- What states can I be in as a member of class X?

As you identify attributes that belong to your objects, you should consider where they belong in the class descriptions. With inheritance, the goal is to place attributes in a superclass as high up in the hierarchy as possible. If the same attribute can be used to describe members of different subclasses, then the attribute belongs in the superclass. Sometimes attribute discovery helps you to revise and refine your class hierarchies.

Choosing Names

Choosing good names for things is an important part of the analysis process. In an object-oriented design, classes, objects, attributes, methods, and source code files are among the things that need names. The names you select should reflect the semantics of the item. Just as a good writer uses the English language carefully and effectively, a good programmer carefully and effectively chooses names.

[2.] Protected can be thought of as a special case of private, in this context.

Picking good names does matter—in analysis, in design, and ultimately in coding. They convey meaning. Using a good name can eliminate the need for explanatory comments, for example. But this means your names must really reflect what the class represents or what the method really does.

Consider the following suggestions for picking names.

Follow the Java conventions for naming described in Chapter 2, especially regarding capitalization.

Classes should be named with common noun phrases, such as `Color` or `Sensor`.

Objects (the Java variables that reference objects) should be named to indicate they are specific instances with identity, such as `theDoorSensor`, `foregroundColor`, or `listOfSensors`.

Methods that modify the state of an object, or cause it to do something, should be named with active verb phrases, such as `drawShape` or `setColor`.

Methods that return state information should indicate a result or use a form of the verb *to be*, such as `getColor` or `isClosed`.

As we noted earlier, the attributes discovered in the OOA phase are public attributes. At this point, we assume other objects are able to access these attributes. The attributes reflect the model, not the implementation design. In practice, you almost never make an attribute directly available to the outside world. Instead, you provide getter and setter methods to access the attributes.

Discover Object Operations

Methods are the services or operations a class defines to implement the behavior of member objects. Methods are how an object interacts with other objects in the system. Discovery of the methods used to implement object behavior is an important OOA activity.

Just as a class has both private and public attributes, it has private and public methods. During the analysis phase, method discovery concentrates on public methods, not on those private methods used internally by a class.

Several kinds of methods are commonly associated with a class. Given the importance of messages in OO systems, the methods that respond to messages may be the most obvious to examine first. They define how other objects interact with members of the class, and how they respond.

Other objects often need to set or get the attributes of an object. Setter and getter methods provide this access. During OOA, these are often implicitly assumed to be available for each public attribute.

Although the relationships among classes and objects are often described statically during analysis and design, in practice the specific relationships between instances of objects are established dynamically as the objects execute. Classes need to provide methods used to build these connections. UML sequence diagrams (see the UML Sequence Diagrams sidebar below) are useful for understanding dynamic relationships among objects.

Remember that during OOA, you are working at a high level of abstraction. Thus, special operations, such as the constructor or other methods involved with implementation details, should not be considered. These are details that can be filled in later in the design process.

You can use the above classifications to help you discover the methods that belong with a given class. Inheritance also makes a difference when describing methods. You want to move methods that describe shared behaviors as high as possible in the hierarchy. You need to identify methods that will be overridden by subclasses.

UML Sequence Diagrams

Once you have some candidate objects, hierarchies, and behaviors identified, it can be useful to understand how the objects can interact with each other. The UML provides sequence diagrams to help this process. A sequence diagram shows example object instances horizontally, lifetimes that stretch vertically, with time flowing from top to bottom.

Sequence diagrams are often used in association with use cases—each scenario depicted in a sequence diagram. They are helpful for understanding how objects interact with each other during particular cases. For example, on the next page is a sequence diagram for the borrow-a-book scenario given in the UML Use Cases sidebar on page 80.

The boxes at the top (aReader, aLibrarian, theLibrary, aBorrowing) represent specific instances of objects. Note that a specific name (for example, theLibrary) is used for the instance, not a class name (for example, LibrarySystem). The names typically use "a" or "the" to indicate some specific instance is being used.

The dashed vertical line below each is the time line. The open box around the timeline indicates the object is in an active operation. The horizontal lines with arrows represent messages to other objects. For example, aReader sends the borrow message to aLibrarian. When an object sends a message to itself, the arrow loops back on the object. Thus, theLibrary sends a message to itself to find the Reader, because theLibrary has the list of readers. The dashed lines to the left represent returns. These need be supplied only when they add clarity to the diagram.

The three diagram types we've used so far—object diagrams, use case diagrams, and sequence diagrams—are the most useful UML diagrams, and the ones you see most often. There are others, which are described in the sidebar More UML Diagrams on page 101.

Note that this example is based on a specific scenario and can be used to help with the final design—which operations will be needed, such as find-Reader, borrow, and so on.

In other cases, sequence diagrams are helpful to understand behavior of existing designs. We will use them to help clarify some of the Java Swing examples in Chapter 5.

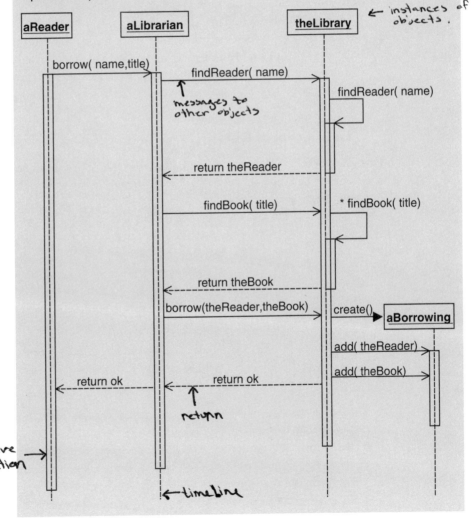

The Essence of Object-Oriented Design

In the strict technical sense, object-oriented design (OOD) takes the results of the object-oriented analysis phase and produces a detailed design suitable for implementation in an object-oriented programming language. In some methodologies, especially those applied to very large software projects, this is close to what happens. However, for smaller projects, the exact line between analysis and design, and even between design and implementation, is not always that clear.

One of the main differences between OOA and OOD is the level of detail required. One of the goals of OOD is to refine the OOA candidate objects into real classes, define the operations and attributes, decide on specific data structures, and account for the target system.

Some OO methodologies separate design and implementation while others blend the process somewhat, relying on quick feedback from the implementation to discover the inevitable design errors and provide quick feedback. While OOA is often done by specialized analysts, the designers and programmers are often the same people.

UML Level of Detail

One of the reasons why the UML is a good tool is that it can be used throughout the development cycle. The level of detail you can view with class diagrams provides a good example.

During the analysis phase, the focus is at a higher level. This means less detail with the UML class diagrams. Thus, an analysis view of the shapes we discussed in Chapter 3 can look like the following.

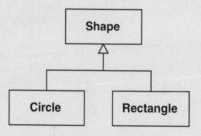

For the design phase, when the details become more critical, the UML allows complete specification of classes. The detail can be so complete, in fact, that some UML tools can generate code from the UML diagrams (and the other way around, too). So at the end of the design phase, the shape class diagrams can show a fine level of detail.

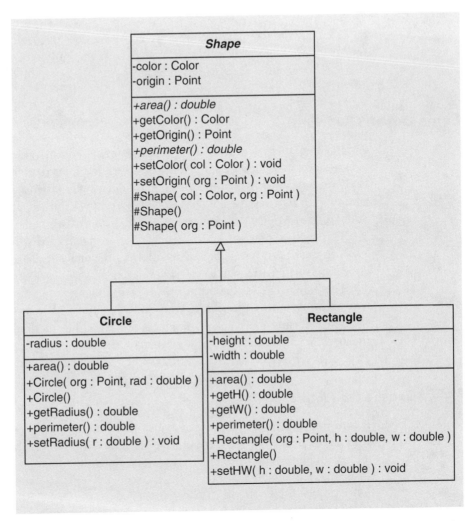

One of the current hot topics in object-oriented software development is the debate about just where to draw the lines between analysis, design, and implementation. In fact, there really is a different answer depending on the overall size of the project. The various development methodologies can be divided into two camps, more or less. For small to medium projects, those with 20 or fewer programmers and time frames of a year or so, there are several lightweight, or agile, methodologies. For larger projects with longer time frames, there are several heavyweight methodologies. Chapter 9 presents overviews of some of these methodologies. Which methodology to use is often a matter of the group or corporate personality.

Even though there are several methodologies to choose from, depending on the size and characteristics of the software being developed, there are still some fundamental design principles that apply to any methodology, and the next section will cover some of these design basics.

Some Design Guidelines

Good design doesn't come easily. It usually requires considerable experience to be able to develop a good design. And it is a certainty that two great designers are likely to come up with two equally good, but different, designs for the same problem. And no two designers would come up with the same list of the most important design principles, although there would certainly be significant overlap.

This section presents some basic design principles. Most of the principles apply to the design phase, but many apply to the analysis phase. Good design is good design, no matter the phase of development.

The only way to get good at design is to design many programs, preferably with someone more experienced, who can help you learn. It is not easy, and even the best and most experienced designers don't get their design completely right the first time. The following guidelines may not be complete, and they aren't the same ones someone else would pick, but they provide a good starting point.

Get the Big Picture

Before you can create a good design, it is important to understand what the software needs to do and what computing resources will be required. Much of this understanding comes from the early planning phase.

Understand the Problem

One of the most important tasks is to understand the problem. This often means frequent talks with the customer. The customer needs to supply the experts necessary for the designers and programmers to understand the problem domain. A good analysis of the problem helps to improve understanding.

Understand the Target Environment

Although the customer is best at providing the information necessary to understand the problem domain, it is the programmers who best understand the target computing environment. It is important to understand the limitations and features of the target computing environment. Sometimes, a software project even requires designing and specifying the hardware involved. The specific programming language used influences the ultimate design.

Think Objects

To get a good object-oriented design, it is critical that the developers think objects. If some members of the development team come from nonobject-oriented environments, they must learn to think objects.

Get Help

Even the best designers can't design great systems without help. The kind of help you need can include expert help to understand the problem domain or to understand the hardware or software required for the project.

Encapsulation

If there is a single most important reason why object-oriented development works, it is encapsulation. Objects by nature encapsulate attributes and behavior, and encapsulation makes software more robust, easier to debug, easier to modify, and easier to maintain over the long term.

Maximize Encapsulation

The more independent each class is, the better. Each class should not provide direct access to any of its internal attributes. It should provide the minimum number of methods for the outside world to carry out its responsibilities. The interface to the outside world should minimize the effects of any changes to the internal design of the class. In other words, maximize the encapsulation of all classes.

Minimize Coupling

As part of maximizing the encapsulation, you should minimize coupling between classes. Classes should depend only on the public interfaces to other classes and not rely on knowing anything about how other classes work. In cases in which classes must be coupled by mutual responsibilities, the effects of the coupling should be minimized for the rest of the world.

Separate the GUI

Separate the implementation of the GUI from the implementation of the application's model. For example, the application must not rely on being able to dynamically retrieve values from GUI controls. Instead, changes in GUI values should update the internal state of the model. You should be able to completely replace the GUI without affecting the rest of the code. The MVC design pattern described in the next chapter helps to separate the GUI.

Designing Classes

Once the need for a class has been identified, these guidelines will help to improve the design of an individual class or a group of related classes.

A Class Needs a Purpose

Every class needs responsibilities. If there are no clear responsibilities and operations required by a class, then it likely should be a part of a different class. If the class doesn't have a purpose, it should not exist.

Classes Versus Attributes

If a class has a well-defined set of attributes that have associated operations that aren't really a part of the class and that could potentially be used independently by other classes, then those attributes and operations are candidates for becoming an independent class. On the other hand, if there is a class with no operations, then its attributes may belong as simple attributes of another class. Because Java does not have the equivalent of a simple C structure, there may be classes in Java that really serve as structures. They may not require any operations but can be used as simple data structures.

Associations Versus Inheritance

Be careful when designing objects with inheritance or aggregation. Frequently, designs use inheritance when simple association or aggregation/composition is a better choice. Remember that all classes in an inheritance hierarchy must pass the *is-a test*. Don't confuse *is-a* with *is-a-member-of*. For example, a Circle *is-a* Shape, but it *is-a-member-of* a Drawing. Thus, a Shape should be a part of a Drawing, but not inherit from it.

A Class Can't Do Everything

Don't make classes too big. The responsibilities of a class should be just those that fit within that class and are not related to any other classes. If a class is trying to do things that really don't relate to its main responsibilities, then those behaviors likely belong in another class.

Inheritance

When designing an inheritance hierarchy, the following guidelines can help yield better designs.

Is-a Test

All classes in an inheritance hierarchy must pass the *is-a test*.

Is-a Is Not Always Enough

The *is-a test* is not always enough. Names can mislead. It is possible for a class to pass the *is-a test* by using just the names of classes, but still not be a good subclass. Besides sharing a general name relationship, a subclass must share common behavior with the superclass. For example, while a room is a rectangular volume, it may not be proper to have a room inherit from a graphical cube class. Remember the *is-a member test*, as well.

Move Attributes and Operations as High as Possible

You should move attributes and operations as high as possible in the hierarchy. If you find two subclasses defining similar attributes or operations that aren't in the superclass, they may be better used if they are moved up to the superclass.

Don't Move Attributes and Operations Too High

Subclasses must take advantage of their superclass. If most of the subclasses don't use operations defined in the superclass, or most are overriding the superclass definition, then the operation may not belong in the superclass.

Find Superclasses

If you have independent classes that have several similar attributes or operations, it is possible that those shared operations could be moved to a new, common superclass. But be sure the new class has something to do.

General Guidelines

The following general guidelines can also help you produce better designs.

The Name Matters

Choosing good names for classes, attributes, methods, and variables is critical for writing good software. The names should be meaningful and help explain the role of the item. Avoid abbreviations. A good descriptive name reduces the need for explanatory comments. It may take a bit more effort to type a long name, but the savings in reduced commenting and ease of reading will more than make up for a little one-time typing effort. Remember, however, that a name that takes most of the line hinders readability.

One Thing at a Time

The operations of a class should accomplish a single well-defined task. Don't combine a getter operation with one that changes the state of the object. Avoid side effects.

Don't Reinvent the Wheel

Avoid solving problems that have already been solved. Reuse existing code whenever possible. Use existing libraries and frameworks whenever possible. Learn about design patterns, and use them when appropriate.

You Won't Get It Right the First Time

No matter how good a designer you are, you will not get the design right the first time.[3] Recognize that there will be problems in the design, and fix them as soon as possible. Fixing problems ultimately results in a better software system that is easier to modify and maintain. Learn about and use refactoring.

Simplicity

Make your design as simple as possible. On one level, this means that you shouldn't try to adopt a fancy solution because you think it will work better. Sometimes a simple linear search works as well as a fancier, but harder-to-code, binary search. On a different level, simplicity doesn't mean using the first thing you think of. Finding a simple, elegant design can require significant effort, but will pay off in the long run.

Your Software Won't Go Away

A software system is often used far beyond its expected lifetime. All software systems should be designed as if they will be used forever. This means designing for the long term. A well-designed system is easier to maintain over time than one that takes shortcuts or makes assumptions about limited lifetime. Remember Y2K.

The Build and Release Phases

At some point in the development process, the planning process leads to the building process. This crossover point varies according to the size of the project and the methodology used. And of course, the ultimate goal of any software project is to release a running system to the customer.

Building the Software

For most programmers, writing code is what it is all about. Many would just as soon forget all the planning stuff and just write code. But experience shows that planning leads to a better product. A good design must be accompanied by good programming practices.

The build phase really consists of three major activities: writing code, testing the pieces of code being worked on (sometimes called unit testing), and then

---

[3.] This fact has led to the recent development of the agile OO methodologies, including XP. XP emphasizes that because a design will inevitably change, you should embrace change and use an adaptive development process. See Chapter 9.

debugging the code. This whole process can be greatly enhanced by choosing the right programming environment and by using the right tools.

Code Reviews and Ownership

The code review is a commonly followed programming practice that is valuable for any project. In a code review, a group of programmers go over a piece of code, line by line. Usually, the author of the code takes part in the review to help explain what the code does.

Code reviews can range from a small session with just two or three programmers to a large group with most of the programming team. Small, informal code reviews can take place almost any time during the development process whereas more-formal reviews, known as code inspections, are an important part of the final quality acceptance process.

Regular code reviews are useful during development because people tend to overlook mistakes in their own code. They are just too close. Code reviews also help to spread expert knowledge throughout a development team. Suggestions and ideas that evolve during review sessions often move the development process several steps forward.

During a code review, it is important to find ways to improve the code without being harsh or judgmental. Everyone involved in a code review can learn from the process, and the author should not be subjected to ridicule or unkind words.

Having regular code reviews helps promote joint ownership of all the code. While individual programmers may have primary responsibility for certain pieces of it, no one should "own" code. Most programs consist of code contributed by many programmers. Eventually, these programmers move on to other projects and have to leave their code behind for the team to work with. Individuals should take pride in contributing a quality piece of code to the team, and not get possessive of code they've written. Having team members who try to maintain personal ownership of their code can lead to serious problems. Group ownership of all code is important for the benefit of all.

Since you're reading this book, it is likely that you will be working in a Java-based environment. As Java has matured, it has become the language of choice for a variety of applications. The language is truly object-oriented and is a perfect target for an object-oriented design. The language is portable across the current major computing platforms, including usually troublesome GUI components. A variety of programming tools is available to enhance the productivity of Java programmers. We will survey some of those tools in Chapter 10.

One recent trend in programming practice has been the emphasis on testing and integration as you go. The tendency in the past was to independently develop fairly large pieces of the code with minimal testing and then to integrate the parts late in the development process. There is considerable practical evidence that it is much better to get small pieces of the code working, perform unit tests as a standard part of the process, and to frequently integrate the different parts of the project.

The practice of constantly testing and integrating makes the traditional release the culmination of many small steps rather than a huge, final visible step in the overall process. Just as the lines between planning and building can get fuzzy, so too can the line between building and releasing. As usual, this often depends on the magnitude of the project.

Releasing the Software

Traditionally, a finished piece of software is turned over to a testing department for final testing and ultimate release to the customer. This testing is called functional testing, and it usually takes a different team and tools than the unit testing used during ongoing development.

One of the most important tasks associated with the release of a system should be the learning phase. Every major project generates many lessons—we used the wrong computer configuration, we used the wrong development tools, this testing and integration stuff really works, we didn't have enough programmers, or the pizza from Pizza Joe's is really bad. It is important that these lessons be used to constantly improve the work environment for the programming team.

Even if constant testing and integration are employed, there is still something special about the real final release date. For one thing, it often means lots of overtime. Sometimes, overtime work is unavoidable. However, this practice should be the exception and not the rule. In spite of the advances in understanding the software development process (which is in part what this book is all about), programming is still very much an art. Programmers can't be productive working more than 40 hours a week for more than a few weeks in a row, and they really need time off to recharge their creative energies. Unfortunately, this fact is still not recognized by many managers of programmers.

Once a project is released to the customer, it usually enters a new phase of its lifetime, the maintenance phase. Often, this means turning the finished code over to a maintenance team while the prime developers move on to other projects (which might be the new and improved version of the current project). Traditionally, the maintenance team consists of the newest, least experienced programmers, a tradition not without some merit. For one thing, if the system has a good design and the programmers produced good code, the maintainers have a good example to learn from. But there should be close contact between the original development team and the maintenance team for as long as possible.

Eventually, however, most software takes on a life of its own, and it is likely that a significant portion of the original development team won't be around a few years down the line. It is this aspect of software reality that makes it all the more critical to use good development practices. It is here that object orientation can provide great paybacks.

More on the UML

We've introduced various UML features as we've needed them. So far, we've used class and object diagrams, use case diagrams, and sequence diagrams. These diagrams are not the only UML diagrams, although they are all we use in this book. The following sidebar, More UML Diagrams, gives brief descriptions of the other diagrams provided by the UML. These other diagrams are used to various degrees, depending on the size of the project and the design methodology.

More UML Diagrams

In addition to the class and object diagrams, use case diagrams, and sequence diagrams already discussed, the UML also provides the diagrams briefly described in this section.

Collaboration Diagram

The collaboration diagram and the sequence diagram we've already discussed are both used to show object interaction. While the sequence diagram shows dynamic interactions, the collaboration diagram shows the static relationships and messages between objects. The collaboration diagram consists of objects, classes the objects belong to, and links and messages with sequence numbers between these objects. Different developers tend to use one or the other of the collaboration and sequence interaction diagrams.

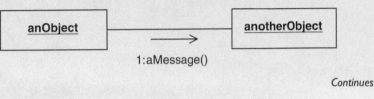

Continues

State Diagram

The state diagram is used when an object has well-defined states and serves as a complement to the class description. It shows all possible states that objects of the class can have, and which events cause the state to change or transition. The transition can also have an action connected to it that specifies what should be done on transitions.

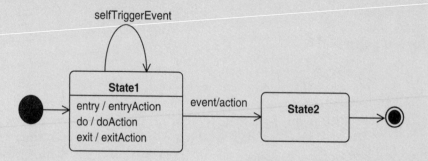

Activity Diagram

Activity diagrams are used to show the flow of activities in a procedure. They show actions and the results of activities. Activity diagrams focus on the high-level view of an entire process. They can also be used to help understand what is happening in a use case. Activity diagrams are useful for showing workflow and in describing the behavior of a system with parallel processing.

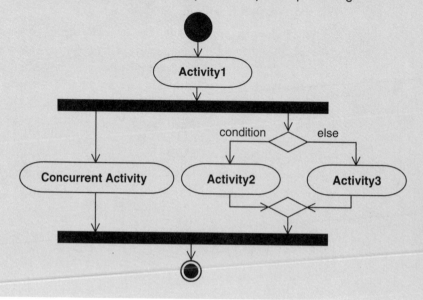

Deployment Diagram

A deployment diagram is used to represent physical relationships among the software and hardware components in a system. It can show how components and objects move around a networked system.

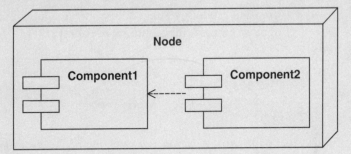

Package

The UML package symbol is used to group various UML items together into a single package. Various diagrams can be grouped, such as classes, use cases, and collaborations. Then the relationships among various packages can be shown.

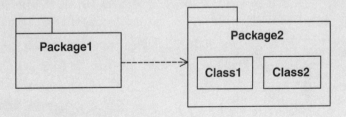

Chapter Summary

- All software can benefit from at least some design.
- There are several object-oriented development methodologies. All include some form of planning, building, and release phases.
- The initial design of a software project should be a collaboration between the customer and the developer.
- Object discovery and development of coherent object hierarchies are two of the major activities of OOA.
- CRC cards and use cases are useful tools for software analysis.

- OOD refines the results of the OOA. OOD takes the target environment into consideration, and turns the classes developed by the OOA into a design that includes most of the details of how the classes are implemented.

- The overall magnitude of a project has great influence on the kind of methodology used and the actual development practices used for the project.

- Continual coding, testing, debugging, and integration can enhance the development process and lead to more-robust and bug-free code.

Resources

OOAD

Object-Oriented Analysis and Design with Applications, Second Edition, Grady Booch, Addison-Wesley, 1994, ISBN 0-805-35340-2. Still the classic OOAD reference.

CRC

A Laboratory for Teaching Object-Oriented Thinking, Kent Beck and Ward Cunningham, 1989, c2.com/doc/oopsla89/paper.html.

The CRC Card Book, David Bellin and Susan Suchman Simone, Addison-Wesley, 1997, ISBN 0-201-89535-8.

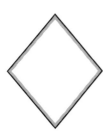

CHAPTER 5

Object-Oriented Graphical User Interfaces with Swing

Up to this chapter, we've concentrated on object-oriented concepts. By now, you should have a good grasp of the basic object-oriented concepts. You should be starting to think objects when it comes to programming in Java. This chapter will cover graphical user interfaces and the Java Swing library, with the same object-oriented perspective.

Graphical user interfaces, or GUIs, are how users interact with programs. Almost any program will have a GUI part to it. Programming with a GUI library, or toolkit as they are commonly called, can be a daunting task. There are dozens of methods to use, user actions to respond to, and conventions to follow when designing the user interface.

However, looking at a GUI toolkit with object-oriented eyes can make the whole process much easier. By getting a fundamental understanding of the relationships among the objects of a GUI toolkit (Java's Swing, in this case) and which goals the GUI objects need to accomplish, the whole task of building GUIs with clean and simple code becomes possible.

In this chapter, we will cover the essence of GUIs. First, we will discuss GUIs in general terms to get the big picture of what they need to do. Next, we will take a big-picture, object-oriented look at Swing. From this perspective, Swing becomes less complex and easier to understand. We will show how to handle user events with Swing in some simple examples. Finally, we will discuss the Model/View/Controller (MVC) design, which is commonly used to structure object-oriented GUI programs. We will develop a small MVC **framework** and build a simple Swing GUI-based MVC application.

> **framework**   A collection of classes designed to provide a set of services for a particular problem area. The designers of a framework should be experts in a problem domain and thus provide a higher-level design that makes it easier for an application using the framework to build an application for that problem domain.

Graphical User Interfaces

GUIs are how most applications interact with the user. The interfaces used by most applications have a lot in common. This is a good thing, because users have come to expect a certain look and feel from their applications. While the visual details may differ, most applications have windows that show views of the data being manipulated, and use menus, tool bars, and dialogs to provide interaction with the user. The user interacts with the program using a pointing device, usually a mouse, and the keyboard.

A Typical Application

The MovieCat application shown in Figure 5.1 is fairly representative of many Java applications. This application is actually the example we develop in Chapter 6, so we are using it here to demonstrate some common GUI attributes.

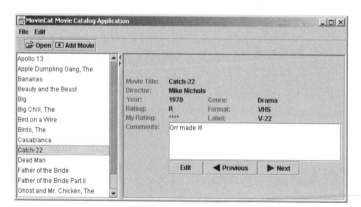

Figure 5.1   Typical GUI—MovieCat app

This application has an outer frame with a title bar at the top. In this case, the title bar has some special icons in addition to the title. The exact look of the title bar and surrounding frame depends on the host environment—Windows versus Motif, for example. This example shows the Java metal look and feel.

Inside the outer frame, there is a menu bar, a tool bar, and a split pane that shows a list on the left and information on the right. The menu bar may be the most standard component, and consists of pull-down menus. The tool bar usually has buttons and other components that are most often used in interacting with the program. The area below is the main window or canvas to the program, where the information is usually displayed. In this case, it is a split window with two views into the data. The left view shows all movies while the right shows the specific movie. In this example, both view panes have additional controls: a list and some command buttons. In other applications, these panes could be drawing canvases, and the interaction could be done using mouse motion and clicks. But many applications follow this general pattern: menu bar, tool bar, view area.

Dialog Boxes

Dialog boxes are another common way to implement user interfaces. They usually pop up in response to some command in the main application window. These can be file choosers, color choosers, or specialized tools. There are two kinds of dialogs: modal and modeless. In a modal dialog, interaction with any other window or dialog is locked out until the user interacts with the dialog. In a modeless dialog, the user can continue to interact with other parts of the application while the dialog remains displayed. Modal dialogs go away once the user enters a command. Modeless dialogs may remain visible and available even while the user interacts with the main program window.

Most GUI toolkits provide a standard set of control components. The exact look and feel of these can vary, but the most common controls include

- **Command buttons** Click to perform command
- **Text labels** Label the controls, give information
- **Text input** Read text input from the user
- **List selection boxes** Scrolling list with item selection
- **Combo boxes** Drop-down lists
- **Radio buttons** Select only one of a group
- **Check boxes** Select an item
- **Spinners and sliders for value entry** Enter a value

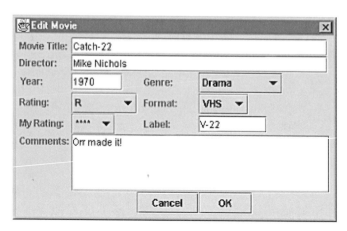

Figure 5.2   Dialog box—MovieCat edit dialog

- **Progress bars** Show progress in a process
- **Decorations** Group controls, make interface look good

Toolkits that support these components usually provide the capability to lay out and group controls within a dialog or other display frame. The dialog in Figure 5.2 is from the MovieCat application. It uses label, text input, combo box, and button controls.

Events

When a user clicks on a button, selects an item from a list, or performs some other command, the program must respond appropriately. The structure of the code for user command processing in GUI applications is based on events. Interaction with an application from the user's viewpoint consists of a series of mouse movements and clicks as well as text and command input through the keyboard. From the programmer's viewpoint, each of these is an event. The important thing about an event is that it can occur at any time, and the program cannot simply stop and wait for the event to happen.

Interaction with an application by the user can generate several kinds of events. Consider mouse events. If the mouse is in the drawing area, each movement generates a mouse movement event. If the user clicks a mouse button, a mouse button event is generated. A keystroke from the keyboard generates a keyboard event.

If the mouse pointer is in a dialog, or over a menu or command button, then movement events are not generated. Instead, button clicks generate command events corresponding to the button or other control.

In a GUI environment, windows are usually not displayed alone. Often, other applications are running, each with its own window(s). The host windowing system typically displays windows with various decorations that let the user manipulate the windows. Sometimes, these manipulations generate events that require a response from the application code. For example, the user can use the mouse to change the size of a window, causing a resize event. When multiple windows are displayed, some can be completely or partially covered by other windows. If the user moves a window so that a different part of the window is displayed, then an expose event is generated, which requires the program to redraw part of the canvas area.

All these events require a response from the application—to carry out the command, to draw something in the canvas area, or to redraw the canvas after a resize or expose event. Some events, however, are handled by the system, not the application. This includes drawing menus and handling dialogs. For example, when a dialog is displayed, the system tracks mouse movements within the dialog and handles redrawing the dialog for expose events. In general, the application is responsible for resize and expose events only for the canvas area.

All these events are asynchronous, and the application must be able to respond immediately to any of them. The most common way to handle events is with what is called an event loop. Somewhere, there is an event loop that detects when the user presses a key, moves the mouse, or clicks a mouse button. This detection is usually done at the system level, not by the program. As part of this process, the GUI toolkit distinguishes among kinds of events—a mouse click on a control or a mouse motion over a drawing area, for example. These events are then passed on to the program for appropriate action. The exact method of handling the event loop and passing the events on to the application code varies from toolkit to toolkit. In Swing, the program doesn't need any direct access to the event loop. In Java, the event loop is really in a separate thread of execution, which is started and controlled by the runtime system. A Java program handles events using what are known as listeners and callbacks. The section "Handling Swing Command Events" discusses events and Swing in more detail.

A Brief Introduction to Swing

The original GUI toolkit provided by Java was called the Abstract Windowing Toolkit (AWT). While there are many existing Java AWT applications, the Swing toolkit has superseded the AWT. Swing is generally more complete and easier to use. It is almost too complete. One of the problems of providing *the* GUI toolkit for a programming language is that it must provide everything, even if most of the features are used by only a small fraction of programmers. The myriad of details and options provided by Swing make it seem more complicated than it is. We will try to focus on the essentials. With the proper perspective, it is possible to get a handle on Swing in just a few pages.

So, let's use our general GUI model to look at how Swing can build applications that fit that model. For the main application, Swing needs to provide the outer window that includes a title bar and special buttons, a menu bar, a tool bar, and a place to hold the main view or views, often a drawing canvas.

 Although Swing has superseded the AWT, it is based upon and uses the AWT. To distinguish similarly named classes in the AWT, Swing has adopted its own naming conventions. For the most part, Swing classes start with a capital J, such as JFrame, JButton, and JSplitPane. However, not all Swing classes start with a J (for example, Box or Timer). It is possible to mix AWT and Swing, but that really is not a good idea.

Swing provides the JFrame as the main class to support "standard" applications. A JFrame is a top-level container that exists mainly to provide a place where other Swing components can paint themselves. (Two other top-level components are also commonly used: JDialog for dialogs, and JApplet for applets.) A JFrame is displayed with the title frame. It has a single component called a JRootPane, which has a menu bar (a JMenuBar), a content pane (typically set to hold something like a general purpose JPanel by the user program), and some other things that don't matter for typical situations. The fact that the JFrame uses a JRootPane isn't usually relevant for many practical situations.

It is easy to create a simple Swing application with JFrame. The sequence of code that creates the practical object structure shown in Figure 5.3 is given in Listing 5.1.

Listing 5.1 Code excerpt
Code to set up JFrame

```
...
// Set up a JFrame for practical use

    JFrame theFrame = new JFrame("Application Name");

    JMenuBar theMenuBar = new JMenuBar();
    // code to define items on Menu, event handlers, etc.
        ...
    theFrame.setJMenuBar(theMenuBar);

    JPanel thePanel = new JPanel();
    // code to define what is on panel, layout manager,
    // define user interface, command control, etc.
    // (non-trivial)
```

```
    . . .
theFrame.setContentPane(thePanel);
theFrame.pack();
theFrame.setVisible(true);
    . . .
```

This code fragment would be found in the definition of some object, and would usually be defined in the top-level class that has the `main` method and that defines the application. It is likely that this code would be found in the order shown here, but would have some additional code in between the steps that uses the parts of the interface. But the steps shown are really at the heart of the matter.

1. Create `JFrame`.

2. Create and define `JMenuBar`.

3. Add `JMenuBar` to `JFrame`.

4. Create `JPanel`.

5. Add whatever you need to the `JPanel`.

6. Add the `JPanel` to the `JFrame` Content Pane.

7. Pack and show the `JFrame`.

In this example, note that the content pane has been set to a `JPanel`, which can be used as a general purpose window to hold buttons, drawing canvases, split

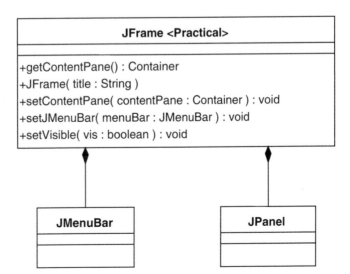

Figure 5.3　The practical structure of JFrame

panes—anything the program needs to display. Thus, to implement a tool bar, the `JPanel` can use a `Border` layout to hold a `JToolBar` at its top and yet another drawing pane or panel in its center.

The key to this whole idea is that the `JPanel` can serve to build practically any interface needed. Swing has several kinds of panes (for example, `JPanel`, `JSplitPane`, `JTabbedPane`) that can serve to hold other Swing components. Associated with each pane is a layout manager. Layout managers control how other Swing components are placed in a pane. Some layout managers are relatively simple to understand; others get quite complicated. But the difficulty is in the details of using a specific layout manager. The concept that each pane has a layout manager is simple.

Once you have this basic object structure down, it is "simply" a matter of selecting which Swing components you need to implement your interface. The basic components, such as `JButton`, are easy to use. Others, such as `JTable`, are harder. And if you need to draw something on a drawing canvas, you will need to use the Java `Graphics` object. How to use `Graphics` is beyond the scope of this book, other than to note that your program is responsible for responding to paint events caused by the drawing pane being resized or exposed.

Defining the GUI and laying out the Swing components is not that difficult. But it is only half the story. For each component with which the user can interact, your program must provide code that makes an appropriate response. These are the events, and the next section, "Handling Swing Command Events," shows how to handle events generated by Swing components.

Remember, one of the hardest parts about using Swing is figuring out which features of a component are most useful and commonly needed, and which are included to give Swing the capability of defining interfaces for every possible situation. Sun's documentation for Java (and the rest of the core Java classes) is consistent and complete. It is really much better than average, but it covers *everything*. The Sun Swing tutorial is more useful. It has many good examples that tend to demonstrate the most useful features of the components. Once you get an idea of what you want to do with a component, the Swing documentation is about the best there is.

Handling Swing Command Events

The components of Java Swing generate events in response to actions. For example, when a user clicks on a button or selects a menu item, Swing generates an `ActionEvent`. The program handles these events by registering an appropriate Listener for each event. Swing generates several kinds of events—`ActionEvents`, `ChangeEvents`, `ItemEvents`, and others. Each kind of event is appropriate for some kind of action in a component. These can be caused by a user click, a list changing its values, a timer going off, and on different things, depending on the nature of the component. All these events can be handled in the same general way.

The general steps are

1. Create a component (such as a `JButton`).

2. Add it to an appropriate place in the GUI (such as a `JPanel`).

3. Register a Listener that gets notified when the component generates an event (such as an `ActionListener` for a user click).

4. Define the callback method that is invoked when the Listener is notified (such as `actionPerformed` for an `ActionListener`).

As with most programming tasks, these steps can be accomplished in many ways. However, two main ways have evolved as Java idioms. One is to define a single listener and determine which component generated the event, using a series of `if` statements. The second method is to use inner classes to respond to events for each Swing component individually. And there are really two variants of using inner classes. The first is to use anonymous inner classes; the other is to define named inner classes.

We will define a simple Java application that displays two buttons (Figure 5.4), and responds to the user click by displaying an appropriate dialog (Figure 5.5). However, this example can be extended to more-complicated user interfaces. We will implement this application three different ways: the single listener approach, the anonymous inner class approach, and the named inner class approach.

Figure 5.4 Simple Swing application

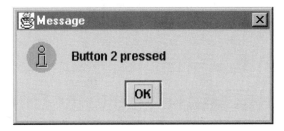

Figure 5.5 Dialog window—response to event

First, we will implement this program using the single listener approach. We define a single class called `Simple1`, which contains all the code needed for this example. All user events (button clicks in this example, but they could be menu picks or any other event) are handled by the callback `actionPerformed` in the single listener class `SimpleListener`. Here's the code.

Listing 5.2 `Simple1.java`
Single listener

```java
/*
 * Simple1.java - an example of handling events.
 *     For this example, we implement a single ActionListener
 *     which is then used to catch all events. A series of ifs
 *     are used to determine which object caused the event.
 */
import java.awt.*;              abstract windowing tool kit.
import java.awt.event.*;
import javax.swing.*;

public class Simple1
{
    private static JFrame frame;     // static so main can use it
    private static JPanel myPanel;   // panel for the contentPane
    private JButton button1;         // Define out here to make
    private JButton button2;         // visible to ActionListener

    public Simple1()                 // Construct, build GUI
    {
        // Create a panel
        myPanel = new JPanel();
        // Create the buttons.
        button1 = new JButton("Button 1");   // Create buttons
        button2 = new JButton("Button 2");

        SimpleListener ourListener = new SimpleListener();
        // Set action listener for both buttons to share
        button1.addActionListener(ourListener);  ← implement argument to transform into anonymous
        button2.addActionListener(ourListener);     inner class listener

        myPanel.add(button1);        // Adds to current JFrame
        myPanel.add(button2);
    }

    private class SimpleListener implements ActionListener
    {
    /*
     * We will use a simple inner class to implement an
     * ActionListener to use to get the button events. We
     * could have instead used the Simple1 class itself to
     * implement ActionListener instead, but this way is
     * more consistent with the other examples.
     */
```

```java
public void actionPerformed(ActionEvent e)
{
    // We will use getActionCommand to get the button
    // name, but we could use getSource() instead and
    // the if tests would then be like:
    // if (e.getSource() == button1)  etc.

    String buttonName = e.getActionCommand();
    if (buttonName.equals("Button 1"))
        JOptionPane.showMessageDialog(frame,
                                "Button 1 pressed");
    else if (buttonName.equals("Button 2"))
        JOptionPane.showMessageDialog(frame,
                                "Button 2 pressed");
    else
        JOptionPane.showMessageDialog(frame,
                                "Unknown event");
    }
}

public static void main(String s[])
{
    Simple1 gui = new Simple1(); // Create Simple1 component

    frame = new JFrame("Simple1");  // JFrame for the panel
    // Standard idiom to catch close event
    frame.addWindowListener(new WindowAdapter() {
        public void windowClosing(WindowEvent e)
        {System.exit(0);} });

    frame.getContentPane().add(myPanel);
    frame.pack();                   // Ready to go
    frame.setVisible(true);
    }
}
```

catches the close event (The button to close the window ⊗)

Let's go over the way this code works. Our simple application consists of a Swing JFrame defined in main. We add a single JPanel to the frame. The panel contains the two JButtons. The variable references to these components—frame, button1, and button2—are defined at the top level of Simple1.[1]

The main method starts by creating the Simple1 object, which then creates the user GUI by defining the JPanel and adding the JButtons. After each button is created, JButton.addActionListener is called for each button instance to

---

[1] Note how this code follows the setup code for JFrames we outlined in Listing 5.1. It creates and adds JButtons to a JPanel (and implements the listeners for the buttons). It then creates a JFrame and sets the content pane to the JPanel just created. The order of creation is not important. This app has no menus, so JMenuBar was not used.

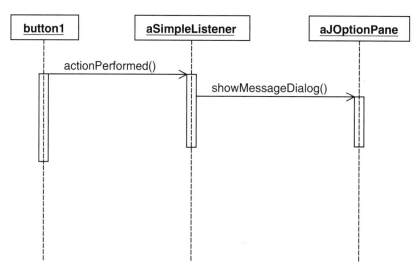

Figure 5.6 Sequence diagram for simple listener

add the single instance of `SimpleListener`. Finally, each button is added to the panel. After the GUI has been created, `main` adds the panel to the frame and displays the results. When a user clicks one of the buttons, the `actionPerformed` callback is called. Inside `if` statements are used to determine which button was pressed, and an appropriate modal dialog box is displayed. The UML sequence diagram in Figure 5.6 shows the sequence of operations when a user clicks on `Button1`.

This simple single listener approach has some problems. Because determining the identity of each event requires either a string comparison (`e.getActionCommand().equals("name")`) or, alternatively, an object comparison (`e.getSource() == button1`), you can't use a `switch`, but must add an `if` for each event. This can result in a long string of `if` statements, and the code can get unwieldy and difficult to read and maintain. For handling a few events, however, this approach is simple.

One solution to this problem is to use anonymous inner classes. Instead of implementing a single named inner class for the listener, you simply use an anonymous class as the argument to `addActionListener`. This places the definition of the event handler with the definition of the control component.

Listing 5.3 `Simple2.java`
Anonymous inner classes for listeners

```
/*
 * Simple2.java - an example of handling events.
 *    For this example, we will use anonymous inner classes to
```

```
 *      implement an ActionListener for each button. This approach
 *      can avoid long switch-type if statements from the approach
 *      used in the Simple1 example.
 */
import java.awt.*;
import java.awt.event.*;
import javax.swing.*;

public class Simple2
{
    private static JFrame frame;       // static so main can use it
    private static JPanel myPanel;      // panel for the contentPane
    private JButton button1;            // Define out here to make
    private JButton button2;            // visible to ActionListeners

    public Simple2()                    // Construct, build GUI
    {
        // Create a panel
        myPanel = new JPanel();
        // Create the buttons
        button1 = new JButton("Button 1");
        button2 = new JButton("Button 2");

        // For each component that needs a listener, define an
        // anonymous inner class to implement ActionListener.
        button1.addActionListener(
            new ActionListener()
            {
                public void actionPerformed(ActionEvent e)
                {
                    JOptionPane.showMessageDialog(frame,
                                    "Button 1 pressed");
                }
            }
        );

        button2.addActionListener(
            new ActionListener()
            {
                public void actionPerformed(ActionEvent e)
                {
                    JOptionPane.showMessageDialog(frame,
                                    "Button 2 pressed");
                }
            }
        );

        myPanel.add(button1);           // Adds to current JFrame
        myPanel.add(button2);
    }
```

(handwritten margin note, right): same as ~~anonymous~~ named.

(handwritten margin note, left): anonymous listener class

```
public static void main(String s[])
{
    Simple2 gui = new Simple2(); // Create Simple2 component

    frame = new JFrame("Simple2");   // JFrame for the panel
    // Standard idiom to catch close event
    frame.addWindowListener(new WindowAdapter() {
        public void windowClosing(WindowEvent e)
        {System.exit(0);} });
    frame.getContentPane().add(myPanel);
    frame.pack();                      // Ready to go
    frame.setVisible(true);
}
}
```

Using anonymous inner classes has some problems. First, the definitions of the classes, and thus the code that handles the events, can be scattered all over the application source code, depending on where the component was defined. Components tend to be defined deep within the nested code, which can make the indentation and appearance of the code a bit awkward. If the required response to the event is complicated, the code for the anonymous class can get long, making it difficult to follow the overall flow and intent of the code that defines the components in the first place. Finally, there are often synonyms for commands defined for a particular user interface. For example, it is common to provide both a tool bar button and a menu item for the same command.

The sequence diagram in Figure 5.7 shows the event sequence with an anonymous listener. The only difference from the previous case is that the anonymous listener is called instead.

Using named inner classes provides a good alternative to anonymous inner classes. All the handlers can be defined in one place. They can have meaningful names. A single handler can be reused by different controls. And the code in

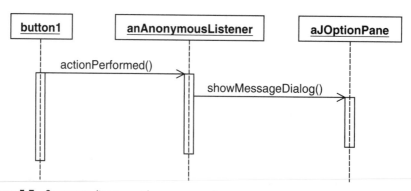

Figure 5.7   Sequence diagram with anonymous listener

which the GUI is defined and laid out is <u>not interrupted by long anonymous class definitions.</u> So here is the simple application again, this time written using named inner classes.

Listing 5.4 `Simple3.java`
Named inner classes for listeners

```
/*
 * Simple3.java - an example of handling events.
 *     For this example, we will use inner member classes to
 *     implement an ActionListener for each button. This approach
 *     can avoid some of the code clutter that anonymous classes
 *     can sometimes cause. It also concentrates the action code
 *     all in one place, and allows synonyms.
 */
import java.awt.*;
import java.awt.event.*;
import javax.swing.*;

public class Simple3 extends JPanel
{
    private static JFrame frame;      // static so main can use it
    private static JPanel myPanel;    // a panel for contentPane
    private JButton button1;          // Define out here to make
    private JButton button2;          // visible to ActionListener

    // Define handlers for each event needed (button1, button2)
    private class Button1Handler implements ActionListener
    {
        public void actionPerformed(ActionEvent e)
        {
            JOptionPane.showMessageDialog(frame,
                                "Button 1 pressed");
        }
    }

    private class Button2Handler implements ActionListener
    {
        public void actionPerformed(ActionEvent e)
        {
            JOptionPane.showMessageDialog(frame,
                                "Button 2 pressed");
        }
    }

    public Simple3()                  // Construct, build GUI
    {
        // Create a panel
        myPanel = new JPanel();
        // Create the buttons
```

[handwritten annotations:]

Named inner classes (outside of constructor)

Same as anonymous

```
        button1 = new JButton("Button 1");
        button2 = new JButton("Button 2");

        // For each component add its ActionListener class
        button1.addActionListener(new Button1Handler());
        button2.addActionListener(new Button2Handler());

        myPanel.add(button1);            // Adds to current JFrame
        myPanel.add(button2);
    }

    public static void main(String s[])
    {
        Simple3 gui = new Simple3();   // Simple3 component

        frame = new JFrame("Simple3");   // JFrame for the panel
        // Standard idiom to catch close event
        frame.addWindowListener(new WindowAdapter() {
            public void windowClosing(WindowEvent e)
            {System.exit(0);} });

        frame.getContentPane().add(myPanel);
        frame.pack();                    // Ready to go
        frame.setVisible(true);
    }
}
```

The sequence diagram in Figure 5.8 now shows that the named listener Button1Handler is used when a user clicks Button1.

In this example, we are responding to the action event generated when the user clicks on one of the buttons. The way these events are handled applies

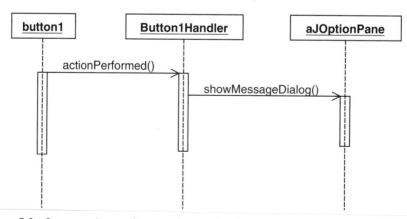

Figure 5.8 Sequence diagram for named inner class listener

equally well to any Swing event: a menu pick, a list selection, and others. Some of these are not `ActionEvents` with `ActionListeners`, but include `Item Events` with `ItemListeners`, `ChangeEvents` with `ChangeListeners`, and so on. The general approaches shown in these examples work for all.

A Bunch of Options

On the whole, the basic features of Swing components are not overly complex. But, you won't always want just the basic features. Most components have many options. Take a `JButton`, for example. The simplest `JButton` has a text label and takes the default look and feel of the GUI. But there are options here. You can make it the default button. You can change the borders; you can change the color; you can add an icon to the button; you can enable or disable the button; you can add a tool tip; you can change its size; you can change the font; and so on. This pattern repeats, with some overlap, for almost every Swing control.

Aside from making it harder to fully understand each component, each of these options is implemented by a specific method call to the Swing component's class. This means that any code that takes full advantage of a component's options can get long. If we set only the options we mentioned for a `JButton`, it would take at least nine lines of code to define the `JButton` object. Repeat this for each control, and the code for defining a GUI can get long and ugly.

There are some solutions to this problem. The definitions for components can be isolated somewhat from the logic. Rather than build a whole interface in the middle of code that has some higher-level meaning, you can place the definitions in some method, such as `createGUI`, then call it from the higher-level code. That still means there are long sequences of repetitive code somewhere.

If you are setting the same component attributes over and over again, you can implement small helper methods that take the attributes as parameters and set them all. Then the code for defining the component would be a single line call to the helper method, rather than many lines.

Even so, defining components of the user interface can be complex and require several lines of code. Even though this can make the code longer and more complex, it does keep it in one place and portable across the systems Java supports.

An alternative is to use software that lets you define GUIs interactively, and then generates all the code automatically. Many Java tools let you do this, in fact. But even that approach has some serious problems, which we will discuss in Chapter 10.

MVC: Model/View/Controller

A commonly used design architecture for GUI applications is called Model/View/ Controller, or MVC. MVC was originally developed for the Smalltalk language, but has found widespread use in designing GUI applications in any object-oriented language. When a GUI application works with an object, it can usually be represented with a model. The model is a complete representation of the object being used by the application, such as a word processing document, a graphical image, a spreadsheet, or a database. The key concept is that the model is self-contained, and its representation is independent of the rest of the program. The model then provides the manipulation methods required for the outside world to use the object the model implements.

An application will then consist of any number of views of the model. There might be an edit view and a print view of a document, or several views of different pages of the document, for example. Each view tracks what it needs to know about its particular perspective of the model, but each view interacts with the same model. Finally, each view has associated with it a user interface implemented as a controller object. This might include command buttons, handlers for the mouse, and so on. When a controller gets a command from the user, it uses appropriate information from the associated view to modify the model. Whenever the model changes, it notifies all views, which then update themselves.

This is an elegant architecture, and is shown in Figure 5.9. Note that there can be as many views as needed. Logically, each view has an associated controller. Typically, there is a single Model class and several View classes with their associated Controller classes. The controller responds to actions from the user, uses whatever information it needs from the associated view, and sends a message to the model to modify itself. When a model changes (and this can be caused by events other than user commands, such as asynchronous events generated by a shared database being modified), it notifies all views, which then update the display.

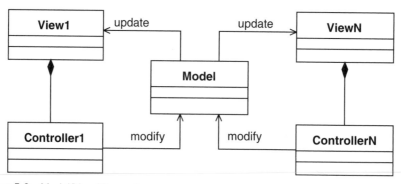

Figure 5.9   Model/View/Controller

In practice, especially in Java, the view and controllers are often combined. This is usually because of the design of the GUI toolkit, such as Swing. Thus a Java MVC program is really a model and associated view/controllers made up of specifications of Swing components and their listeners.

No matter what the actual implementation of the view/controller is, the main idea of MVC is to separate the model from its display and the user interface. There are many advantages to this approach. The model can be designed completely independently of how it will be displayed. With such an independent model, there is great flexibility in how views can be designed to display the model. New views can be created and the whole user interface changed, without affecting the model.

MVC with Java

In the original Smalltalk MVC concept, each of the classes—model, view, controller—was an integral part of the Smalltalk implementation. Other programming languages, and specifically Java, do not provide integrated MVC classes. However, the concept of MVC is still valid and provides a good way to implement GUI programs.

As we discussed earlier, a graphical interface in Swing is usually built by using several Swing components and defining the appropriate listeners for each component. Thus, it is often easier to define a combined view/controller class when working with Swing. There can be a pure, Swing-free implementation of the model class. Views then consist of implementations of the different views of the model using Swing components, and the controllers are implemented using the required Swing listener interface. Thus, the controllers are really the required listeners for the various Swing components used in the views. The controllers are included with the associated view code. It is possible to use a controller class that further separates the controllers from the views, and we will develop such a controller class in the next section.

While MVC is most commonly used for full GUIs, it can be applied to other designs. At their lowest level, many of the individual Swing components are implemented using MVC. This provides a great deal of programming flexibility for using Swing components; the programmer can provide a new look and feel, for example, by replacing the standard Swing views. However, this flexibility is not required or used by the vast majority of Swing applications. Nor should the low-level MVC implementation of Swing be confused with an MVC implementation of an application that uses Swing. Swing provides nothing that makes it easier to implement an MVC application, even though its own low-level implementation uses MVC.

CRC Cards for MVC

The MVC design lends itself as a good example for CRC cards. Note in this example how the view and controller cards overlap, showing their close collaboration. The model is placed under the view and controller, showing their supervision. These cards show only the minimum responsibilities to help clarify the model. Note that when using any tool, such as CRC cards or the UML, the tool should be used to make it easier to understand the design, which often means showing only the details that are relevant.

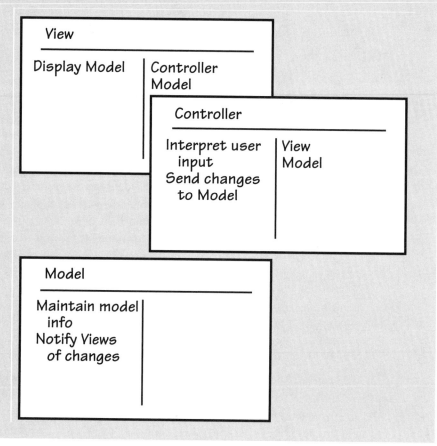

In the next section, we will present the design of a small Swing-based MVC framework. This framework combines many of the aspects of Swing that we've covered. It defines a top-level application class that uses a JFrame to build the foundation of the application, which includes a menu bar, tool bar, and a JPanel to construct views. It implements model, view, and controller classes that can be used to construct a full MVC application. And it provides methods that make it easier to use and define controls within the views.

A Small Swing MVC GUI Framework

Now we are ready to put everything from this chapter together in a small Swing-based MVC framework. Even though it is small, this framework is suitable as a starting point for even large Java MVC applications.

Recall the definition of a framework at the beginning of this chapter. One of the goals of a framework, even a simple one, is to make it easier for a programmer to develop an application that requires the services of the framework. In this case, the goal of our simple framework is to make it easier to develop a Swing GUI application that uses the MVC design.

We begin by considering what services the framework must include to build a "standard" GUI application as described in Graphical User Interfaces on page 106. Such a standard app included an outer frame that contained a title bar, a menu bar, a tool bar, and a drawing area that could be used for views. The existing Swing `JFrame` class almost meets these requirements, so let's define a top-level application class based on `JFrame`. Most frameworks have a name; we'll call our framework the `Wmvc` framework for the Wampler MVC framework. All classes in this framework will start with `Wmvc`. This kind of naming convention is commonly used with frameworks and libraries.

WmvcApp Class

The top-level application class is called `WmvcApp`. A user application derives its top-level application class from `WmvcApp`. The basic structure of the `Wmvc` framework is shown in Figure 5.10. The class diagram for `WmvcApp` shows the most important services it provides. `WmvcApp` allows the user app class to build an application easily. The app defines the elements of the menu bar, tool bar, and drawing panes. The user app defines menus by creating `JMenu` objects and adding items to those menus, using the `Wmvc` menu controllers, and finally adding the menus to the menu bar with `WmvcApp.addMenu`. Tool bar items are defined and added to the tool bar, using `Wmvc` controller objects. `WmvcApp` provides a `JPanel` for the app to define whatever it needs for views.

`WmvcApp` provides the basic functionality needed to build simple, "standard" applications. It simplifies the job of the programmer. The details of defining a tool bar and a `JPanel` are hidden.

`WmvcApp` has another job—to support the MVC model. Although the structure of an MVC program is clear, the MVC structure must hang off of something. In the `Wmvc` framework, the `WmvcApp` class provides the foundation on which to build the MVC structure. Because all the views must access the model,

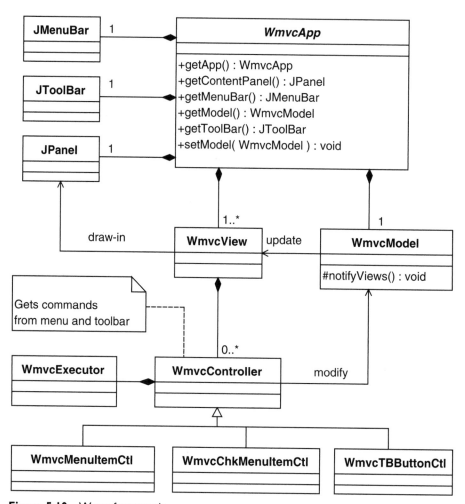

Figure 5.10   Wmvc framework

WmvcApp provides the services setModel() and getModel() to give them access to the model. It provides a class method to get access to the WmvcApp object itself. WmvcApp does not provide direct support for views. Instead, views are created in the derived WmvcApp class directly. The Thermometer example later will help make this clear.

The details of creating the tool bar and drawing canvas are found in the WmvcApp.java code. In addition to the services already discussed, WmvcApp provides a standard way to handle closing an application. When the user presses the close button on the title bar, the method appClosing is called, and exits by default. The user app can control closing behavior by overriding appClosing.

There is a method to cause the app window to be displayed after it has been defined (showApp()). Since the programmer must derive an app class from Wmv-cApp, it has been declared abstract.

 We've introduced the note symbol in Figure 5.10. It is used to show notes that help explain the diagram. Note how UML diagrams don't have to give all the details. Sometimes they show only the overall relationships among classes with no details of the attributes or operations. Other times, they show only relevant operations. Finally, they can show the full details, including all attributes and operations.

Listing 5.5 WmvcApp.java
Top level base class for Wmvc Application

```java
/*
 * WmvcApp - The main Application Class for Wmvc
 * Copyright (c) 2001, Bruce E. Wampler
 */

import java.awt.*;
import java.awt.event.*;
import javax.swing.*;

public abstract class WmvcApp
{
    private static WmvcApp theApp = null;        // Singleton

    // Model

    protected static WmvcModel theModel = null;

    // GUI interface parts
    private static JFrame theFrame = null;   // The topmost frame
    private static JMenuBar theMenuBar = null;
    private static JToolBar theToolBar = null;
    private static JPanel theContentPanel = null;

    public static JFrame getFrame() { return theFrame; }
    public static JMenuBar getMenuBar() { return theMenuBar; }
    public static JToolBar getToolBar() { return theToolBar; }
    public static JPanel getContentPanel()
        { return theContentPanel; }
    public static WmvcModel getModel() { return theModel; }
    public static void setModel(WmvcModel m) { theModel = m; }

    public static WmvcApp getApp()
    {
        return theApp;
    }
}
```

```java
// Only one constructor. Could have alternates:
//        public WmvcApp()
//        public WmvcApp(String aName)
public WmvcApp(String aName, boolean cMenu, boolean cTool)
{
    if (theApp != null)
        return;
    theApp = this;
    initializeWmvc(aName,cMenu,cTool);
}

private void initializeWmvc(String aName, boolean cMenu,
                            boolean cTool)
{
    // Step 1 - set up the main JFrame
    theFrame = new JFrame(aName);

    // handle closing cleanly
    theFrame.setDefaultCloseOperation(
                            JFrame.DO_NOTHING_ON_CLOSE);
    theFrame.addWindowListener(new WindowAdapter()
      {
          public void windowClosing(WindowEvent e)
          {
              if (theApp.appClosing())
                  System.exit(0);
          }
      });

    // Step 2 - the menu bar
    if (cMenu)              // add a MenuBar?
    {
        theMenuBar = new JMenuBar();
        theFrame.setJMenuBar(theMenuBar);
    }

    // Step 3 - the JPanel (may or may not have a tool bar)

    theContentPanel = new JPanel();              // A JPanel
    theContentPanel.setLayout(new BorderLayout());
    theContentPanel.setPreferredSize(
            new Dimension(400, 300));

    if (cTool)              // add a Tool Bar?
    {
        theToolBar = new JToolBar();
        theContentPanel.add(theToolBar,BorderLayout.NORTH);
    }

    // Note: we could add a status bar (another ToolBar) at
    // the bottom by using BorderLayout.SOUTH
```

```
            theFrame.setContentPane(theContentPanel);
    }

    public static void addMainPane(JComponent pane)
    {
        // This will add the "user" pane to the content pane
        theContentPanel.add(pane,BorderLayout.CENTER);
    }

    public static void addMenu(JMenu menu)
    {
        if (theMenuBar == null)
            return;
        theMenuBar.add(menu);
    }

    public static void showApp()
    {
        theFrame.pack();
        theFrame.setVisible(true);
    }

    public boolean appClosing()
    {
        return true;   // Default behavior - close automatically
    }
}
```

WmvcView, WmvcController, WmvcModel Classes

The MVC classes themselves are not too complicated. One of the most important responsibilities of these classes is to allow the model to update all the views, whenever it changes. This is implemented by using the Java `Observable`/ `Observer` classes.[2] `WmvcView` implements the `update` method of the `Observer` Java interface as `updateView`. Each view then registers itself with the model, using the `WmvcModel` method `addView`, which uses the `addObserver` method defined by the Java `Observable` class that `WmvcModel` extends. When the model changes, the model object uses `notifyViews` to send a message to all views that have registered with the model. The `Observable` class initiates calling the `updateView` method of each registered view. The `Wmvc` classes insulate the application programmer from the details of using the `Observable` class and provide a naming convention more meaningful to use with the MVC design.

---

[2] The Observable class implements the Observer design pattern. Design patterns are discussed in more detail in Chapter 7. The examples that follow use other design patterns, which we will note.

Listing 5.6 WmvcModel.java
Wmvc Model base class – the Model

```java
/*
 * WmvcModel - An MVC model superclass for the Wmvc framework
 * Copyright (c) 2001, Bruce E. Wampler
 */

import java.util.*;

public class WmvcModel
    extends     Observable
{
    // not a huge class, but provides implementation of
    // Observer pattern using MVC naming

    public WmvcModel()
    {
        super();
    }

    public void addView(WmvcView view)
    {
        addObserver((Observer) view);
    }

    public void deleteView(WmvcView view)
    {
        deleteObserver((Observer) view);
    }

    public void notifyViews()
    {
        setChanged();
        notifyObservers();
    }
}
```

Listing 5.7 WmvcView.java
Wmvc View base class—the View

```java
/*
 * WmvcView - An MVC view superclass for the Wmvc framework
 * Copyright (c) 2001, Bruce E. Wampler
 */

import java.util.*;

public class WmvcView
    implements  Observer
{
    // implement the single Observer class
    public void update(Observable observed, Object value)
```

```
    {
        updateView();
    }

    public void updateView()
    {
        // no-op by default
    }
}
```

Wmvc includes the WmvcController class. This class makes it easier to build controllers for menu items and tool bar buttons.[3] The WmvcController class serves as a base class for subclasses that support specific menu bar and tool bar controls. This example has been simplified to implement only basic text and checkbox menu items (WmvcMenuItemCtl and WmvcChkMenuItemCtl) and simple buttons (WmvcTBButtonCtl) for the tool bar. Additional subclasses of Wmvc-Controller would be required to support additional Swing components on the tool bar, but have not been implemented to help simplify the example. Note that WmvcController is intended to simplify working with the menu bar and the tool bar. Controllers for Swing components inside the individual views would need to be implemented using Swing listeners defined within the view code. It would be possible, however, to design other WmvcController implementations for components not on the menu or tool bars. As we noted earlier, using MVC with Java often means a combined view/controller.

The WmvcController supports functionality for subclasses that implement menu items and tool bar controls. The basic support includes handling tool tips and providing the implementation for the WmvcExecutor class. There is a subclass for each type of Swing component: normal menu, check-box menu, and tool bar button. It would be simple to support other Swing components by adding new subclasses of WmvcController. There are many details "hidden" in this code to simplify the use of these components.

Listing 5.8 WmvcController.java
The Controller

```
/*
 * WmvcController - implements a general-purpose Swing-based
 * Controller using the Command pattern - for Wmvc framework
 * used to simplify Swing controls
 *
 * (c) 2001, Bruce E. Wampler
 */
```

---

[3] WmvcController is implemented using the Command design pattern. See Chapter 7.

```java
import java.awt.*;
import java.awt.event.*;
import javax.swing.*;
import javax.swing.event.*;

public class WmvcController
        implements     ActionListener,
                       ItemListener
{
    protected JComponent myComponent;
    private WmvcExecutor wmvcExecutor;   // The Executor object

    // This constructor is use by the subobjects
    public WmvcController(JComponent comp,     // the component
                          String tip,
                          WmvcExecutor wExec)
    {
        myComponent = comp;
        wmvcExecutor = wExec;
        if (tip != null)
            myComponent.setToolTipText(tip);
    }

    public WmvcExecutor getWmvcExecutor()
        { return wmvcExecutor; }

    /* ------------------------------------------------------
     * Implement the Listeners for components.
     * Each listener will send a message to the appropriate
     * execute method from the associated WmvcExecutor. Type
     * of event determines the signature of the execute method.
     */

    // implement the ActionListener
    public void actionPerformed(ActionEvent event)
    {
        if (wmvcExecutor != null)
            wmvcExecutor.execute(event);
    }

    // implement ItemListener
    public void itemStateChanged(ItemEvent event)
    {
        if (wmvcExecutor != null)
            wmvcExecutor.execute(event);
    }
}
```

The following are subclasses of WmvcController that implement menu items, checked menu items, and tool bar buttons.

Listing 5.9 `WmvcMenuItemCtl.java`
Controller subclass for JMenuItem

```
/*
 * WmvcMenuItemCtl - implements JMenuItem controller
 * (c) 2001, Bruce E. Wampler
 */
import java.awt.*;
import java.awt.event.*;
import javax.swing.*;
import javax.swing.event.*;

public class WmvcMenuItemCtl extends WmvcController
{

    private JMenu myMenu;
    private JMenuItem menuItem;

        // Constructor for JMenu item: Standard JMenuItem
    public WmvcMenuItemCtl(JMenu menu,      // JMenu I go with
                      String text,          // Button's text
                      String icon,          // the icon's name
                      char mnemonic,        // Button's mnemonic
                      String accel,         // accelerator
                      WmvcExecutor wExec)
    {
        super((JComponent)new JMenuItem(), null, wExec);

        myMenu = menu;
        menuItem = (JMenuItem) myComponent;

        if (text != null)
            menuItem.setText(text);
        if (mnemonic != ' ' && mnemonic != 0)
            menuItem.setMnemonic(mnemonic);
        if (accel != null)
          {
            KeyStroke ks = KeyStroke.getKeyStroke(accel);
            menuItem.setAccelerator(ks);
          }
        if (icon != null)
          {
            Icon theIcon = new ImageIcon(icon);
            menuItem.setIcon(theIcon);
          }
        menuItem.addActionListener(this);  // Add listeners
        menuItem.addItemListener(this);
        menu.add(menuItem);                     // Finally, add to menu
    }

    public void setEnabled(boolean enable)
```

```
    {
        menuItem.setEnabled(enable);
    }

    public JMenu getJMenu() { return myMenu; }
    public JMenuItem getJMenuItem() { return menuItem; }
}
```

Listing 5.10 WmvcChkMenuItemCtl.java
Controller subclass for JCheckBoxMenuItem

```
/*
 * WmvcChkMenuItemCtl - implements JCheckBoxMenuItem controller
 * (c) 2001, Bruce E. Wampler
 */

import java.awt.*;
import java.awt.event.*;
import javax.swing.*;
import javax.swing.event.*;

public class WmvcChkMenuItemCtl extends WmvcController
{
    private JMenu myMenu;
    private JCheckBoxMenuItem checkBoxItem;


    // Constructor for JMenu item:  JCheckBoxMenuItem
    public WmvcController(JMenu menu,        // JMenu I go with
                          String text,       // Button's text
                          String icon,       // the icon's name
                          char mnemonic,     // Button's mnemonic
                          String accel,      // accelerator
                          boolean checked,   // initial state
                          WmvcExecutor wExec)
    {
        super((JComponent)new JCheckBoxMenuItem(), null, wExec);

        myMenu = menu;
        checkBoxMenuItem = (JCheckBoxMenuItem) myComponent;
        if (text != null)
            checkBoxItem.setText(text);
        if (mnemonic != ' ' && mnemonic != 0)
            checkBoxItem.setMnemonic(mnemonic);
        if (accel != null)
          {
            KeyStroke ks = KeyStroke.getKeyStroke(accel);
            checkBoxItem.setAccelerator(ks);
          }
```

```
            if (icon != null)
              {
                Icon theIcon = new ImageIcon(icon);
                checkBoxItem.setIcon(theIcon);
              }

            checkBoxItem.setState(checked);

            checkBoxItem.addActionListener(this);   // Add listeners
            checkBoxItem.addItemListener(this);
            myMenu.add(checkBoxItem);          // Finally, add to menu
        }

    public boolean getState()
    {   return checkBoxItem.getState();
    }
    public void setState(boolean checked)
    {   checkBoxItem.setState(checked);
    }
    public void setEnabled(boolean enable)
    {   checkBoxItem.setEnabled(enable);
    }
    public JMenu getJMenu() { return myMenu; }
    public JCheckBoxMenuItem getJCheckBoxMenuItem()
    {   return checkBoxItem;
    }
}
```

Listing 5.11 WmvcTBButton.java
Controller subclass for JButton for tool bar

```
/*
 * WmvcTBButtonCtl - implements JButton controller for tool bar
 * (c) 2001, Bruce E. Wampler
 */

import java.awt.*;
import java.awt.event.*;
import javax.swing.*;
import javax.swing.event.*;

public class WmvcTBButtonCtl extends WmvcController
{
    private JButton myButton;

    // Constructor for JToolBar item:  JButton
    public WmvcTBButtonCtl( String text,        // Button's text
                            String icon,        // the icon's name
                            String tip,         // tool tip
                            WmvcExecutor wExec)
    {
        super((JComponent)new JButton(), tip, wExec);
```

```
        myButton = (JButton) myComponent;

        if (text != null)
           myButton.setText(text);
        if (icon != null)
          {
            Icon theIcon = new ImageIcon(icon);
            myButton.setIcon(theIcon);
          }

        myButton.addActionListener(this);       // add listener
        WmvcApp.getToolBar().add(myButton);      // add to bar
    }

    public void setEnabled(boolean enable)
    {   myButton.setEnabled(enable);
    }
    public JButton getJButton() { return myButton; }
}
```

WmvcExecutor is the implementation specification for the Command design pattern. In the context of this MVC framework, Executor seems to be a more appropriate name, even though it is based on the Command pattern. It is used and functions much like a standard Swing listener.

Listing 5.12 WmvcExecutor.java
The Executor (Command pattern) used with WmvcController

```
/*
 * WmvcExecutor - Support class for implementation
 *   of the WmvcController class.
 * (c) 2001, Bruce E. Wampler
 */

import java.awt.event.*;
import javax.swing.event.*;

public class WmvcExecutor
{
    // an execute for each type of event we might have
    public void execute(ActionEvent event)
    {
    }
    public void execute(ItemEvent event)
    {
    }
    public void execute(ChangeEvent event)
    {
    }
}
```

Now that we've examined the implementation of the Wmvc framework, we present a small example that uses the framework.

A Simple Application Based on Wmvc

We will use a small application called Thermometer to illustrate how the Wmvc framework can be used (see Figure 5.11). This application displays a temperature value in both degrees Fahrenheit and degrees Celsius. It provides buttons on the tool bar to allow the user to move the temperature up and down.

The model, called ThermometerModel, is simple. It is an integer value representing the Fahrenheit temperature. It has a getter to get the current temperature and a setter to set a new temperature. Whenever the temperature changes, the model notifies all views.

There are three views. The two most obvious are the display views that display the temperature in Fahrenheit and in Celsius. The third view doesn't actually display the temperature. It is a control view that reacts to menu and tool bar commands. This nondisplay view is just a controller, but it is implemented as a view/controller to fit within the MVC design. The two display views are really two objects of the class TemperatureView. These views don't have a controller. The nondisplay view is called MainView, and it uses the WmvcController class to implement the controller.

Figure 5.12 is the UML diagram of the Thermometer application. Note that this diagram is somewhat simplified to show the logical structure of the app. We don't show the WmvcApp, WmvcModel, or WmvcView classes as they are unneeded detail. The update, modify, and draw-in associations have been removed to simplify the diagram.

The code for the application is quite simple. That was the goal of designing the Wmvc framework to begin with. Listing 5.13 shows the Thermometer class, which is the app class derived from WmvcApp. Thermometer defines the app by creating the model, creating the views, and adding the Fahrenheit and Celsius views to a JSplitPane.

Figure 5.11   Thermometer app

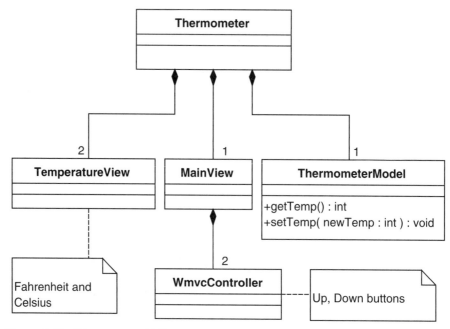

Figure 5.12   Thermometer UML

Listing 5.13   `Thermometer.java`
Thermometer subclass of WmvcApp

```
/*
 * Thermometer - A simple test for Wmvc framework
 * Copyright (c) 2001, Bruce E. Wampler
 */

import java.awt.*;
import javax.swing.*;

public class Thermometer extends WmvcApp
{
    private MainView mainView;
    private TemperatureView fView;
    private TemperatureView cView;

    public Thermometer(String name)        // constructor
    {
        super(name, true, true);       // Create with menu, toolbar

        // **** First, create the model
        setModel( (WmvcModel) new ThermometerModel() );
```

```
    // **** Next, create the view/controllers
    mainView = new MainView();        // won't use any panels
    fView = new TemperatureView('F');   // Fahrenheit, left
    cView = new TemperatureView('C');   // Celsius, right

    // ****  Create a split pane, add list and item views
    JSplitPane splitPane = new JSplitPane(
        JSplitPane.HORIZONTAL_SPLIT, fView.getPanel(),
        cView.getPanel());
    splitPane.setOneTouchExpandable(false); // details
    splitPane.setDividerLocation(150);

    WmvcApp.addMainPane(splitPane); // add splitter
}

public static void main(String[] args)
{
    final Thermometer theThermometer =
            new Thermometer("Thermometer App");

    WmvcApp.getContentPanel().setPreferredSize(
            new Dimension(300, 60)); // not big
    WmvcApp.showApp();

    ((ThermometerModel) (WmvcApp.getModel())).setTemp(70);
}
}
```

The model for this application is extremely simple. It has one attribute: the temperature. The views and controller interact with the model, using setTemp and getTemp. The model updates views when setTemp changes the value.

Listing 5.14 ThermometerModel.java
Model subclass

```
/*
 * ThermometerModel - implements model. Handles changes.
 * Copyright 2001, Bruce E. Wampler
 */

import java.util.*;

public class ThermometerModel
    extends      WmvcModel
{
    private int theTemp;
    public int getTemp() { return theTemp; }

    public ThermometerModel()
```

```
    {
        theTemp = 0;
    }

    public void setTemp(int newTemp)
    {
      theTemp = newTemp;
      notifyViews();              // not much to the model!
    }
}
```

The `MainView` defines the menu items and the tool bar items. Since it doesn't
have to change anything when the model changes, it uses the default `WmvcView`
update method, which doesn't do anything.

Listing 5.15 `MainView.java`
Main view subclass

```
/*
 * MainView - Top level view/controller for the Thermometer
 *
 * This is the main view/controller.
 * Copyright (c) 2001, Bruce E. Wampler
 */

import java.util.*;
import java.awt.*;
import java.awt.event.*;
import javax.swing.*;

public class MainView extends WmvcView
{
    private ThermometerModel myModel; // local model reference

    public MainView()
    {
        myModel = (ThermometerModel) WmvcApp.getModel();
        myModel.addView(this);
        JMenu fileMenu = new JMenu("File");

        // File->Up
        WmvcMenuItemCtl fileUp = new WmvcMenuItemCtl(fileMenu,
            "Up",null, 'U',
            null /* no accel */, new WmvcExecutor()
            {
                public void execute(ActionEvent event)
                {
                    myModel.setTemp(myModel.getTemp()+1);
                }
            });
```

```
    // File->Down
    WmvcMenuItemCtl fileDown = new WmvcMenuItemCtl(fileMenu,
        "Down",null, 'D',
        null /* no accel */, new WmvcExecutor()
        {
            public void execute(ActionEvent event)
            {
                myModel.setTemp(myModel.getTemp()-1);
            }
        });

    // File->Exit
    WmvcMenuItemCtl fileExit = new WmvcMenuItemCtl(fileMenu,
        "Exit", null, 'x',
        null /* no accel */,  new WmvcExecutor()
        {
            public void execute(ActionEvent event)
            {
                if (WmvcApp.getApp().appClosing())
                  System.exit(0);
            }
        });

    WmvcApp.addMenu(fileMenu);       // Add to app menu

    // ToolBar: Up
    WmvcTBButtonCtl toolUp = new WmvcTBButtonCtl(
        "    Up    ",null,"Up one degree F",
        fileUp.getWmvcExecutor() /* same as file up */);

    // ToolBar: Down
    WmvcTBButtonCtl toolDown = new WmvcTBButtonCtl(
        " Down ",null,"Down one degree F",
        fileDown.getWmvcExecutor() /* same as file up */);
    }
}
```

There is one view class for both the Fahrenheit and Celsius views. The constructor determines which scale is to be used. It overrides the WmvcView update method to handle the change notification from the model.

Listing 5.16 TemperatureView.java
View subclass for Fahrenheit and Celsius views

```
/*
 * TemperatureView - a view for C or F temps.
 * Copyright (c) 2001, Bruce E. Wampler
 */

import java.util.*;
import java.awt.*;
```

```java
import javax.swing.*;

public class TemperatureView extends WmvcView
{
    private JPanel myPanel;
    private ThermometerModel myModel;           // local copy
    private char myScale;

    private static JLabel lblF = new JLabel("Fahrenheit: ");
    private static JLabel lblC = new JLabel("Celsius: ");
    private JLabel fldTemp;

    public JPanel getPanel() { return myPanel; }

    public TemperatureView(char scale)
    {
        myModel = (ThermometerModel)WmvcApp.getModel();
        myModel.addView(this);                  // adds update for mvc

        myScale = scale;                        // remember my scale

        myPanel = new JPanel();                 // surrounding Panel
        myPanel.setPreferredSize( new Dimension(390, 40));

        if (scale == 'F' || scale == 'f')
        {
            myPanel.add(lblF);                  // F degrees
        }
        else
        {
            myPanel.add(lblC);                  // C degrees
        }
        fldTemp = new JLabel(" ");
        fldTemp.setForeground(Color.black);     // temp in black
        myPanel.add(fldTemp);
    }

    public void updateView()
    {
        int val = myModel.getTemp();
        if (myScale == 'C')
            val = (int) (((double)(val-32))/1.8); // not rounded
        fldTemp.setText(Integer.toString(val));
    }
}
```

UML Sequence Diagram for Thermometer

Figure 5.13 is the UML sequence diagram corresponding to the user clicking the Up button. The sequence diagram shows how the Wmvc framework implements MVC to send messages to the views.

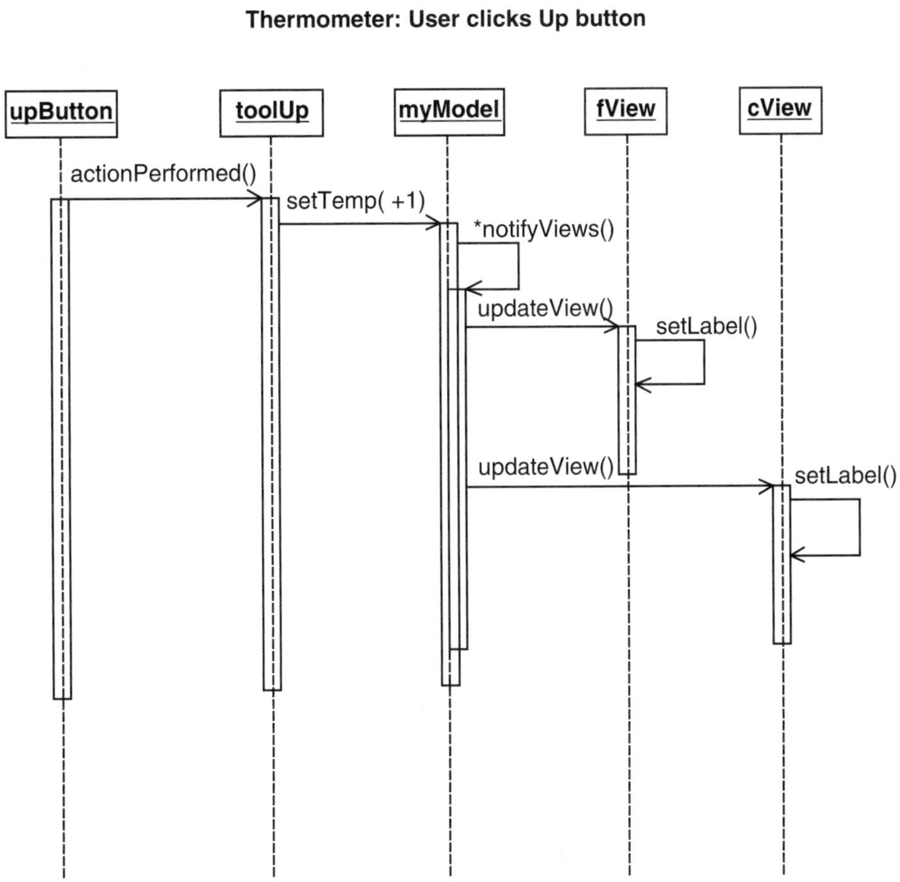

Thermometer: User clicks Up button

Figure 5.13 UML sequence diagram—Up button pressed

When the user clicks the Up button, the object corresponding to the Up button, called upButton in the diagram, sends an actionPerformed message to the Up button controller, toolUp.[4] The toolUp controller then sends a setTemp message to the model, myModel, to increase the temperature by 1. After changing its internal state appropriately, myModel then sends the notifyViews message. This is effectively a message to itself (using the Observer design pattern), which then causes the update method of each view to be called. The views then change their labels appropriately.

---

[4]. The Up button object, which we call upButton, is created as a WmvcController object. The framework hides the button object from the application. The corresponding controller is called toolUp.

Chapter Summary

- A "typical" GUI-based application has an outer frame, a title bar, a menu bar, a tool bar, and a drawing area. Applications can have dialogs with control components, such as buttons and lists.

- Swing is Java's GUI toolkit. The `JFrame`, `JDialog`, and `JApplet` are the normal top-level container components used to build applications, dialogs, and applets. Events are handled in Swing by defining listeners with callbacks to respond to the events.

- MVC, Model/View/Controller, is an object-oriented design pattern useful for GUI applications.

- Wmvc is a small, Swing-based Java GUI framework that combines the Swing `JFrame` with an implementation of MVC. It demonstrates all the basics for building good object-oriented Swing-based GUI applications in Java.

Resources

Swing

Creating a GUI with JFC/Swing, from Sun: `java.sun.com/docs/books/tutorial/uiswing/index.html`.

The JFC Swing Tutorial: A Guide to Constructing GUIs, Kathy Walrath, Mary Campione, Addison-Wesley, 1999, ISBN: 0-201-43321-4.

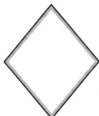

CHAPTER 6

A Case Study in Java

The goal of this chapter is to put everything from the previous chapters together to develop a small Java application. We will start with a specification for the program, go through a simplified OOAD process, and finally build the program with Java and Swing.

For this case study, we will develop a small home video movie catalog. Here is the specification for the application.

> The application, which we will call MovieCat, will allow a collector to create a catalog of a home movie collection. The movies can be collected from several sources in different media formats. The movies can be either original commercial copies or copies recorded at home. The movies can be on VHS tape, DVD, VCD, SVCD, Hi8, or miniDV. The user should be able to categorize the movies into classes, such as action, comedy, family, and the like. MovieCat should include the rating of the movie (G, PG-13, and so forth), as well as a personal evaluation by the user. The information included in the catalog should include the title, director, and year the movie was made. Because people often record multiple movies on one tape, MovieCat should be able to track which tape a movie is recorded on. Finally, MovieCat should have a general comment field in which the user can enter any other information about the movie. To help simplify the program, it won't have to keep track of actors, awards, or other specific information. The application

should use Java and have a GUI that is simple and easy to use. The user will want to browse for movies in the collection (but, at least for now, not search for specific titles or other parts), add new movies, and edit or delete existing movies.

This is a simple application, so the specification can be simple. Because MovieCat will perform a function that is familiar to everyone, maintaining a list of a movie collection, there is not a lot of specialized expertise required to build this application. It might be useful to talk to a movie buff to find out what information is most interesting to track, but most of us have seen movie reviews and books of listed and rated movies, so this is really common knowledge.

Analysis of MovieCat

Before we design MovieCat code, we will perform an analysis.

Use Cases

MovieCat is a small, simple application, so it won't require an extensive analysis. First, we present the use cases. There aren't very many. In fact, the last sentence of the specification reveals the likely use cases: browse for movies, add new movies, edit existing movies, and delete movies. Figure 6.1 shows the UML use case diagram.

The next step is to produce a written description of each use case with the accompanying scenarios. MovieCat is simple. There is only one actor, the Collector. There is not much that can go wrong when using this program, so the scenarios are short. We won't bother with a formal use case write-up; we'll just show the scenarios that go with each use case.

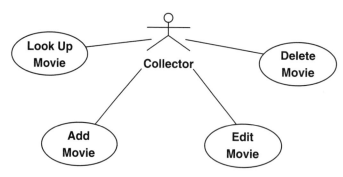

Figure 6.1   MovieCat use cases

Scenario for Look Up Movie

1. Collector chooses movie catalog.

2. Collector browses list of movies.

3. When the collector is at the beginning or end of the list, browsing will wrap around to bottom or top.

Scenario for Add Movie

1. Collector chooses movie catalog.

2. Collector selects add movie.

3. Collector edits new movie entry.

4. Collector commits or abandons new movie.

5. On commit, movie is added in alphabetical order of the title to the list of movies.

Scenario for Edit Movie

1. Collector chooses movie catalog.

2. Collector browses for movie to edit.

3. Collector edits movie.

4. Collector commits or abandons edits.

5. On commit, the entry is replaced in the correct alphabetical order.

Scenario for Delete Movie

1. Collector chooses movie catalog.

2. Collector browses for movie to delete.

3. Collector deletes movie.

These scenarios reflect some decisions that were made while writing them. For example, the original specification did not say anything about the order of the movie list. The scenarios indicate that the movie catalog is kept in alphabetical order. The specification of the steps required to edit or delete a movie reveal that editing and deleting movies involves many of the same steps required to simply browse.

Even though there are only four simple use cases, they do reveal important aspects of what needs to be done. Larger applications would have many more use cases, some more complicated, some just as simple. The use cases lead to the scenarios. Scenarios are often more complicated than this example, and represent a more detailed contract between the customer and the developer for certain features or functionality. In a more critical application, for example, the Edit Movie scenario would need to be more detailed. We simply specify "edits movie." If we were editing a record in a financial application, for instance, the scenario would have to cover each field of the record. What are the legal values of the field? What fields are required? What if the user makes an entry error? A complete scenario would cover each possible situation. The level of detail required for each scenario depends on many things, but writing scenarios helps to ensure that everyone understands what the system is supposed to do.

We've been informal in our presentation of the MovieCat use cases and scenarios. Sometimes, this informal approach and a few pieces of paper or a white board are all that is needed. More-formal OO methodologies have more-formal rules for specifying use cases and their associated scenarios, and provide specific software tools to create and track them.

Now that we have the MovieCat use cases and their scenarios, we can continue with the OOA. The next step is to analyze the problem to discover objects, attributes, and operations.

Object, Attribute, and Operation Discovery

In Chapter 4, we looked at some of the basic steps of analysis, including object discovery, attribute discovery, and operation discovery. Because the MovieCat problem is so simple, we can combine these steps. In a larger problem, the steps would more likely be done as separate tasks, although there is always some overlap.

Examining the problem specification for nouns and verbs is one of the most effective ways to begin object, attribute, and operation discovery. Here we list the nouns and verbs in the MovieCat problem description.

Nouns
Reading the problem description gives the following list of nouns: application, collector, catalog, movie collection, movie, formats, classes, rating, evaluation, user, title, director, year, tape, comment field, information, Java, and GUI. Table 6.1 discusses each noun and presents candidate classes and attributes.

The analysis of the nouns from the problem statement has given us three candidate objects or classes: MovieCat, MovieModel, and Movie. We discovered several attributes of a Movie. We identified a whole/part hierarchy between the MovieModel and Movie. Finally, we have some views to identify.

Table 6.1   Analysis of Nouns in the MovieCat Problem Description

Nouns	Discussion	Candidate Classes and Attributes
Application	The application is the main thing we are talking about. Since this application is a GUI app, we will use the Wmvc framework presented in Chapter 5. Thus, our application will derive from `WmvcApp`.	`MovieCat`
Collector	The collector is the user of the system and is outside it. If this system were intended to be used by several collectors, this might represent a useful candidate object, but not in our case.	
Catalog	Creating a catalog is one of the primary goals of this application. However, catalog and movie collection are really the same thing.	
Movie Collection	This is the real thing—what we will be modeling. The concept of a movie collection fits well with the MVC notion of a model, so we will call it the model.	`MovieModel`
Movie	A movie collection is made up of movies. So we have discovered an object, `Movie`, and a hierarchy, part of a collection.	`Movie`
Format	This is the format of the tapes. It seems to be simply an attribute of a movie.	`Movie.format`
Class	This is the category of a movie. A better name is genre, and it is an attribute of a Movie.	`Movie.genre`
Rating	A Movie attribute.	`Movie.rating`
Evaluation	A Movie attribute.	`Movie.evaluation`
User	Another name for the collector. Outside the system.	
Title	A Movie attribute.	`Movie.title`

Continues

Table 6.1   Analysis of Nouns in the MovieCat Problem Description *(Continued)*

Nouns	Discussion	Candidate Classes and Attributes
Director	A Movie attribute.	`Movie.director`
Year	A Movie attribute.	`Movie.year`
Tape	A Movie attribute. It will be an ID or label on a tape.	`Movie.label`
Comment Field	A Movie attribute.	`Movie.comments`
Information	In this context, the content of the comment field.	
Java	Sometimes the customer will specify the environment or language. This is a design constraint, not an object or an attribute.	
GUI	We already discussed the GUI as part of the application. We will use the Wmvc framework and Swing to build the GUI. Because of this decision, we know there will also be some views we still have to identify.	

We also decided to use the Wmvc framework. This level of decision is usually more a design decision. Sometimes, however, candidates for libraries or support databases come up in the analysis because such decisions can affect the ultimate design. Next, we examine the verbs from the problem description.

Verbs

Reading the problem description gives the following list of verbs: create catalog, collected, categorize, track, browse, add new, edit, and delete. Because this list is short, we will just discuss the verbs instead of creating a table.

The first four verbs—create catalog, collected, categorize, and track—have to do with how the collector uses MovieCat. The verbs don't add any hints about the objects involved. The remaining verbs, browse, add new, edit, and delete, are the same actions we've already discussed in the use cases and scenarios.

We know that browsing, adding, editing (which is equivalent to replacing an existing movie with a "new," edited version), and deleting movies are important activities, and will no doubt show up as operations on the `MovieModel` and individual `Movies`. We noted in the discussion of the noun GUI that we still need to identify the views we need. The verbs browse and edit yield probable views: a view of the movie collection to browse with an associated detailed view of an individual movie, and an edit view to edit existing movies or add information for new movies. So, the new candidate views would be a `MovieListView`, a `MovieItemView`, and a `MovieEditView`.

Evaluation

Now that we have some candidate objects, attributes, and operations, we can evaluate what we have before going on to the design phase. In our analysis, the `MovieModel` and `Movie` classes were covered in the most detail. Figure 6.2 is a UML diagram to summarize `MovieModel` and `Movie`. All the operations and attributes included in the diagrams come directly from the analysis we just did.

Note that the UML class diagrams in the figure represent analysis diagrams, not design or implementation class diagrams. The level of detail we are looking at is different, and specific implementation details such as public attributes instead of setters and getters for the `Movie` class are not relevant in analysis. We have not yet specified types for the attributes, either. This is a detail best left for design and implementation.

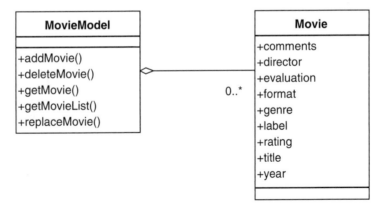

Figure 6.2   MovieModel and Movie class diagrams—analysis

Design of MovieCat

The results of our analysis for MovieCat can lead directly to a specific design. The goal of the design phase is to cover the details and come up with a design that can be turned into the final implementation in code. This means that not only do we consider what the program will do and what its main organization is, but also that we specify the details—the programming language, the hardware, the libraries we will use, and all the other details needed to get a working implementation.

As part of the analysis, we decided to use the MVC design to build Movie-Cat. One of the advantages of MVC is that it allows you to design a model that is completely independent of the rest of the application. In this section, we will focus mainly on designing the model, which is made up of the `MovieModel` and `Movie` classes. We already have the analysis class diagrams for those two classes in Figure 6.2.

Movie Class

Let's start by refining the `Movie` class. The analysis diagram for `Movie` shows all the attributes as public values. In the actual implementation, these public attributes should be made private, with appropriate methods supplied to get and set their values, as needed.

Attributes can be variables of simple Java primitive type, or they can be variables that reference objects of some class. Most of the attributes associated with a `Movie` seem to be simple Java `Strings`. This would include `comments`, `director`, `label`, and `title`. `Year` could be a `String` or an `int`; we will use `String`.

The other attributes, `evaluation`, `format`, `genre`, and `rating`, represent a list of possible values. For example, `rating` would be one of G, PG, PG-13, R, NC-17, X, or NR. One obvious way to represent this would be as an array of `Strings` with all the different values. But any movie will have only one of these values. So an alternative representation could be to define integer constants that represent a particular rating. In fact, partly because of the different ways we will view a `Movie`, we'd like to be able to use either representation—an `int` or a `String`.

One way around this dilemma is to use small helper classes for the `evaluation`, `format`, `genre`, and `rating` attributes. These helper classes would be similar, and they would allow us to represent the value of the attribute as an `int` but easily convert between the `int` and a `String`. And we'd like to know all the possible values (which might change over time because a new rating might be added) for use in a list or combo box. The helper classes won't have much behavior, and they can be implemented as class (that is, `static`) variables and methods. Each class provides methods to map between the `int` and `String` representations, and will return the full `String` list of possible values. To keep them `static`, a separate class is used for each attribute (this is a Java limitation). A main advantage of designing the attributes this way is that it isolates all the representational information in the class definition. We could easily add new genres or modify the letter codes for the ratings, without affecting how the rest of the program works.

What other responsibilities should the `Movie` class have? Who will use a `Movie` object? We know that we want to edit a `Movie` object. An editor should work with a copy of a `Movie`, so the `Movie` class should be `cloneable`. And it is common practice for objects that have their values saved in a file to be able to read and write themselves, so we should add `readMovie` and `writeMovie` methods. Finally, we should define a constructor.

The `Movie` class is somewhat atypical because it is so data dominated. It has more setters and getters than is typical of most classes, but that is not out of the ordinary for a data-oriented class. `Movie` still has significant responsibilities, such as reading and writing `Movie` objects. Data-oriented classes are not necessarily bad, and many applications require one or several such classes.

Figure 6.3 is the final detailed UML object diagram for the `Movie` class.

This class diagram shows the list-like attributes (`genre`, and so forth) as `ints`. `Movie` saves the representations as `ints`, and then uses the helper classes to get the `String` values.

The UML for the helper classes is shown in Figure 6.4. Note that the diagrams show the values for the `Strings`. The UML uses <u>underlines</u> to indicate class attributes and methods.

MovieModel Class

The analysis diagram of the `MovieModel` class in Figure 6.2 on page 151 shows five methods for the views to interact with the model. In the design phase, we need to decide if those five are all the methods we really need. We need to consider exactly which information about a list of movies the views will require to be able to completely display their views.

We will have at least three views: a list view, a view of the current movie, and an edit view. First, note that the phrase *current movie* implies that there is a single movie that is the one to be displayed in the current movie view. This is a new attribute for `MovieModel`. The current movie view needs access to the current `Movie` object, which will then be used by the view to get all the values it needs to display. The list view requires access to the full list of movies, the ability to get or set the movie that is the current movie, and to find out if the list has changed. The edit view requires access to either a blank movie object or a copy of the current movie. It then adds a new movie, replaces the current movie, or deletes the current movie.

The user will want to be able to open an existing movie list file or save the current movie list to a file. MovieCat should save the movie list only if it has changed, so `MovieModel` needs to track whether it has changed. Since the `MovieModel` is part of the MVC design, it must implement the `notifyViews` method. These responsibilities belong in the `MovieModel` object.

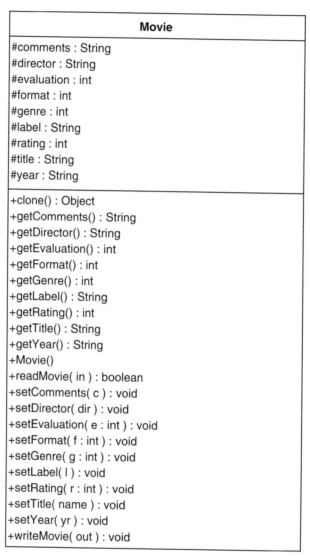

Figure 6.3   Movie class

Figure 6.5 is the UML for the MovieModel class that includes all the responsibilities we just discussed. Note the FILE_ID attribute. This is a constant that will be used to identify MovieCat files.

The private Vector theList is the list of the Movie objects and represents the implementation of the aggregation relationship between MovieModel and Movie.

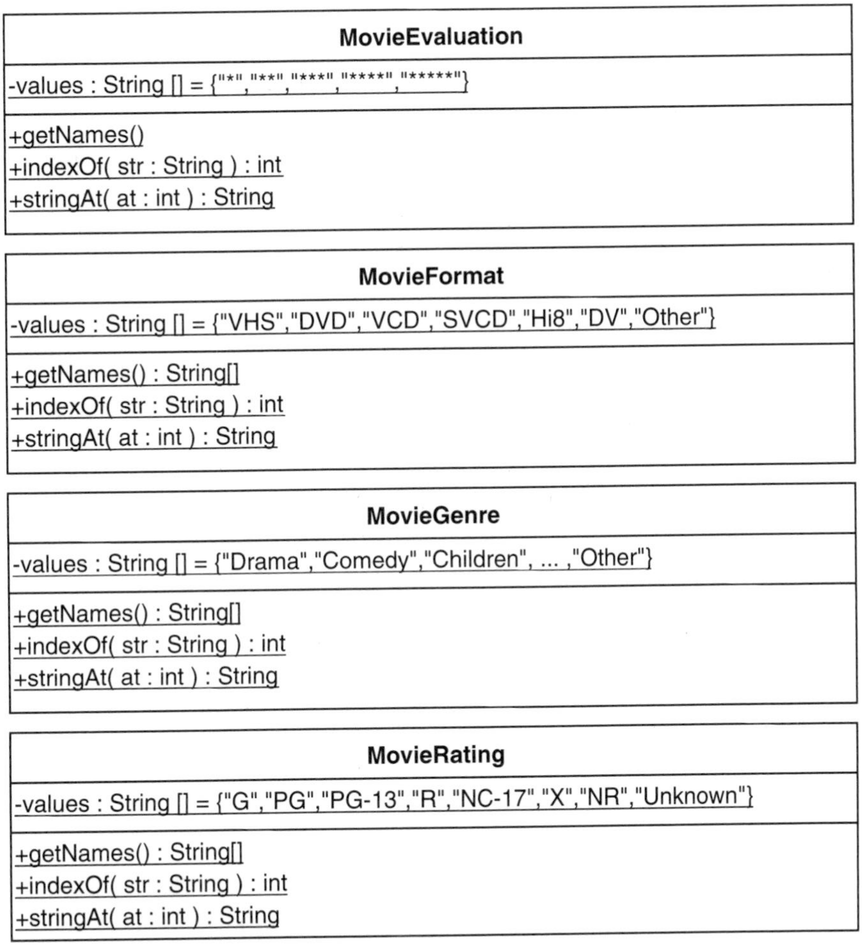

MovieEvaluation
-values : String [] = {"*","**","***","****","*****"}
+getNames() +indexOf(str : String) : int +stringAt(at : int) : String

MovieFormat
-values : String [] = {"VHS","DVD","VCD","SVCD","Hi8","DV","Other"}
+getNames() : String[] +indexOf(str : String) : int +stringAt(at : int) : String

MovieGenre
-values : String [] = {"Drama","Comedy","Children", ... ,"Other"}
+getNames() : String[] +indexOf(str : String) : int +stringAt(at : int) : String

MovieRating
-values : String [] = {"G","PG","PG-13","R","NC-17","X","NR","Unknown"}
+getNames() : String[] +indexOf(str : String) : int +stringAt(at : int) : String

Figure 6.4   Movie helper classes

View Classes

In the analysis, we identified three candidate view classes: list, item, and edit. In the Thermometer example in Chapter 5, we used another view, called the Main-View, to implement the controllers for the menu and tool bar commands. We also use a MainView for MovieCat.

Before designing the view classes, it would be a good idea to know what the GUI should look like. Good GUI design is somewhat of an art form. A full treatment is beyond the scope of this book, but we will briefly cover the MovieCat GUI design. One of the first steps in any design is to sketch out a rough design

MovieModel
-currentMovieIndex : int
-editsMade : boolean
-@FILE_ID : int = 48879
-listChanged : boolean
-myFile : File
-theList : Vector
+addMovie(movie : Movie) : void
+closeMovies() : boolean
+deleteCurrentMovie() : void
+getCurrentMovie() : Movie
+getCurrentMovieIndex() : int
+getEditsMade() : boolean
+getFile() : File
+getListChanged() : boolean
+getMovieListIterator() : ListIterator
+getNumberOfMovies() : int
+MovieModel()
#notifyViews() : void
+openMovies(file) : boolean
+replaceCurrentMovie(movie : Movie) : void
+saveMovies() : boolean
+saveMoviesAs(file : File) : boolean
+setCurrentMovieIndex(movieNumber : int) : void

Figure 6.5 MovieModel UML

with paper and pencil. Depending on which software tools you have available, you might then generate some trial GUIs using a GUI designer tool. These rapid prototyping tools can quickly give you a fair idea of what might work for your application.

The MovieCat app has simple GUI requirements. Because we are using the Wmvc framework, we won't use any GUI prototyping tool. The GUI for MovieCat was initially designed with pencil and paper, then mapped directly to the corresponding Swing components. Figure 6.6 shows the final version of the MovieCat GUI. We will use it instead of the original pencil layouts to discuss the design of the MovieCat view classes.

The screen shot of MovieCat shows three views; the main view is the view/controller for the menu and tool bars. It doesn't show any movie information. The JPanel provided by the Wmvc framework is used to hold a JSplitPane. The list view is in the left pane, and the item view is in the right pane. The user browses the movie list by using the scrolling functions of the list view.

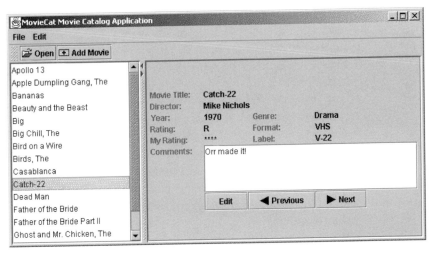

Figure 6.6   MovieCat app

What about the edit view? One choice would have been to use the item view for the editor as well. One problem with this approach is that it is too easy for the user to accidentally make changes. A better design is to have the editor as a separate popup dialog. The layout of the dialog is similar to the item view but uses editable components so that the user can change or create a movie entry. The editor dialog is invoked by the Edit button in the item view, or by the Add Movie button on the tool bar. There are synonyms for these commands in the Menu.

Figure 6.7 shows the MovieCat movie editor dialog.

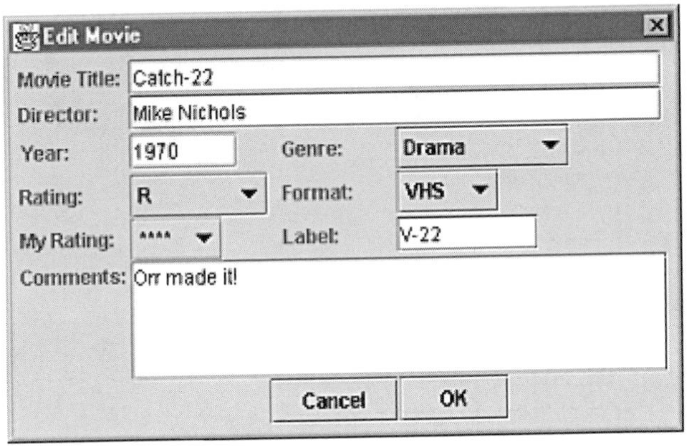

Figure 6.7   MovieCat editor dialog

Because we are using Wmvc and Swing, the design of the view classes is a matter of selecting the appropriate Swing components to implement the required functionality that has been specified. The MVC design architecture dictates the logical structure of the views. We won't show detailed UML diagrams of the view classes.

The Wmvc framework requires one more class, the main app class. Let's call the class MovieCat; its main purpose is to create the model and the views. Its design is really dictated by the Wmvc framework.

One of the advantages of using a framework, even a small one like Wmvc, is that it can greatly simplify the design. Wmvc defines a specific framework based on MVC, and provides some basic Swing building blocks. The basic Wmvc architecture makes the design of the views, main app, and even the model simpler than it might have been with a design from scratch. Once we designed the MovieModel class, it was not difficult to design the views.

Putting It All Together

We now have all the parts of MovieCat designed. Figure 6.8 has a UML class diagram for the full MovieCat application, but without the Wmvc details. The UML shows how all the parts fit and interact with each other.

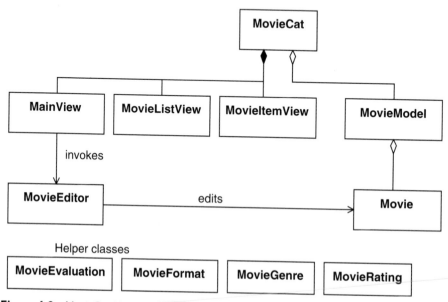

Figure 6.8 MovieCat UML for design

Implementation of MovieCat

Now that we have the design for MovieCat, we can write the code. The following listings[1] show the complete implementation of the MovieCat application. Each listing is introduced by a short description of the class.

MovieCat Class

We start with the main `MovieCat` class. It isn't always easy to know in what order to examine source code, but it is often good to start with the main application class.

`MovieCat.java` is the top-level app class derived from `WmvcApp`. This class has the `main` method that gets things rolling. It creates the parts of the app in the `MovieCat` constructor.

After creating the `MovieModel` object, the constructor creates the three views. Finally, it creates a `JSplitPane` with two `JScrollPanes` to hold the `MovieListView` and `MovieItemView` views. The `JSplitPane` is then added to the MainPane provided by Wmvc.

The last thing the `MovieCat` class does is to call `showApp`, which causes the GUI to be displayed, and the Java event loop thread to start.

Listing 6.1 `MovieCat.java`
MovieCat main app class

```
/* MovieCat - A simple Movie Catalog Application
 * Copyright (c) 2001, Bruce E. Wampler
 */

import java.awt.*;
import javax.swing.*;

public class MovieCat extends WmvcApp
{
    private MainView mainView;
    private MovieListView listView;
    private MovieItemView itemView;

    public MovieCat(String name)        // constructor
    {
        super(name, true, true);     // Create with menu, toolbar

        // **** First, create the model
        setModel( (WmvcModel) new MovieModel() );
```

[1.] Note that some of these listings have a few awkward line breaks caused by the need to fit the page size of this book. The full source code is included on the book's CD.

```
        // **** Next, create the view/controllers
        mainView = new MainView();        // won't use any panels
        listView = new MovieListView(); // list view for left
        itemView = new MovieItemView(); // item view for right

        // **** Create a split pane, add list and item views
        JScrollPane listPane =
            new JScrollPane(listView.getPanel());
        JScrollPane itemPane =
            new JScrollPane(itemView.getPanel());
        JSplitPane splitPane =
            new JSplitPane(JSplitPane.HORIZONTAL_SPLIT,
                listPane, itemPane);
        splitPane.setOneTouchExpandable(true);   // details
        splitPane.setDividerLocation(200);
        Dimension minimumSize = new Dimension(100, 50);
        listPane.setMinimumSize(minimumSize);
        itemPane.setMinimumSize(minimumSize);

        WmvcApp.addMainPane(splitPane); // add splitter
    }

    public boolean appClosing()
    {
        return mainView.closingCurrentMovie(true);
    }

    public static void main(String[] args)
    {
        final MovieCat movieCat =
            new MovieCat("MovieCat Movie Catalog Application");

        WmvcApp.getContentPanel().setPreferredSize(
            new Dimension(640, 300)); // make bigger than default
        movieCat.showApp();                // pop it up
    }
}
```

Movie Class

Since the Movie class is used by almost all the other classes, it is the next class we will examine. The Movie class follows the design shown in the UML in Figure 6.3 on page 154. Each attribute is implemented as a protected value, and setters and getters are provided for each attribute. There is a clone method to support cloning.

The readMovie and writeMovie classes are the most interesting. Java provides a rich library for doing I/O. One alternative to consider when writing and reading objects to a file is to use Java's Serializable feature, which allows you to read or write an entire object with a single statement. This is very convenient and easy to use. A problem with Serializable objects, however, is that each saved object represents the exact form of an object. If you change the class definition of the object in any way, such as adding a new attribute variable, the serialized form also changes, and you are no longer able to read previous versions of the object.

Because it is likely that the definition of the Movie class will change, readMovie and writeMovie use Java's DataInputStream and DataOutputStream. Each attribute is handled separately. If the definition of Movie ever changes, it would be simple to write a program to convert the format of an old saved movie database to that of the latest version.

Listing 6.2 Movie.java
Movie class

```
/* Movie - Defines and manipulates a Movie object for MovieCat
 * Copyright (c) 2001, Bruce E. Wampler
 */

import java.io.*;

public class Movie
    implements Cloneable
{
    protected String title;
    protected String director;
    protected String year;
    protected int genre;
    protected int rating;
    protected int format;
    protected int evaluation;
    protected String label;
    protected String comments;

    public void setTitle(String name) { title = name; }
    public String getTitle() { return title; }
    public void setDirector(String dir) { director = dir; }
    public String getDirector() { return director; }
    public void setYear(String yr) { year = yr; }
    public String getYear() { return year; }
    public void setGenre(int g) { genre = g; }
    public int getGenre() { return genre; }
    public void setRating(int r) { rating = r; }
    public int getRating() { return rating; }
    public void setFormat(int f) { format = f; }
    public int getFormat() {return format;}
    public void setEvaluation(int e) { evaluation = e; }
    public int getEvaluation() { return evaluation; }
    public void setLabel(String l) { label = l; }
    public String getLabel() { return label; }
    public void setComments(String c) { comments = c; }
    public String getComments() { return comments; }
```

```java
public Movie()
{
    title = new String(""); director = new String("");
    year = new String("");        genre = 0;
    rating = 0;                    format = 0;
    label = new String("");        evaluation = 0;
    comments = new String("");
}

// override Object.clone()
public Object clone()
{
    Movie c = null;
    try
    {
        c = (Movie)super.clone();        // copy ints
        c.title = new String(title);     // String doesn't
        c.director = new String(director); // have clone so
        c.label = new String(label);     // make copy of
        c.comments = new String(comments); // each String
    }
    catch (CloneNotSupportedException e)
    {
        System.out.println(
                "Should never happen: Movie clone failed.");
    }
    return c;
}

public boolean readMovie(DataInputStream in)  ⟵
    throws IOException
{
    try                // read one MovieCat record
    {
        title = new String(in.readUTF()); 2.
        director = new String(in.readUTF());
        year = new String(in.readUTF());
        genre = in.readInt();
        rating = in.readInt();
        format = in.readInt();
        evaluation = in.readInt();
        label = new String(in.readUTF());
        comments = new String(in.readUTF());
        return true;
    }
    catch (EOFException e)  // all records read
    {
        in.close();
        return false;
    }
}
```

```
public void writeMovie(DataOutputStream out)
    throws IOException
{
    out.writeUTF(title);
    out.writeUTF(director);
    out.writeUTF(year);
    out.writeInt(genre);
    out.writeInt(rating);
    out.writeInt(format);
    out.writeInt(evaluation);
    out.writeUTF(label);
    out.writeUTF(comments);

}
}
```

MovieModel Class

The MovieModel class closely follows the UML design shown in Figure 6.5 on page 156. There are some details worth covering.

The attributes listChanged and editsMade serve slightly different purposes. The listChanged is needed to interact with the MovieListView when the list of movies changes in any way. The editsMade tracks whether any changes have been made to any of the movies in the movie list, and is used to determine if the movie list needs to be saved when the application closes.

The movie list aggregation is implemented using a Java Vector. A Vector is a standard collection class provided by the Java library, and it makes handling the list almost trivial. One of the features of a Vector is the iterator[2] it provides. The iterator is used twice in the MovieModel class.

MovieModel provides the high-level methods needed to read and write an entire movie list. These methods, in turn, rely on the Movie methods readMovie and writeMovie. MovieModel adds an ID tag to the beginning of the movie list file so that the format of the file can be checked and identified.

Listing 6.3 MovieModel.java
The MovieModel class

```
/* MovieModel - implements the movie model. Handles changes.
 * Copyright 2001, Bruce E. Wampler
 */

import java.io.*;
import java.util.*;
import java.awt.*;
```

---

[2]. The iterator is another design pattern used for accessing every item in a collection of objects.

```java
import java.awt.event.*;
import javax.swing.*;

public class MovieModel
    extends      WmvcModel
{
    private int currentMovieIndex;
    private Vector theList;
    private final int FILE_ID = 48879;   // 0xBEEF

    // need two changed flags - one if a new entry has been
    // added that is true only until the views update, and a
    // global one that remains true if anything has changed
    // until the list is saved
    private boolean listChanged;    // true until views updated
    private boolean editsMade;              // true until saved
    private File myFile;

    public ListIterator getMovieListIterator()
        { return theList.listIterator();}
    public boolean getListChanged() { return listChanged; }
    public boolean getEditsMade() { return editsMade; }
    public int getCurrentMovieIndex()
        { return currentMovieIndex; }
    public int getNumberOfMovies() { return theList.size(); }
    public File getFile() { return myFile; }

    public MovieModel()
    {
        editsMade = false;
        listChanged = false;
        theList = new Vector();
        myFile = null;
    }

    public void setCurrentMovieIndex(int movieNumber)
    {
        if (theList == null || theList.size() == 0) // valid?
            return;
        // Validate number passed in, wrap appropriately
        if (movieNumber < 0)
            movieNumber = theList.size() - 1;
        if (movieNumber >= theList.size())
            movieNumber = 0;

        currentMovieIndex = movieNumber;   // change the movie
        notifyViews();                             // update
    }

    public void addMovie(Movie movie)
    {
        if (movie == null)                  // some validation
            return;
```

```
        editsMade = true;           // we've made some changes
        listChanged = true;

        ListIterator it = getMovieListIterator();
        int nextI = 0;

        while (it.hasNext())
        {
            // Assume list is sorted, so as soon as we find the
            // first entry that is > than this one, we insert
            // it before that one.

            nextI = it.nextIndex();     // index of next entry
            Movie m = (Movie) it.next();
            String adding = movie.getTitle();
            String curName = m.getTitle();
            if (adding.compareToIgnoreCase(curName) <= 0)
                break;                  // curName > adding
        }

        if (!it.hasNext())      // add at end (also if 1st time)
        {
            theList.add(movie);
            // make it current movie
            setCurrentMovieIndex(theList.size() - 1);
        }
        else                    // add it before nextI
        {
            theList.add(nextI,movie);
            setCurrentMovieIndex(nextI);
        }
    }

    public void deleteCurrentMovie()
    {
        if (theList.size() <= 0)
            return;

        editsMade = true;       // we've made some changes
        listChanged = true;

        theList.removeElementAt(currentMovieIndex);
        setCurrentMovieIndex(currentMovieIndex);
    }

    public void replaceCurrentMovie(Movie movie)
    {
        if (movie == null)
            return;

        theList.setElementAt(movie,currentMovieIndex);
        editsMade = true;       // we've made some changes
```

```java
        listChanged = true;
        notifyViews();
}

public boolean saveMovies()
{
    return saveMoviesAs(myFile);
}

public boolean saveMoviesAs(File file)
{
    if (file != null)
    {
        try
        {
            DataOutputStream out = new DataOutputStream(
                    new BufferedOutputStream(
                        new FileOutputStream(file)));
            out.writeInt(FILE_ID);
            ListIterator it = getMovieListIterator();
            while (it.hasNext())
            {
                Movie m = (Movie) it.next();
                m.writeMovie(out);
            }
            out.flush(); out.close();
            myFile = file;           // remember name
        }
        catch (IOException e)
        {
            JOptionPane.showMessageDialog(
                WmvcApp.getFrame(),
                "Error opening file: " + e,
                    "MovieCat Error",
                JOptionPane.ERROR_MESSAGE);
            return false;
        }
    }
    else
        return false;

    editsMade = false;              // no edits now!
    return true;
}

public boolean openMovies(File file)
{
    if (file != null)
    {
        myFile = file;              // remember the name
        try
```

```
                    {
                        DataInputStream in = new DataInputStream(
                                new BufferedInputStream(
                                    new FileInputStream(file)));
                        // check if file was made by us
                        if (in.readInt() != FILE_ID)
                        {
                            in.close();
                            myFile = null;
                            JOptionPane.showMessageDialog(
                                WmvcApp.getFrame(),
                                file.getName() +
                                " is not a valid MovieCat file.",
                                "MovieCat Error",
                                JOptionPane.ERROR_MESSAGE);
                            return false;
                        }
                        for ( ; ; )        // do until catch EOF Exception
                        {
                            Movie m = new Movie();
                            if (!m.readMovie(in))   ← see pg 162
                                break;
                            theList.add(m);
                        }
                    }
                    catch (IOException e)
                    {
                        JOptionPane.showMessageDialog(
                            WmvcApp.getFrame(),
                            "Error reading file: " + e,
                                "MovieCat Error",
                            JOptionPane.ERROR_MESSAGE);
                        myFile = null;
                        return false;
                    }

                    editsMade = false;          // no edits to start
                    listChanged = true;
                    notifyViews();
                    return true;
                }
                else
                    return false;
            }

            public boolean closeMovies()
            {
                // Just close - Views responsible to save before closing
                myFile = null;                  // reset to empty values
                theList.clear();
                editsMade = false;              // no edits now!
                listChanged = true;
```

```
        notifyViews();
        return true;
    }

?   public Movie getCurrentMovie()
    {
        if (currentMovieIndex < 0
                    && currentMovieIndex >= theList.size())
            return null;
        else if (theList.size() == 0)
            return null;
        else
            return (Movie)theList.elementAt(currentMovieIndex);
    }

    public void notifyViews()
    {
        super.notifyViews();
        // updating views makes list correct
        listChanged = false;
    }
}
```

MainView Class

The MainView class handles defining and implementing the commands on the main menu and tool bars. Because we are using Wmvc, this process is greatly simplified.

To handle some of the commands, MainView uses dialog boxes. Some are standard Java dialogs (for example, JOptionPane, JFileChooser). It also uses the MovieEditor dialog class.

MainView does not display any part of the movie list. Because it only handles control functions, it does not need to provide the update method used by the MVC design.

Listing 6.4 MainView.java
MainView handles menu and tool bars

```
/* MainView - Top level view/controller for the MovieCat
 *
 * This is the main view/controller.
 * The main view/controller interacts with the model for
 * the global commands like open and save list in a file.
 * Copyright (c) 2001, Bruce E. Wampler
 */

import java.io.*;
import java.util.*;
import java.awt.*;
```

```java
import java.awt.event.*;
import javax.swing.*;
import javax.swing.filechooser.*;

public class MainView extends WmvcView
{
    private JFileChooser fc;        // instance of a file chooser
    private MovieEditor theMovieEditor; // instance of editor
    private MovieModel myModel; // local copy of model reference

    public MainView()
    {
        myModel = (MovieModel) WmvcApp.getModel();
        myModel.addView(this);

        // Create file chooser dialog. We will tell it to open
        // in the "user.dir" directory, which will usually be
        // the "current directory" when the program is started.
        // This will let the user use the "Start In" setting
        // on Windows, for example.

        fc = new JFileChooser(  // file chooser in current dir.
                new File(System.getProperty("user.dir")));

        createControls(); // Create controls - menus,toolbar

        theMovieEditor = MovieEditor.getInstance();  // editor
        theMovieEditor.initialize();
    }

    public boolean closingCurrentMovie(boolean ask)
    {
        // Check if current movie has changed, ask if want to
        // save. Returns true if saved or didn't want to save,
        // false if save fails or user cancels.
        if (myModel.getEditsMade())    ← pg 164
        {
            if (ask)                // interactive closing
            {
                switch (JOptionPane.showConfirmDialog(
                        WmvcApp.getFrame(),
                        "The movie list has changed since you "
                        + "last saved it.\n"
                        + "Save the current movie list?",
                        "Movie List Has Changed",
                    JOptionPane.YES_NO_CANCEL_OPTION))
                {
                    case JOptionPane.NO_OPTION:
                        return true;   // don't save, but done
                    case JOptionPane.CANCEL_OPTION:
                    case JOptionPane.CLOSED_OPTION:
                        return false;
                    default:
```

```java
                        break;              // YES
                }
                if (myModel.getFile() == null)
                {
                    int retV =
                        fc.showSaveDialog(WmvcApp.getFrame());
                    if (retV == JFileChooser.APPROVE_OPTION)
                    {
                        File file = fc.getSelectedFile();
                        if (!myModel.saveMoviesAs(file))
                            return false;
                        else
                        {
                            myModel.closeMovies();
                            return true;
                        }
                    }
                    else
                        return false;
                }
            }
            myModel.saveMovies();
            myModel.closeMovies();
        }
        return true;
    }

    private void createControls()
    {
        // This is the Controller for this view. It creates the
        // menu & toolbar and implements all the control code,
        // mostly in anonymous WmvcExecutor classes.

        // MenuBar: File
        JMenu fileMenu = new JMenu("File");

        // File->Open Movie List
        WmvcMenuItemCtl fileOpen = new WmvcMenuItemCtl(fileMenu,
            "Open Movie List","images/open-16.gif", 'O',
            null /* no accel */, new WmvcExecutor()
            {
                public void execute(ActionEvent event)
                {
                    if (!closingCurrentMovie(true))
                        return;

                    int retV =
                        fc.showOpenDialog(WmvcApp.getFrame());
                    if (retV == JFileChooser.APPROVE_OPTION)
                    {
                        File file = fc.getSelectedFile();
                        myModel.openMovies(file);
                    }
```

```
            }
    });

    // File->Save Movie List
    WmvcMenuItemCtl fileSave = new WmvcMenuItemCtl(fileMenu,
        "Save Movie List","images/save-16.gif", 'S',
        null /* no accel */, new WmvcExecutor()
        {
            public void execute(ActionEvent event)
            {
                if (myModel.getFile() == null)
                {
                    JOptionPane.showMessageDialog(
                    WmvcApp.getFrame(),
                     "No movie file name specified.\n"
                    + "Use \"Save MovieList As\" instead.",
                    "No file name specified",
                    JOptionPane.ERROR_MESSAGE);
                }
                else
                    myModel.saveMovies();
            }
    });

    // File->Save Movie List
    WmvcMenuItemCtl fileSaveAs = new WmvcMenuItemCtl(
        fileMenu,
        "Save Movie List As","images/gray.gif",
        'A', null /* no accel */, new WmvcExecutor()
        {
            public void execute(ActionEvent event)
            {
                int retV =
                    fc.showSaveDialog(WmvcApp.getFrame());
                if (retV == JFileChooser.APPROVE_OPTION)
                {
                    File file = fc.getSelectedFile();
                    myModel.saveMoviesAs(file);
                }
            }
    });

WmvcApp.addMenu(fileMenu);        // Add to app menu

// MenuBar: Edit
JMenu editMenu = new JMenu("Edit");

// Edit->Edit Current Movie
WmvcMenuItemCtl editEdit = new WmvcMenuItemCtl(editMenu,
    "Edit Current Movie","images/gray.gif", 'E',
    null /* no accel */,  new WmvcExecutor()
    {
        public void execute(ActionEvent event)
```

```
            {
                Movie edited = theMovieEditor.showDialog(
                    WmvcApp.getFrame(),
                    myModel.getCurrentMovie());
                myModel.replaceCurrentMovie(edited);
            }
        });

    // Edit->Add New Movie
    WmvcMenuItemCtl editNew = new WmvcMenuItemCtl(editMenu,
        "Add New Movie","images/addmovie-16.gif", 'A',
        null /* no accel */, new WmvcExecutor()
        {
            public void execute(ActionEvent event)
            {
                Movie blank = new Movie();
                Movie newMovie = theMovieEditor.showDialog(
                    WmvcApp.getFrame(), blank);
                myModel.addMovie(newMovie);
            }
        });

    // Edit->Remove Current Movie
    WmvcMenuItemCtl editRemove = new WmvcMenuItemCtl(
        editMenu,
        "Remove Current Movie","images/delx.gif", 'R',
         null /* no accel */, new WmvcExecutor()
        {
            public void execute(ActionEvent event)
            {
                myModel.deleteCurrentMovie();
            }
        });

    WmvcApp.addMenu(editMenu);        // Add to app menu

    // ToolBar: Open
    WmvcTBButtonCtl toolOpen = new WmvcTBButtonCtl(
        "Open","images/open-16.gif",
        "Open an Existing Movie List",
        fileOpen.getWmvcExecutor()); // reuse fileopen exec

    // ToolBar: Add
    WmvcTBButtonCtl toolAdd = new WmvcTBButtonCtl(
        "Add Movie", "images/addmovie-16.gif",
        "Add a new movie",
        editNew.getWmvcExecutor()); // reuse editNew exec
    }
}
```

MovieListView Class

The MovieListView class implements the movie list browser shown in the left side of the split pane. It uses a Java JList in a JPanel to do this. The JList is created in the constructor and is handled by the valueChanged method of the ListSelectionListener implemented by the class. When the user selects a different movie from the list, MovieListView sends a message to the MovieModel to change the current movie, which then causes the MVC notifyViews to be called to update all the views.

Some code uses the updating attribute, which is needed to avoid some interaction between MVC update messages and list change messages coming from the JList object.

Listing 6.5 MovieListView.java
MovieListView implements the movie list browser

```
/*
 * MovieListView - the list View of the MovieCat model.
 *  This view implements the view of the movie list
 * Copyright (c) 2001, Bruce E. Wampler
 */

import java.util.*;
import java.awt.*;
import java.awt.event.*;
import javax.swing.*;
import javax.swing.event.*;

public class MovieListView
    extends WmvcView
    implements  ListSelectionListener    // for JList
{
    // need updating to avoid interaction between update and
    // valueChanged listener
    private static boolean updating = false;
    private JPanel listPanel;
    private JList jlist;

    private MovieModel myModel;
    private DefaultListModel movieList;

    public JPanel getPanel() { return listPanel; }

    public MovieListView()
    {
        // Build list view which is simply a JList in a JPanel
        myModel = (MovieModel)WmvcApp.getModel();
        myModel.addView(this);  // add view to model list
```

```
        movieList = new DefaultListModel(); // first allocation
        movieList.addElement("No Movie List Opened");

        listPanel = new JPanel();
        listPanel.setLayout(new BorderLayout());

        jlist = new JList(movieList);
        jlist.setSelectionMode(
                    ListSelectionModel.SINGLE_SELECTION);
        jlist.setSelectedIndex(0);
        jlist.addListSelectionListener(this); // valueChanged

        listPanel.add(jlist,BorderLayout.CENTER);
    }

    public void updateView()
    {
        // Called when model changes
        updating = true;
        // if list changed, don't need to refresh here
        if (myModel.getListChanged())
        {
            movieList.ensureCapacity(
                            myModel.getNumberOfMovies() + 8);
            movieList.clear();

            // See if just the selection changed
            // copy titles from movie list to view list
            ListIterator it = myModel.getMovieListIterator();
            while (it.hasNext())
              {
                Movie m = (Movie) it.next();
                movieList.addElement(m.getTitle());
              }
        }
        // Always update selected item
        // Note that by using the DefaultListModel, these will
        // trigger valueChanged, so we need the updating value
        jlist.setSelectedIndex(myModel.getCurrentMovieIndex());
        jlist.ensureIndexIsVisible(
                            myModel.getCurrentMovieIndex());
        updating = false;
    }

    // Implement ListSelectionListener
    public void valueChanged(ListSelectionEvent e)
    {
        if (e.getValueIsAdjusting()) // Still adjusting?
            return;

        JList theList = (JList)e.getSource();
        if (! theList.isSelectionEmpty())
        {
```

```
                    int index = theList.getSelectedIndex();
                    // now set the model to use the selected movie name
                    if (!updating)
                        myModel.setCurrentMovieIndex(index);
                }
            }
        }
```

MovieItemView Class

Although the MovieItemView class seems long, it is not complex. Most of its bulk comes from the code needed to set up the Swing component layout. The view consists of JLabel, JTextArea, and JButton components laid out in a GridBagLayout.

It turns out that the helper classes for the list-like Movie attributes are the most useful in this MovieItemView class and the MovieEditor class. By providing the helper classes, MovieItemView and MovieEditor can use the String values provided by the helper classes rather than define their own String arrays or use long switch statements to determine the values of those attributes for display in the GUI.

MovieItemView also defines the protected setAndAdd method to help simplify defining the various components added to the view panel.

Listing 6.6 MovieItemView.java
MovieItemView shows details of each Movie

```
/*
 * MovieItemView - the item View for the MovieCat model.
 * This implements a view of a single item - the current movie.
 * Copyright (c) 2001, Bruce E. Wampler
 */

import java.util.*;
import java.awt.*;
import java.awt.event.*;
import javax.swing.*;

public class MovieItemView
        extends         WmvcView
        implements      ActionListener  // for buttons
{
    protected GridBagLayout gridbag;
    protected GridBagConstraints c;

    private JPanel itemPanel;
    private MovieModel myModel;          // local copy
```

```java
// Various components needed for constructing the view
// We use private statics of each of these since there will
// be only one instance of the itemView

private static JLabel lblTitle=new JLabel("Movie Title: ");
private static JLabel fldTitle = new JLabel(" ");
private static JLabel lblDirector=new JLabel("Director: ");
private static JLabel fldDirector = new JLabel(" ");
private static JLabel lblYear = new JLabel("Year: ");
private static JLabel fldYear = new JLabel(" ");
private static JLabel lblRating = new JLabel("Rating: ");
private static JLabel fldRating = new JLabel(" ");
private static JLabel lblGenre = new JLabel("    Genre: ");
private static JLabel fldGenre = new JLabel(" ");
private static JLabel lblFormat = new JLabel("    Format: ");
private static JLabel fldFormat = new JLabel(" ");
private static JLabel lblLabel = new JLabel("    Label: ");
private static JLabel fldLabel = new JLabel(" ");
private static JLabel lblEvaluation =
                          new JLabel("My Rating: ");
private static JLabel fldEvaluation = new JLabel(" ");
private static JLabel lblComments=new JLabel("Comments: ");

private static JTextArea textArea;
private static JButton bPrevious;
private static JButton bNext;
private static JButton bEdit;

public JPanel getPanel() { return itemPanel; }

protected void setAndAdd(JComponent comp,
    int gx, int gy, int gheight, int gwidth, double wx)
{
    // to simplify laying out the gridbag
    c.anchor = c.WEST;
    c.gridx = gx; c.gridy = gy;
    c.gridheight = gheight; c.gridwidth = gwidth;
    c.weightx = wx;
    gridbag.setConstraints(comp,c);
    itemPanel.add(comp);
}

public MovieItemView()
{
    myModel = (MovieModel)WmvcApp.getModel();
    myModel.addView(this);          // adds update

    // We will use a GridBag for simple layout of itemView

    itemPanel = new JPanel();        // surrounding Panel
    gridbag = new GridBagLayout();
    c = new GridBagConstraints();
```

```
itemPanel.setLayout(gridbag);
itemPanel.setBorder(BorderFactory.createEmptyBorder(
                                        5, 5, 5, 5));

// Set data fields to black foreground
fldTitle.setForeground(Color.black);
fldDirector.setForeground(Color.black);
fldYear.setForeground(Color.black);
fldRating.setForeground(Color.black);
fldGenre.setForeground(Color.black);
fldFormat.setForeground(Color.black);
fldLabel.setForeground(Color.black);
fldEvaluation.setForeground(Color.black);

// Movie Title: _____
setAndAdd(lblTitle, 0, 0, 1, 1, 1.0);
setAndAdd(fldTitle, 1, 0, 1, c.REMAINDER, 0.);

// Director: _____
setAndAdd(lblDirector, 0, 1, 1, 1, 1.0);
setAndAdd(fldDirector, 1, 1, 1, c.REMAINDER, 0.0);

// Year: _____       Genre: _____
setAndAdd(lblYear,  0, 2, 1, 1, 1.0);
setAndAdd(fldYear,  1, 2, 1, 1, 0.0);
setAndAdd(lblGenre, 2, 2, 1, c.RELATIVE,0.0);
setAndAdd(fldGenre, 3, 2, 1, c.REMAINDER,0.0);

// Rating: _____     Format: _____
setAndAdd(lblRating,  0, 3, 1, 1, 1.0);
setAndAdd(fldRating,  1, 3, 1, 1, 0.0);
setAndAdd(lblFormat,  2, 3, 1, c.RELATIVE, 0.0);
setAndAdd(fldFormat,  3, 3, 1, c.REMAINDER, 0.);

// My Rating: _____     Label: _____
setAndAdd(lblEvaluation,  0, 4, 1, 1, 1.0);
setAndAdd(fldEvaluation,  1, 4, 1, 1, 0.);
setAndAdd(lblLabel,       2, 4, 1, c.RELATIVE, 0.0);
setAndAdd(fldLabel,       3, 4, 1, c.REMAINDER, 0.);

// Comment box:
setAndAdd(lblComments,  0,5,1,1, 0.0);
textArea = new JTextArea(4,30);
JScrollPane textScroll = new JScrollPane(textArea);
setAndAdd(textScroll, 1,5,4,c.REMAINDER, 0.0);

// Command Buttons
bEdit =   new JButton(" Edit  ");
bEdit.setActionCommand("edit");
bEdit.addActionListener(this);
bEdit.setToolTipText("Edit current movie");
setAndAdd(bEdit, 1,9,1,1, 0.0);
```

```java
    bPrevious = new JButton("Previous");
    bPrevious.addActionListener(this);
    bPrevious.setActionCommand("previous");
    bPrevious.setIcon(new ImageIcon("images/left-16.gif"));
    bPrevious.setToolTipText("Go to previous movie");
    setAndAdd(bPrevious, 2,9,1,1, 0.0);

    bNext =      new JButton("Next");
    bNext.setActionCommand("next");
    bNext.addActionListener(this);
    bNext.setIcon(new ImageIcon("images/right-16.gif"));
    bNext.setToolTipText("Go to next movie");
    setAndAdd(bNext, 3,9,1,1,0.0);
}

public void updateView()
{
    // When model changes - update each fld component
    Movie m = myModel.getCurrentMovie();

    fldTitle.setText(m.getTitle());
    fldDirector.setText(m.getDirector());
    fldYear.setText(m.getYear());
    fldLabel.setText(m.getLabel());
    textArea.setText(m.getComments());

    fldRating.setText(MovieRating.stringAt(m.getRating()));
    fldGenre.setText(MovieGenre.stringAt(m.getGenre()));
    fldFormat.setText(MovieFormat.stringAt(m.getFormat()));
    fldEvaluation.setText(
            MovieEvaluation.stringAt(m.getEvaluation()));
}

// Implement ActionListener
public void actionPerformed(ActionEvent e)
{
    // Since only three buttons, easier to use one listener
    if (e.getActionCommand().equals("edit"))
    {
        Movie edited =
            MovieEditor.getInstance().showDialog(
                WmvcApp.getFrame(),
                myModel.getCurrentMovie());
        myModel.replaceCurrentMovie(edited);
    }
    else if (e.getActionCommand().equals("previous"))
    {
        myModel.setCurrentMovieIndex(
            myModel.getCurrentMovieIndex()-1);
    }
    else if (e.getActionCommand().equals("next"))
```

```
            {
                myModel.setCurrentMovieIndex(
                    myModel.getCurrentMovieIndex()+1);
            }
        }
    }
```

MovieEditor Class

The MovieEditor class extends the Swing JDialog class to implement a modal dialog to edit Movies. Much of its code is very similar to the MovieItemView because it follows the same layout of Movie attributes. It uses JComboBox components to allow the user to select from a list of attributes, and JTextField components to allow the String values to be edited.

There is no interaction between the MovieModel and the MovieEditor. MovieEditor dialogs are created by the MainView and MovieItemView classes in response to user commands. The edited Movie object from the MovieEditor is handled appropriately by those classes.[3]

Listing 6.7 MovieEditor.java
MovieEditor lets user edit a movie

```
/* MovieEditor - edits a Movie object for MovieCat
 * Copyright (c) 2001, Bruce E. Wampler
 */

import java.awt.*;
import java.awt.event.*;
import javax.swing.*;

public class MovieEditor
    extends      JDialog
    implements   ActionListener
{
    // Implement MovieEditor with Singleton pattern
    private static MovieEditor theMovieEditor = null;
    private Movie editedMovie = null;

    protected GridBagLayout gridbag;
    protected GridBagConstraints c;

    private JPanel itemPanel;

    // Various components needed for constructing the view
    // We use private statics of each of these since there will
    // be only one instance of the editor
```

[3.] Only one copy of the MovieEditor will exist. Thus, MovieEditor was implemented using the Singleton design pattern.

```java
private static JLabel lblTitle=new JLabel("Movie Title: ");
private static JTextField fldTitle = new JTextField(30);
private static JLabel lblDirector=new JLabel("Director: ");
private static JTextField fldDirector = new JTextField(30);
private static JLabel lblYear = new JLabel("Year: ");
private static JTextField fldYear = new JTextField(6);
private static JLabel lblRating = new JLabel("Rating: ");
private static JComboBox fldRating;
private static JLabel lblGenre = new JLabel("  Genre: ");
private static JComboBox fldGenre;
private static JLabel lblFormat = new JLabel("  Format: ");
private static JComboBox fldFormat;
private static JLabel lblLabel = new JLabel("  Label: ");
private static JTextField fldLabel = new JTextField(8);
private static JLabel lblEvaluation =
                            new JLabel("My Rating: ");
private static JComboBox fldEvaluation;
private static JLabel lblComments=new JLabel("Comments: ");

private static JTextArea textArea;
private static JButton bPrevious;
private static JButton bNext;
private static JButton bUpdate;
private static JButton bRevert;

private Movie movie;        // for a local copy

protected void setAndAdd(JComponent comp,
int gx, int gy, int gheight, int gwidth)
{
    // to simplify laying out the gridbag
    c.anchor = c.WEST;
    c.gridx = gx; c.gridy = gy;
    c.gridheight = gheight; c.gridwidth = gwidth;
    gridbag.setConstraints(comp,c);
    itemPanel.add(comp);
}

static public MovieEditor getInstance()
{
    if (theMovieEditor == null)
    {
        theMovieEditor = new MovieEditor();
    }
    return theMovieEditor;
}

public MovieEditor()
{
    // call JDialog constructor
    super(WmvcApp.getFrame(), "Edit Movie", true);
}
```

```java
public void initialize()
{
    // We will use a GridBag for simple layout of itemView
    itemPanel = new JPanel();           // surrounding Panel

    gridbag = new GridBagLayout();
    c = new GridBagConstraints();
    itemPanel.setLayout(gridbag);

    itemPanel.setBorder(BorderFactory.createEmptyBorder(
                                        5, 5, 5, 5));

    // Movie Title: _____
    setAndAdd(lblTitle, 0, 0, 1, 1);
    setAndAdd(fldTitle, 1, 0, 1, c.REMAINDER);

    // Director: _____
    setAndAdd(lblDirector, 0, 1, 1, 1);
    setAndAdd(fldDirector, 1, 1, 1, c.REMAINDER);

    // Year: _____      Genre: _____
    setAndAdd(lblYear,  0, 2, 1, 1);
    setAndAdd(fldYear,  1, 2, 1, 1);
    setAndAdd(lblGenre, 2, 2, 1, c.RELATIVE);
    fldGenre = new JComboBox(MovieGenre.getNames());
    setAndAdd(fldGenre, 3, 2, 1, c.REMAINDER);

    // Rating: _____     Format: _____
    setAndAdd(lblRating,  0, 3, 1, 1);
    fldRating = new JComboBox(MovieRating.getNames());
    setAndAdd(fldRating,  1, 3, 1, 1);
    setAndAdd(lblFormat,  2, 3, 1, c.RELATIVE);
    fldFormat = new JComboBox(MovieFormat.getNames());
    setAndAdd(fldFormat,  3, 3, 1, c.REMAINDER);

    // My Rating: _____     Label: _____
    setAndAdd(lblEvaluation,  0, 4, 1, 1);
    fldEvaluation = new JComboBox(
                            MovieEvaluation.getNames());
    setAndAdd(fldEvaluation,  1, 4, 1, 1);
    setAndAdd(lblLabel,       2, 4, 1, c.RELATIVE);
    setAndAdd(fldLabel,       3, 4, 1, c.REMAINDER);

    // Comment box:
    setAndAdd(lblComments,  0,5,1,1);
    textArea = new JTextArea(4,30);
    JScrollPane textScroll = new JScrollPane(textArea);
    setAndAdd(textScroll, 1,5,4,c.REMAINDER);

    // Command Buttons

    bRevert =    new JButton(" Cancel ");
    bRevert.setActionCommand("revert");
```

```java
        bRevert.addActionListener(this);
        setAndAdd(bRevert, 2,9,1,1);

        bUpdate =   new JButton("   OK   ");
        bUpdate.setActionCommand("update");
        bUpdate.addActionListener(this);
        setAndAdd(bUpdate, 3,9,1,1);

        Container contentPane = getContentPane();
        contentPane.add(itemPanel,BorderLayout.CENTER);
        pack();
    }

    public Movie showDialog(Component comp, Movie m)
    {
        if (theMovieEditor == null || m == null)
            return null;
        editedMovie = null;

        movie = (Movie)m.clone();// make a copy to work with

        // Set box to current fields
        fldTitle.setText(movie.getTitle());
        fldDirector.setText(movie.getDirector());
        fldYear.setText(movie.getYear());
        fldLabel.setText(movie.getLabel());
        fldRating.setSelectedIndex(movie.getRating());
        fldGenre.setSelectedIndex(movie.getGenre());
        fldFormat.setSelectedIndex(movie.getFormat());
        fldEvaluation.setSelectedIndex(movie.getEvaluation());
        textArea.setText(movie.getComments());

        setLocationRelativeTo(comp);
        setVisible(true);

        // will now wait here until actionPerformed
        // calls setVisible(false)

        return editedMovie;
    }

    // Implement ActionListener
    public void actionPerformed(ActionEvent e)
    {
        if (e.getActionCommand().equals("update"))
        {
            movie.setTitle(fldTitle.getText());
            movie.setDirector(fldDirector.getText());
            movie.setYear(fldYear.getText());
            movie.setLabel(fldLabel.getText());
            movie.setRating(fldRating.getSelectedIndex());
            movie.setGenre(fldGenre.getSelectedIndex());
            movie.setFormat(fldFormat.getSelectedIndex());
```

```
                    movie.setEvaluation(
                                   fldEvaluation.getSelectedIndex());
                    movie.setComments(textArea.getText());
                    editedMovie = movie;
                    setVisible(false);
               }
               else if (e.getActionCommand().equals("revert"))
               {
                    editedMovie = null;
                    setVisible(false);
               }
          }
     }
```

Movie Helper Classes

The helper classes are all nearly identical. Logically, the classes could have been derived from a single superclass. However, to maximize the ease of using these helper classes (specifically, making them completely static with no need for constructors), they were implemented as individual classes.

Listing 6.8 MovieEvaluation.java
Helper class for evaluation attribute

```
/* MovieEvaluation -  very simple helper class
 * Copyright 2001, Bruce E. Wampler
 */
public class MovieEvaluation
{
    private static String[] values =
       {
         "*", "**", "***", "****", "*****"
       };

    public static int indexOf(String str)
    {
        for (int ix = 0 ; ix < values.length ; ++ix)
            if (values[ix].equals(str))
                return ix;
        return 0;
    }
    public static String stringAt(int at)
    {
        if (at < 0 || at >= values.length)
            return "-";
        return values[at];
    }
    public static String[] getNames()
    {
        return values;
    }
}
```

Listing 6.9 MovieFormat.java
Helper class for format attribute

```java
/* MovieFormat -  very simple helper class
 * Copyright 2001, Bruce E. Wampler
 */
public class MovieFormat
{
    private static String[] values =
      {
        "VHS", "DVD", "VCD", "SVCD", "Hi8", "DV", "Other"
      };

    public static int indexOf(String str)
    {
        for (int ix = 0 ; ix < values.length ; ++ix)
            if (values[ix].equals(str))
                return ix;
        return 0;
    }
    public static String stringAt(int at)
    {
        if (at < 0 || at >= values.length)
            return "Other";
        return values[at];
    }
    public static String[] getNames()
    {
        return values;
    }
}
```

Listing 6.10 MovieGenre.java
Helper class for genre attribute

```java
/* MovieGenre -  very simple helper class
 * Copyright 2001, Bruce E. Wampler
 */
public class MovieGenre
{
    private static String[] values =
      {
        "Drama", "Comedy", "Children", "Family", "Action",
        "Sci-Fi", "Documentary", "Other"
      };

    public static int indexOf(String str)
    {
        for (int ix = 0 ; ix < values.length ; ++ix)
            if (values[ix].equals(str))
                return ix;
        return 0;
    }
```

```java
    public static String stringAt(int at)
    {
        if (at < 0 || at >= values.length)
            return "Other";
        return values[at];
    }
    public static String[] getNames()
    {
        return values;
    }
}
```

Listing 6.11 MovieRating.java
Helper class for rating attribute

```java
/* MovieRating -  very simple helper class
 * Copyright 2001, Bruce E. Wampler
 */
public class MovieRating
{
    private static String[] values =
        {
          "G", "PG", "PG-13", "R", "NC-17", "X", "NR", "Unknown"
        };

    public static int indexOf(String str)
    {
        for (int ix = 0 ; ix < values.length ; ++ix)
            if (values[ix].equals(str))
                return ix;
        return 0;
    }
    public static String stringAt(int at)
    {
        if (at < 0 || at >= values.length)
            return "Unknown";
        return values[at];
    }
    public static String[] getNames()
    {
        return values;
    }
}
```

Review

At the end of the development of any software, one of the most important steps is to review the project and then apply lessons learned to the next round of development. The MovieCat application is not a completely typical case. While it does have a useful purpose, it was designed mostly as a good, short case study for this book, and it meets that goal. It lent itself to an elegant yet simple analysis. It had some nontrivial design issues. It provided an example of using MVC to build a real application, and it could be implemented with a reasonable amount of code to include in a book.

There are still some aspects of MovieCat we can review. For one thing, the program is not really complete. There are several features that could be added for the next release. In fact, the MovieCat app presented in this chapter is not unlike a real-world app; now that we have an initial release version, we need to see what should be added for the second release.

What is missing from MovieCat? The following are some features that might be added.

- More attributes, including actors, writers, awards, language, aspect ratio, and others

- Multiple categories for genre

- Printing

- Searching

- IMDb (Internet Movie DataBase gives complete information about most movies) connectivity

- Import/Export of movie list

- Movie images and clips

How hard would these be to add? Evaluating how easy it would be to modify an existing program is a good measure of how well designed it is. Let's examine a couple of items from the list.

How about adding more attributes? Adding them to the Movie class should be simple. All the attributes we've discussed could easily map to either a String or a new helper class. There would be some problems associated with adding new Movie attributes.

First, we would have to provide a conversion program to convert from the original file format to a new one. This might mean that we would want to revisit the whole issue of file format. Perhaps we would be better off with a format that would not require conversion from one version of MovieCat to the next.

Second, we would have to modify the code for both the MovieItemView and MovieEditor classes to account for the new attributes. However, the Swing GridBagLayout we've used lends itself to easily modifying component layout, and adding the new code would not be much more difficult than writing the original. The fact that all the new attributes are isolated in the Movie class makes the process easier.

What about adding searching capability? This should be easy. We could use two approaches. In either case, the user interface would be most easily added to the `MainView` class. First, we could add a search method to the `MovieModel` class and then use it from the `MainView` interface. A second approach would be to use the iterator provided by the `MovieModel` and implement the search within `MainView`. Keeping the search within `MovieModel` would make the system less sensitive to future changes, but it would limit the searches to whatever the `MovieModel` class provides. Building a search based on the iterator would allow the most flexibility regarding fields that could be used for the search, but it would be sensitive to changes. Either way can easily be added to the current MovieCat code.

Some other changes, such as adding images or IMDb connectivity would require a significant effort to understand which image formats are available, or how to connect and use the IMDb. The effort to add either might equal or exceed the original effort, but it would still fit within the existing design.

The same seems true for the other features. The isolation of the model from the GUI, and the use of MVC, makes it easy to add features to MovieCat.

Chapter Summary

- This chapter uses the material from previous chapters to build a small application.

- A short specification for the MovieCat application was provided.

- The problem was analyzed, and we produced several candidate objects and some analysis-level UML class diagrams.

- The analysis was refined, and we designed several classes for the final implementation. We produced detailed UML class diagrams for some of the classes.

- The design was implemented in Java and Swing.

- We evaluated the resulting design.

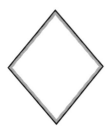

CHAPTER 7

Design Patterns

Design patterns have become an essential part of object-oriented design and programming. They provide elegant and maintainable solutions to commonly encountered programming problems. Before the mid-1990s, design patterns were seldom mentioned. Now it is difficult to find a current article or book about designing software that doesn't mention design patterns. An understanding of design patterns has become a critical part of any object-oriented programmer's toolbox.

A key event in the spread of design patterns was the publication and popular acceptance of the book *Design Patterns: Elements of Reusable Object-Oriented Software*, by Erich Gamma, Richard Helm, Ralph Johnson, and John Vlissides (often called the Gang of Four or just GoF). Currently, design patterns are used mostly for software architecture and design, but the concept of patterns is moving to other areas of software development as well.

The goal of this chapter is to give you a good feeling for what design patterns are and why they can lead to better-designed object-oriented programs. Read one of the design pattern books listed in Resources at the end of the chapter for more complete coverage of design patterns.

What Are Design Patterns?

A big challenge in developing software is to avoid reinventing the wheel. Libraries and frameworks help you to reuse useful tools for many software systems. The tools provided by libraries and frameworks solve common but low-level problems.

Design patterns deal with solving common design problems at a higher level. They do not provide code that can be used for one problem. Rather, they help to generate a design solution for a software problem that has come up repeatedly over many software projects. A design pattern provides a description of a design solution that can be adapted and applied to a specific situation.

The Gang of Four book *Design Patterns* describes 23 patterns arranged into three groups. The groups help classify how the patterns are used. Creational patterns help make a system independent of how the objects it uses are created. Structural patterns are concerned with how classes and objects are organized and composed to build larger structures. Behavioral patterns deal with the assignment of responsibilities to objects and communication between objects.

Using Design Patterns

The complexity of different design patterns ranges from simple to hard. For example, the Iterator design pattern is so simple and basic that it has become an essential feature of the standard Java object collections library. Others, such as the Composite pattern, are more complex and require more experience to recognize their usefulness.

Most of the patterns are not inherently difficult or complex. In fact, good software designers have been using the solutions described by the patterns for years, but without formally recognizing that they could be described as general design guidelines. One of the goals of developing design patterns has been to pass on the experience and knowledge of pattern authors to other programmers to help them produce better designs.

Using design patterns takes some experience. You must have at least a basic understanding of all the patterns available, and then be able to recognize when you have a design situation that can be helped by using a pattern. Often, this requires nothing more than reading through the patterns to see if any fit the case at hand. When a pattern fits, it tends to ring a little bell of recognition. The longer you work with patterns, the easier they become to use.

For the rest of this chapter, we will cover how design patterns are described in the GoF book, go over each of the basic GoF patterns, and finally show how a few patterns have been used in the Wmvc framework and the MovieCat application.

Design Pattern Description Template

The GoF developed a description template in their book that defines their patterns. The GoF template has also been adopted for descriptions of patterns found in other sources. Table 7.1 covers the sections included in the GoF pattern description template.

Table 7.1　Gang of Four Pattern Description Templates

Section	Description
Pattern Name and Classification	The name of the pattern and its classification (creational, structural, or behavioral)
Intent	A short statement about what the pattern does
Also Known As	Alternate well-known names for the pattern
Motivation	An illustrative design problem that shows how the pattern can solve the problem
Applicability	Situations in which the pattern can be used
Structure	A graphical (UML) representation showing the classes in the pattern
Participants	The classes that participate in the pattern and their responsibilities
Collaborations	How the participants collaborate
Consequences	Benefits and trade-offs of using the pattern
Implementation	Hints, pitfalls, and techniques that can be used to help implement the pattern
Sample Code	Code illustrations of using the pattern
Known Uses	Examples of the pattern used in real systems
Related Patterns	Other patterns closely related to the current one

The Gang of Four Patterns

Design Patterns presents descriptions of 23 patterns. Since it was published, other software designers have developed and defined new patterns. (See Resources at the end of the chapter for a list of other pattern resources.) However, the GoF *Design Patterns* remains the standard reference, and this section presents a brief description. The last section presents an example of how patterns can be used in the design of a real software system, in this case, Wmvc and MovieCat.

Creational Patterns

There are five creational patterns.

Abstract Factory

An *Abstract Factory* is a class used to create instances of other objects that are related to or depend on each other, such as creating GUI components for various GUI toolkits. The Abstract Factory lets the application see a unified component while it creates the appropriate concrete object for a given look and feel.

Builder

The *Builder* pattern is used by a Director class to construct different complex objects based on a specific requirement, such as creating a text converter object that can convert text to various formats, depending on how the converter is built.

Factory Method

A *Factory Method* provides a common interface for creating subclasses. The Factory Method is defined in the top-level class definition, but instantiation of the subclasses determines which specific instance of the Factory Method is used.

Prototype

The *Prototype* pattern can reduce the number of different classes by creating new object instances based on a copy or clone of an original prototype instance. The copies can then be modified to carry out their various responsibilities.

Singleton

There are often situations in which you need one and only one instance of a class. Rather than rely on the programmer to create only one instance of a class, the *Singleton* pattern creates only one instance of a class and makes that instance accessible by other objects.

Structural Patterns

There are seven structural patterns.

Adapter

The *Adapter* pattern is used to adapt an interface of one class so that it can be used by another class that originally could not use it. The adapter is sometimes called a Wrapper. For example, Adapters, or Wrappers, are often written for existing libraries so that a new application can use the library.

Bridge

A *Bridge* is used to decouple an abstraction from its implementation. The Bridge pattern is often used to build drivers, such as a printer driver, which connects an application program to a real printer. It is possible to vary the abstraction and the implementation independently.

Composite

The *Composite* pattern is used to compose whole/part hierarchies into a tree structure that lets the client treat either individual objects or compositions of those objects uniformly. An example is a graphical object, which can be made up of individual graphics (such as a line or a square) or other graphical objects (a picture in a picture).

Decorator

The goal of the *Decorator* pattern is to add more responsibilities to an object dynamically, and thus avoid subclassing. An example would be adding scrolling to a text view. The scrolling object surrounds the text view, handles the mechanics of the scroll bar, and then tells the text view to display itself appropriately.

Facade

The *Facade* pattern provides a higher-level unified interface to a set of objects in a subsystem. The extra layer provides a simpler interface to the subsystem and helps to avoid coupling between classes.

Flyweight

The *Flyweight* pattern helps to efficiently use a large number of small objects with sharing. An example is sharing representation of individual characters in a document formatting program.

Proxy

The *Proxy* pattern is similar to the Adapter in that it provides an interface layer between objects. An Adapter changes the interface; a Proxy doesn't. Instead, it controls access to one object from another.

Behavioral Patterns

There are eleven behavioral patterns.

Chain of Responsibility

The *Chain of Responsibility* pattern allows a sender to issue a request to a series or chain of objects, allowing each object a chance to handle the request. The receiving objects pass the request along until some object handles the request.

One example is a context-sensitive help system that passes a request for help along a chain until the appropriate object can provide the help.

Command

The *Command* pattern provides a way to encapsulate a command request as an object without the object that issues the command knowing what the response is, such as a GUI menu system that issues a command in response to a menu selection. Any menu command can issue a request to a Command object in a uniform way without having to know how the object handles the command.

Interpreter

The *Interpreter* pattern recognizes that it is sometimes better to define a language with a grammar, and to provide an interpreter for that language. An object that can recognize and respond to a regular expression search pattern is an example.

Iterator

The *Iterator* pattern provides a means to access all the elements of some collection of objects sequentially, without exposing the collection's internal representation. The Iterator is so common and useful that Java provides iterators for its collection objects as a standard feature.

Mediator

The *Mediator* pattern defines an object that knows how to use several other objects, and provides a means for those objects to refer to each other using the Mediator rather than directly. This increases encapsulation and decreases coupling.

Memento

The *Memento* pattern captures and saves the current state of an object, without violating its encapsulation. For example, an editor program would use the Memento pattern to save the state of whatever was being edited so that it could be restored via an undo command.

Observer

The *Observer* pattern is used when any number of objects (Observers) need to be notified automatically whenever another object (the Observable) changes its state.

State

The *State* pattern allows an object to change its behavior depending on how its internal state is changed. An example is a network-monitoring object that changes its behavior depending on whether the network connection is open or closed.

Strategy

The *Strategy* pattern defines a family of interchangeable algorithms. The client is able to use the object that implements the Strategy, without necessarily knowing which Strategy is used or how it differs from other Strategies. An example might be a Strategy that implements different sort algorithms, with each algorithm appropriate for a different kind of data.

Template Method

The *Template Method* defines an operation as a superclass whose implementation is deferred to subclasses. This lets the subclasses redefine an operation, without affecting how the method is used.

Visitor

The *Visitor* pattern performs an operation on some structure of objects. The Visitor allows new operations to be defined, without changing any elements that are part of the structure. An example would be visiting each leaf of a tree of objects to perform some operation.

Example Design Patterns Used by Wmvc and MovieCat

Because design patterns can be so useful, it should be no surprise that several design patterns can show up even in small applications. The Wmvc framework and the MovieCat applications we covered in Chapters 5 and 6 use several patterns. Let's discuss some of the details of using the patterns in this section.

MVC

The GoF book, *Design Patterns*, doesn't call Model/View/Controller a design pattern. Instead, it uses MVC as a higher-level design that can be implemented using patterns. However, in other sources, MVC itself is called a design pattern.

Since we've covered MVC is some detail already, we won't cover it again here. However, let's look at how the Wmvc framework uses two GoF design patterns for its implementation.

Observer Pattern

The Observer pattern is an easy way to make the model update all the views when it changes state. Wmvc uses the Observer pattern for its implementation. To better understand Observer, let's start with an excerpted version of the full pattern description from *Design Patterns*. This fairly complete excerpt should help give you a good idea of what a pattern description is. *[Comments about text we've omitted from the full pattern description are shown in square brackets, in italic.]*

Excerpt from *Design Patterns*

OBSERVER   Object Behavioral

Intent

Define a one-to-many dependency between objects so that when one object changes state, all its dependents are notified and updated automatically.

Also Known As

Dependents, Publish-Subscribe.

Motivation

The need to maintain consistency among related objects is a common side effect of partitioning a system into a collection of cooperating classes. You don't want to achieve consistency by making the classes tightly coupled, because that reduces their reusability.

[A description of a GUI toolkit.]

The Observer pattern describes how to establish these relationships. The key objects in this pattern are **subject** and **observer**. A subject may have any number of dependent observers. All observers are notified whenever the subject undergoes a change in state. In response, each observer queries the subject to synchronize its state with the subject's state.

This kind of interaction is also known as **publish-subscribe**. The subject is the publisher of notifications. It sends out these notifications without having to know who its observers are. Any number of observers can subscribe to receive notifications.

Applicability

Use the Observer pattern in any of the following situations:

- When an abstraction has two aspects, one dependent on the other. Encapsulating these aspects in separate objects lets you vary and reuse them independently.

- When a change to one object requires changing others, and you don't know how many objects need to be changed.

- When an object should be able to notify other objects without making assumptions about what these objects are. In other words, you don't want these objects tightly coupled.

Structure

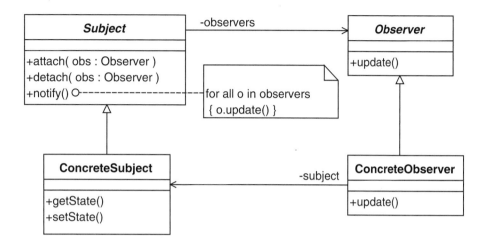

Participants

- Subject

    - knows its observers. Any number of Observer objects may observe a subject.
    - provides an interface for attaching and detaching Observer objects.

- Observer

    - defines an updating interface for objects that should be notified of changes in a subject.

- ConcreteSubject

    - stores state of interest to ConcreteObserver objects.
    - sends a notification to its observers when its state changes.

- ConcreteObserver

    - maintains a reference to a ConcreteSubject object.
    - stores state that should stay consistent with the subject's.
    - implements the Observer updating interface to keep its state consistent with subject's.

Collaborations

- ConcreteSubject notifies its observers whenever a change occurs that could make its observers' state inconsistent with its own.

- After being informed of a change in the concrete subject, a Concrete-Observer object may query the subject for information. ConcreteObserver uses this information to reconcile its state with that of the subject.

[*Sequence diagram shown in original.*]

Consequences

The Observer pattern lets you vary subjects and observers independently. You can reuse subjects, without reusing their observers, and vice versa. It lets you add observers, without modifying the subject or other observers.

[*A discussion of further benefits and liabilities of the Observer pattern.*]

Implementation

[*A discussion of issues related to the implementation of the pattern. Since Observer is already provided by the Java library, the implementation details are not relevant.*]

Sample Code

[*An example of implementing the Observer pattern.*]

Known Uses

The first and perhaps best-known example of the Observer pattern appears in Smalltalk Model/View/Controller (MVC), the user interface in the Smalltalk environment. MVC's Model class plays the role of Subject, while View is the base class for observers. [*More examples are given.*]

Related Patterns

[*Two patterns related to the example are given.*]

Observer Pattern in Wmvc

We know from reading the *Design Patterns* excerpt that Observer is useful for MVC. But how is Observer really used by Wmvc?

It turns out that Wmvc can simply use the Observer supplied by the Java library and doesn't have to implement it. *Design Patterns* includes a discussion of implementation for each pattern, but in this case, that's already done. We just need to figure out how to use Observer to implement MVC.

First, let's look at the specifics of the Java Observer implementation. It defines a class called `Observable` that corresponds directly to the `Subject` class in the pattern description. It also provides the `Observer` interface, which corresponds to the `Observer` class in the pattern. This makes sense. Since an `Observer` needs only one method, `update`, an interface works well for this, and it allows the different observers to be derived from other classes. The `Observable` (Subject) needs to provide several services to implement the pattern. The Java `Observable` class has named the `Subject attach` method `addObserver`, and the `Subject detach` method `deleteObserver`. The `Subject notify` is named `notifyObservers`. There are some other methods provided to make using `Observable` easier. Figure 7.1 shows the relevant details in UML.

Now we are ready to see how Wmvc uses `Observable`. In MVC, what is the Subject, or `Observable`? It is the model. So, we extend `Observable` in `Wmvc-Model`. The observers are the views, so we implement `Observer` in `WmvcView`. To stay consistent with the MVC model, we provide the functionality of the xObservable methods, renamed as xView methods (for example, `addView` instead of `addObserver`). While it is often best to use the names described in a pattern, it sometimes makes more sense to rename them to fit the actual problem. Finally, the ConcreteSubject and ConcreteObservers are new classes derived from `WmvcModel` and `WmvcView`. Figure 7.2 shows how everything fits together.

Command Pattern in Wmvc

One of the goals of the Wmvc framework is to provide an easy-to-use interface to menu bar and tool bar commands. Even though the details of implementing a menu item, a tool bar button, or other Java Swing components are different, Wmvc provides a uniform interface to each component. This uniform interface is provided using the Command design pattern. Figure 7.3 shows the structure of the Command pattern as given in *Design Patterns*.

As we noted earlier, the Command pattern provides a way to encapsulate a command request as an object, without the object that issues the command needing to know what the response is. In the case of Wmvc, it is the Swing library

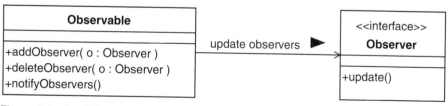

Figure 7.1 Java Observer

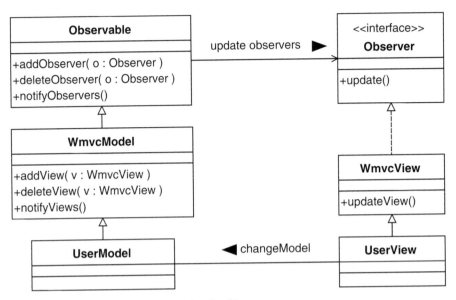

Figure 7.2   Wmvc implementation using the Observer pattern

that issues a command after user input, and it is a Wmvc application that encapsulates the command response.

Within Wmvc, the class `WmvcExecutor` implements the Command class of the pattern. Wmvc uses the name Executor rather than Command because it makes more sense within the framework. Design patterns are outlines of solu-

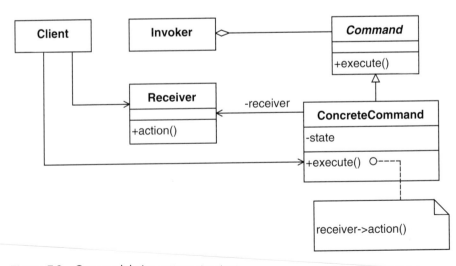

Figure 7.3   Command design pattern structure

tions to problems that can be adapted and applied to specific problems. In this case, we adapted the name.

Within the `WmvcExecutor` class is the `execute()` method, which is invoked by the Swing system in response to user input. This is the behavior encapsulated by the Command pattern. Each command object (Swing component) invokes the `execute()` method and is protected from knowing what happens inside `execute`.

Other Patterns Used in Wmvc and MovieCat

The `MovieEditor` is implemented as a Singleton pattern. The Singleton pattern makes sure there is only one `MovieEditor` object created. We want only one editor active at a time.

The `MovieModel` class uses the Iterator pattern to provide access to all the movies. This access is used by `MovieListView` to get the movies for the list. The Iterator is also used within `MovieModel` itself to find the correct place to add a new movie object.

Chapter Summary

- Design patterns have become an important part of designing object-oriented software.

- The primary reference is the Gang of Four *Design Patterns* book.

- Patterns are defined using a description template.

- There are 23 basic patterns arranged into three classification groups.

- Wmvc and MovieCat use several patterns, including Observer, Command, Singleton, and Iterator.

Resources

Java™ *Design Patterns: A Tutorial*, James W. Cooper, Addison-Wesley, 2000, ISBN 0-201-48539-7.

Design Patterns, Erich Gamma, Richard Helm, Ralph Johnson, John Vlissides, Addison-Wesley, 1995, ISBN 0-201-063361-2.

Patterns in Java, A Catalog of Reusable Design Patterns Illustrated with UML, Volume 1, Mark Grand, Wiley, 1998, ISBN 0471258393.

Pattern Hatching: Design Patterns Applied, John Vlissides, Addison-Wesley, 1998, ISBN 0-201-43293-5.

Patterns home page: `hillside.net/patterns/patterns.html`.

CHAPTER 8

Refactoring

Up to this point, we've focused on using object orientation to design and develop new programs. Understanding objects and using object-oriented techniques is one of the best ways to develop programs that are easy to understand, easy to write, and perhaps most important, easy to modify and maintain.

The fact is, most programming involves maintaining and modifying existing code. If the existing code is not written in an OO language, then using object orientation probably won't help much with changing it. If the existing code is written in an OO language, there is hope. Unfortunately, as we've noted before, just because a program uses Java or C++ doesn't mean it uses OO techniques. And even if the program started out with a decent OO design, if it has been maintained and modified over time, it is likely to have lost some of its initial elegance.

So what are you going to do? One of the most recent object-oriented techniques to be formalized and developed into an essential programming tool is called refactoring. While programmers have always spent some time cleaning up their code, refactoring takes this a bit further. Refactoring is a disciplined approach to improving the design of existing code. With it, the overall design and structure of an existing program is improved while its observable functionality remains unchanged. Once its design has been improved, it is easier to maintain.

Software maintenance usually has one of two goals. The first is to fix bugs; the second is to add features. While the goal of refactoring is neither of these, it can greatly improve how easy it is to do either. At first, it may seem a waste to refactor code without adding new functionality. However, trying to modify a poorly constructed program can take far more time and effort than first refactoring and then modifying. Refactoring can reveal flaws in the structure of the existing code that are the underlying causes of bugs or incorrect behavior.

Ward Cunningham and Kent Beck were two of the first software experts to recognize the importance of refactoring and to help develop it into a formal technique. The principal refactoring resource is *Refactoring: Improving the Design of Existing Code*, by Martin Fowler. Although refactoring can be useful for almost any kind of object-oriented programming, it is an essential part of the Extreme Programming (XP) methodology (see Chapter 9).

What Is Refactoring?

Refactoring should be considered a basic principle of programming and does not require any special methodology. Over time, as code is changed, it tends to deteriorate. Changes are often made on the fly, under time pressure, without regard for the overall structure of the code. This can lead to code entropy. Refactoring helps to undo code entropy.

The Basic Refactoring Process

While the basic refactoring process is not that complicated, experience with programming helps (especially object-oriented programming). The main goal of refactoring is to improve the overall design and structure of an existing program, without changing its observable behavior. This means that you don't refactor and add functionality at the same time. Once the refactoring has been done, it is then easier to add functionality.

The first step in refactoring is to understand the existing code. As part of the process of reading the code, you will almost certainly find problems with it. Refactoring isn't just about finding problems and making small improvements. It is a well-defined and structured technique for improving the code. Each individual refactoring may make only a small difference, but the cumulative effect of applying many refactorings can result in greatly improved overall quality, readability, and design of the code.

Refactorings

The developers of refactoring have identified a list and descriptions of known refactorings that can help improve code. Many of these refactorings are listed and described in Fowler's book, and more can be found on the refactoring Web site, `www.refactoring.com`. As you become more experienced, many specific refactorings will become familiar, and you will start to recognize cases in code that can benefit from the technique.

Reduce Risk of Change

Any time you change code, it is risky. You can introduce new bugs. You can change the behavior of the program. You can break things. By using disciplined refactoring, you can reduce the risks involved in making changes. This is a major difference between a simple code cleanup and the formal refactoring process. By carefully following the refactoring process, you reduce the risk of making changes and, at the same time, improve its design and make it easier to change in the future.

Don't Change Functionality

One of the first rules of refactoring is: Do not change the functionality of the existing code. By functionality, in this context, we mean the outside observed behavior of the code. The program should behave exactly the same before and after the refactoring. If the behavior changes, it will be impossible to know for sure that the refactoring hasn't broken other things as well. If you need to change the behavior, do that as a separate step. Improve the code with refactoring, then make the change.

One Thing at a Time

To be sure you don't change behavior, it is important to apply only one refactoring at a time. While going over the code, you may often find several things that can benefit from refactoring. But to reduce the risk of making changes, refactoring requires that you make only one change at a time.

Test Each Step

Perhaps the most important principle of refactoring is to thoroughly test the program after each refactoring. This is how you reduce the risk of change—by ensuring that you haven't changed functionality or broken other parts of the program. Besides the identification of a large set of known refactorings, the combination of preserving functionality, of making only one change at a time, and of testing after each step is one of the most important contributions of refactoring.

Summary

The following list summarizes the refactoring process.

1. Review code to identify refactorings.

2. Apply only one refactoring at a time, without changing functionality.

3. Test the refactoring.

4. Repeat to find more refactorings.

When Do You Refactor?

To use refactoring effectively, it is important to know just when to refactor. You don't always need to refactor working code. There are some guidelines for deciding when to refactor.

First, when you plan to add some functionality to a program, be prepared to refactor. As we've noted before, one important benefit of object-oriented program design is that the code is easier to maintain and modify. So when it comes time to add new functionality to a program, it is important that code be as well-designed as possible. This is precisely the goal of refactoring. Refactoring should be applied to the code until its design has improved enough to make it easy to modify. Then, after the refactoring, new functionality should be much easier to add.

Refactoring is also useful when you need to find bugs. Part of finding a bug is understanding a program. The fact that a program has bugs often means that the code isn't clear enough to spot them in the first place. Refactoring while you are going over code to hunt for bugs improves the quality of the code and even reduces the number of bugs.

One important part of almost every project is the code review. For code reviews with just two or three programmers (probably the most productive kind), refactorings can be suggested and applied as the group goes over the code and gets better at understanding its design. In fact, the pair programming of Extreme Programming can be considered pair code reviews, and refactoring is an important part of XP.

Code Smells

Kent Beck and Martin Fowler have also developed a list of what they call "code smells" to help determine when to refactor. If you sniff these out in existing code, refactoring is in order. Here's a brief list of some of the smells they've identified.

- **Duplicate code** Duplicate code means you need to extract some methods.

- **Long method** Too long is hard to understand. Extract methods.

- **Large class** A class that does too much needs to be split.

- **Long parameter list** A long list makes it hard to read. Consider passing objects.

- **Divergent change** This is code degradation as a result of too many chaotic changes to a class.

- **Shotgun surgery** Shotgun surgery means too many undisciplined changes to classes and attributes.

- **Feature envy** One class is interested in too many details of another class.

- **Data clumps** Data that is used together everywhere should be in a class of its own.

- **Primitive obsession** A program can use too many primitive data types that should really be part of a class.

- **Switch statements** Switch statements can mean you are not using polymorphism effectively.

- **Parallel inheritance hierarchies** Repeating class definitions in parallel classes is more duplication to eliminate.

- **Lazy class** A class should do enough to pay its own way or be eliminated.

- **Speculative generality** Designing for future flexibility before it is needed can increase complexity unnecessarily.

- **Message chain** Too many messages in a chain are hard to follow.

- **Middleman** Sometimes, it is better to work with an object directly.

- **Inappropriate intimacy** Classes shouldn't need to know too much about each other.

- **Incomplete library class** Sometimes, you can't get it all and need to do some yourself.

- **Data class** Classes need something to do.

- **Refused bequest** Subclasses should use most of what their parents give them.

- **Comments** Could a comment be eliminated by providing a better name for a method or variable?

When Not to Refactor

Knowing when not to refactor is also important. One of the main reasons not to refactor is when the code is so bad that it needs to be rewritten from scratch. Eventually, code can become so outdated, so difficult to understand, or so buggy that it would be more cost-effective to start over than to try to fix it or add new features.

This decision can also apply to code that is written in a non-object-oriented language. Most refactorings apply to object-oriented languages. Obviously, these refactorings have limited use for non-OO languages. It may be time to rewrite the program using an OO language.

Some Refactorings

The identification of refactorings gives you a catalog of things to look for in existing code. Each refactoring has been given a name, much like the design patterns we discussed in Chapter 7. There are many more refactorings than there are design patterns, and most refactorings are much simpler and easier to understand.

In this section, we will go over a few refactorings. It is not the goal here to make you into a master of refactoring, but to give you an idea of some of the specifics. Just as design patterns belong in every good programmer's toolbox, refactoring has its place there as well.

Refactoring Categories

More than 70 specific refactorings have been identified in Fowler's book, and many more are identified on the refactoring Web site, with more added all the time. The refactorings have been organized into the following categories. Specific individual refactorings are shown in *italics*. This summary mentions only a fraction of the total number.

Composing Methods

One common problem comes from code that has methods that are too long. The Composing Methods group of refactorings is intended to help reduce the size of methods and to help improve the readability of the code by replacing sequences of code with calls to methods that are built from the original code. Refactorings in this category include *Extract Method*, *Inline Method*, and *Replace Temp with Query*.

Moving Features Between Objects

During object design, it is important to decide where to place various responsibilities. Sometimes, responsibility can be placed in the wrong class. Some classes end up with too many responsibilities. Such refactorings as *Move Method*, *Move Field*, and *Extract Class* can be used to help put responsibilities where they belong.

Organizing Data

Sometimes objects can be used instead of simple data items. Refactorings such as *Replace Data Value with Object* or *Replace Array with Object* can make working with a class easier. They can also clarify what the data item is being used for and make it easier to work with.

Simplifying Conditional Expressions

Conditional expressions can be some of the most complicated and confusing parts of any program to understand. Such refactorings as *Decompose Conditional* or *Consolidate Duplicate Conditional Fragments* can be used to simplify code.

Making Method Calls Simpler

Defining the interface to a class can be difficult. Just what the methods are named and how they are called can lead to confusion or simplicity. Refactorings such as *Rename Method*, *Add Parameter*, and others from this category can help improve the interface to a class.

Dealing with Generalization

One guideline we discussed for good object design was moving methods as high up the inheritance hierarchy as possible. Getting methods and subclasses in just the right place is the goal of this category of refactorings. Some of them include *Pull Up Method*, *Push Down Method*, *Extract Subclass*, and *Extract Superclass*. All are meant to help refine the inheritance hierarchy.

Some Specific Refactorings

In Fowler's book, each individual refactoring description includes the name of the refactoring, a short description of the problem, a short description of the solution, a more detailed discussion of the motivation for using the refactoring, and a discussion of the mechanics for carrying out the refactoring.

Currently, refactoring is mostly a manual operation. It is up to the programmer to identify specific refactorings and then actually rewrite the code. As this book is written, a few refactoring software tools that can help with some of the mechanical aspects of the different refactorings are emerging. The refactoring Web site, `www.refactoring.com`, keeps information about the latest refactoring tools.

The following descriptions of some refactorings are neither complete nor intended to imply that they are the most important refactorings. They were chosen simply to illustrate some typical refactorings from each category.

Extract Method

Extract Method is used when you have a code fragment that has meaning when taken by itself. That code is extracted and turned into a method whose name clearly explains the purpose of the method. Short, well-named methods can make code clearer. A well-named method can eliminate the need for a comment. Sometimes, you can even find duplicated code that belongs in a method.

Replace Temp with Query

Replace Temp with Query is used when you find a temporary variable used to hold the results of an expression. By extracting the expression into a method and then replacing all references to the temp with the method call, the meaning can be clearer, and you can reuse the method in other places.

Move Method

If you find a method is being used more often by another class than the one where it is defined, you can use Move Method to move the method to the other class. You remove the original definition, and invoke the new method from the original class.

Extract Class

If you find you have one class doing work that should really be done by two, use Extract Class. You can create a new class and move the relevant methods and attributes from the old class into the new one.

Decompose Conditional

One way to improve complicated conditional statements is to extract the code that makes up the *then* and *else* parts into methods with meaningful names. This reduces the complexity, makes the statements more meaningful to read, and often results in methods that can be reused.

Rename Method

Rename Method is one of the simplest refactorings, yet it can lead to code that is much easier to understand. If the name of a method (or even a variable) does not indicate its purpose, then it should be renamed so that it is meaningful.

Pull Up Method

If you find methods in different subclasses that have identical results, you can use Pull Up Method to move them to the superclass. Eliminating this duplicate behavior makes the code easier to maintain and understand.

Extract Subclass

If a class has methods that are used by only some of the instances of that class, those instances should have their own subclass. Extract Subclass is used to extract those features into a new subclass.

Chapter Summary

- Refactoring is a programming tool that can improve the design of existing code.

- A major goal of refactoring is to reduce the risk of change by providing a well-defined approach to improving code.

- Several things indicate you need to refactor, including "code smells."

- There are many refactorings in several categories.

Resources

Refactoring: Improving the Design of Existing Code, Martin Fowler, Addison-Wesley, 1999, ISBN 0-201-48567-2.

Refactoring Web site: `www.refactoring.com`.

CHAPTER 9

Software Development Methodologies Today

Although object-oriented programming languages have been available for a long time, it was only in the late 1980s and early 1990s that object-oriented software development emerged as a mature technology. Before then, structured development techniques and methodologies dominated.

In the early 1990s, there were several competing object-oriented analysis and design methodologies to choose from. Most of these methodologies had one thing in common: They were designed for large-scale software projects. In addition, each methodology had its own set of principles and its own graphical design notation.

One early methodology was known as Coad/Yourdon Object-Oriented Systems Design. Coad/Yourdon's design notation was among the easiest to learn and use of any of the methodologies. Although some of its features resembled older, structured methodologies in their approach to the software life cycle, it had many outstanding concepts for object design, including its approach to object discovery and evaluation. Many of the principles discussed in Chapter 4 are derived from Coad/Yourdon.

An early methodology from the early 1990s was the Booch Method, designed by Grady Booch. It, too, had many sound object-oriented design concepts, as well as its own design notation (often called Booch Clouds). Today, Booch's book, *Object-Oriented Analysis and Design*, remains a classic OO reference.

Two other methodologies are worth mentioning. James Rumbaugh developed a methodology called the Object Modeling Technique, or OMT, which has heavily influenced the design of the UML. Ivar Jacobson developed the Objectory methodology, based largely on the use case.

In the mid-1990s, James Rumbaugh and Ivar Jacobson joined Grady Booch (together often known as the Three Amigos) at Rational Software to unify their methodologies. One of the first results of this collaboration was the UML, followed by the Rational Unified Process (or RUP, as it is commonly called). RUP is discussed in the next section.

RUP has emerged as the dominant object-oriented design methodology. Unfortunately, many projects don't use any kind of methodology. One reason may be that RUP is best suited for large projects with good management teams in place. Another is that until recently, there wasn't much in the way of alternate development methodologies.

Fortunately, this is changing. Several new methodologies more suited to small-scale projects have emerged. And just as there were many competing heavyweight OO development methodologies in the early 1990s, the turn of the millennium has seen the rise of several competing lightweight methodologies.

In the next section, we will briefly discuss the Rational Unified Process. Following that, we will look at some of the smaller, agile methodologies, especially Extreme Programming. Finally, we will go over open source development, which really can be considered an alternate development methodology.

Methodologies for Large-Scale Projects

It is a fact that large software projects require significant planning and management. The largest projects, which involve tens or even hundreds of programmers, can take years to finish. Any software project that involves people numbering in the tens, and time frames of a year or more, really needs a well-defined development process.

Today RUP is the main heavyweight methodology in widespread use. Although the main principles of RUP may be used by themselves as a development process, they are almost exclusively associated with Rational Software, which has a large number of software tools to help with RUP-based development.

Let there be no doubt about what RUP is. It is a very good development process, most suitable for large software projects, although it can be adapted for smaller projects. It has many strong points to recommend its procedures and philosophies, and it is somewhat adaptable to various project needs.

However, it is large and comprehensive, which means it requires extensive training to use properly. Rational Software is the principal supplier of the software tools for RUP. It can cost several thousand dollars for each developer seat.

The whole process is heavily documentation-oriented and requires significant management resources.

This is not to imply that there is anything wrong with RUP. It is the gold standard of OO methodologies. It was developed by some of the best software methodologists around. It has been shown to work for a wide variety of software projects. What is not clear, though, is whether such a heavyweight process is best, or even needed, for smaller projects.

Overview of the Unified Process

In many ways, RUP is not that different from the basic software development process we discussed in Chapter 4. It starts with significant planning, includes analysis and design, and finishes with building and releasing. One strength of RUP is its ability to make all these steps part of an overall process that includes support for both the management and the software engineering sides of the process. The whole process is iterative, with the goal of producing some tangible result at the end of each iteration.

Basic Concepts

One way to look at RUP is to view it as a two-dimensional process, as shown in Figure 9.1. Overall, a software development cycle is made up of four phases: inception, elaboration, construction, and transition. There are activities, or workflows, that are parts of each cycle, including business modeling, requirements, analysis and design, implementation, test, and others.

The entire process is iterative. Each phase itself consists of one or more of the four phase cycles. Thus, the main construction phase may consist of several cycles, each producing a more complete product than the last. One goal of RUP is to produce some kind of product at the end of each cycle.

The vertical lines between each phase in Figure 9.1 are milestones. Progress on the project is tracked using these milestones.

The horizontal lines associated with each workflow help indicate when the activity is carried out during the development cycle. While Figure 9.1 shows the time line of each workflow, there is also an intensity associated with each workflow not shown by the *'s in this diagram. For example, the Analysis and Design workflow involves the most effort at the beginning of the development cycle, in inception and elaboration, while the Implementation workflow is most intense in the construction phase.

This view of development also can be used to help control the project from a high-level management viewpoint and from a lower-lever engineering viewpoint. Top-level management can view the whole project as one big cycle of the four

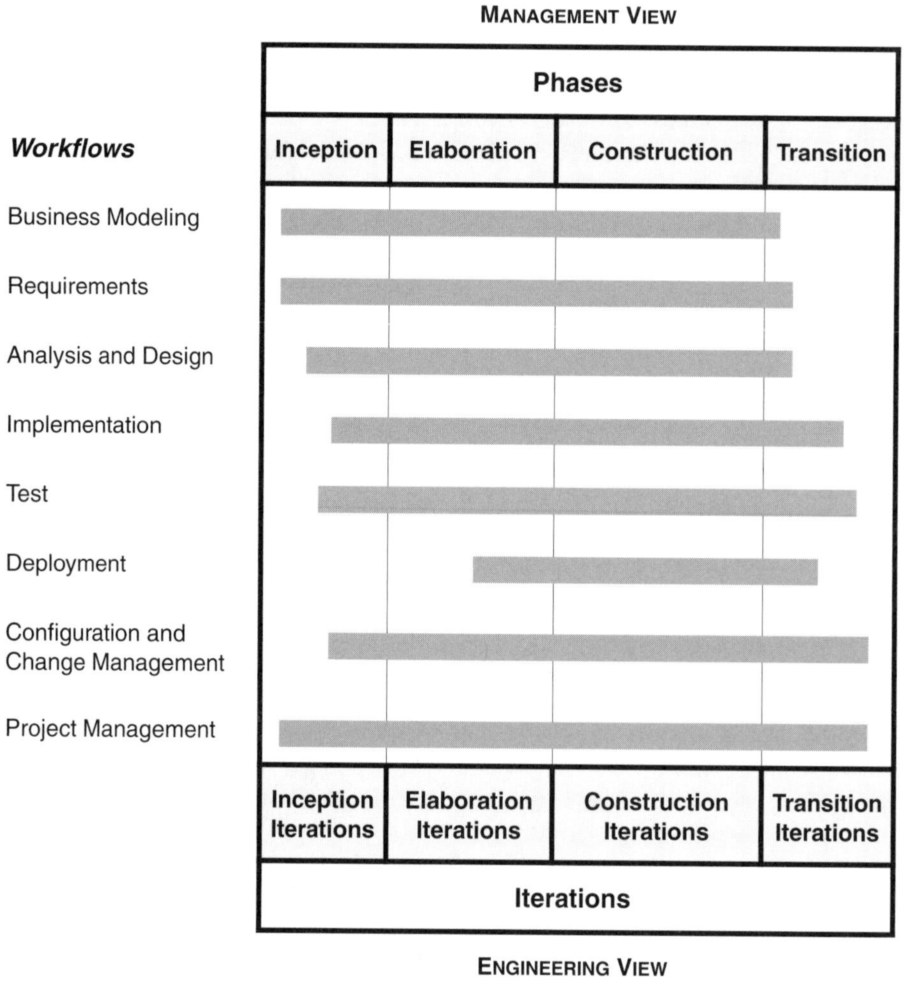

MANAGEMENT VIEW

	Phases			
Workflows	**Inception**	**Elaboration**	**Construction**	**Transition**
Business Modeling				
Requirements				
Analysis and Design				
Implementation				
Test				
Deployment				
Configuration and Change Management				
Project Management				
	Inception Iterations	**Elaboration Iterations**	**Construction Iterations**	**Transition Iterations**
	Iterations			

ENGINEERING VIEW

Figure 9.1   Overview of RUP

phases, whereas the engineering view can see the iterative cycles that really make the project work. Different levels of management can use different milestones to track project progress.

RUP is designed to be flexible. Support tools available from Rational Software can be used to modify the process to fit a particular project. The number of iterations involved, the timing of milestones, and the total number of people involved can be handled flexibly. And because the process is inherently iterative, there is some flexibility built in to handle changing requirements.

One problem associated with any activity involving tens or hundreds of people is that the process can get too rigid and impersonal. With many people involved, there often is a management bureaucracy and an emphasis on producing documentation to track project progress. This may be inevitable when dealing with that many people. However, it can also be impersonal and frustrating for programmers, who like to think of their work as having a high level of creativity.

Agile Methodologies for Small Projects

It isn't only large projects that need a development methodology. Any software project can benefit. Although a heavyweight methodology like RUP may be adaptable to smaller projects, most small projects simply cannot afford the training and management overhead needed to make using one effective. For projects with up to 10 or 15 programmers, what is needed is a lightweight methodology that is small, easy to learn and use, and doesn't require extensive management support. Methodologies need to recognize the talents of the programmers involved, and treat everyone as a member of a team working toward a common goal.

The Agile Alliance

In February 2001, an amazing meeting took place at Snowbird in Utah. Seventeen people, representatives from several development methodologies (including Extreme Programming, SCRUM, DSDM, Adaptive Software Development, Crystal, Feature-Driven Development, Pragmatic Programming, and others who saw a need for alternatives to heavyweight methodologies) met to find some common ground. Getting 17 software gurus to agree on anything was nothing short of a miracle. The group formed the Agile Alliance and produced a manifesto and set of basic principles that is posted on the www.agilealliance.org Web site.

There is a place for lightweight, agile methodologies and for large, heavyweight methodologies. Because the principles set forth by the Agile Alliance are important, and because the alliance wants its message to be freely disseminated, the manifesto and principles are reproduced here from the Agile Alliance Web site.[1]

[1.] © 2001, the signatories on the following page. This declaration may be freely copied in any form, but only in its entirety through this notice.

Manifesto for Agile Software Development

We are uncovering better ways of developing software by doing it
and helping others do it. Through this work we have come to value:

Individuals and interactions over processes and tools

Working software over comprehensive documentation

Customer collaboration over contract negotiation

Responding to change over following a plan

That is, while there is value in the items on
the right, we value the items on the left more.

Kent Beck	James Grenning	Robert C. Martin
Mike Beedle	Jim Highsmith	Steve Mellor
Arie van Bennekum	Andrew Hunt	Ken Schwaber
Alistair Cockburn	Ron Jeffries	Jeff Sutherland
Ward Cunningham	Jon Kern	Dave Thomas
Martin Fowler	Brian Marick	

Principles: The Agile Alliance

We follow these principles:

Our highest priority is to satisfy the customer through early and
continuous delivery of valuable software.

Welcome changing requirements, even late in development.
Agile processes harness change for the customer's competitive advantage.

Deliver working software frequently, from a couple of weeks to
a couple of months, with a preference to the shorter timescale.

Business people and developers must work
together daily throughout the project.

Build projects around motivated individuals.
Give them the environment and support they
need, and trust them to get the job done.

The most efficient and effective method of conveying information to and
within a development team is face-to-face conversation.

Working software is the primary measure of progress.

Agile processes promote sustainable development.
The sponsors, developers, and users should be able to
maintain a constant pace indefinitely.

Continuous attention to technical excellence and good design enhances agility.

Simplicity—the art of maximizing the amount of work not done—is essential.

The best architectures, requirements, and designs
emerge from self-organizing teams.

At regular intervals, the team reflects on how to become more
effective, then tunes and adjusts its behavior accordingly.

At press time, several development methodologies fell into the agile development philosophy. The one garnering the most attention is Extreme Programming, or simply XP. We will discuss some of the major features of XP in the next section, then briefly discuss some of the other agile methodologies in following sections.

Extreme Programming

Extreme Programming comes mainly from the work of Kent Beck and Ward Cunningham, who have been leaders in the object-oriented programming world for some time. The main reference is Kent Beck's book, *Extreme Programming Explained: Embrace Change.*

As the title of the book indicates, one of the main tenets of XP is to embrace change. The traditional development process puts analysis and design at the beginning, and hopes to get it right. This is partly based on the assumption that making changes in software is more expensive the later in the development they occur. It costs far more to fix some flaw in the design after the software is mostly written than to discover and fix the flaw early in the design process.

The problem in locking in a design early is that the requirements almost always change as the project progresses. If nothing else, both the customer's and developer's understanding of the problem increases, making things obvious that weren't obvious at the beginning. XP says software requirements will change, so embrace that change. Use a development process that makes it easy to change software and reduces the cost of doing so.

With this in mind, XP has developed a set of practices that define the process. Four basic values help make these practices work: communication, simplicity, feedback, and courage.

Communication is critical between the developer and the customer, between management and the programmers, and among the programmers themselves. Problems in software systems can often be traced to some missed communication. With an emphasis on communication, discovery of problems comes as early as possible.

Simplicity is another important XP value. Do not overdesign. The software should be as simple as possible to meet the most important business requirements. This means doing what needs to be done now, not maybe later. Often, code written for future possibilities won't ever be used, possibly because requirements will have changed. By focusing on what needs to be done now, everyone's understanding of how the system works and what it can do can be maximized.

Communication and simplicity also help with the third XP value, feedback. Feedback is important so that all can know what the current state of the system is. Which tests are working; which have failed? How far along is the project, and how do the current capabilities meet the customers expectations? All this feedback keeps the project on track.

The final XP value is courage—the courage to change, courage to act when flaws are found, and courage to trust that XP practices will work. Many parts of XP are indeed radical when compared with traditional development methodologies, and it does take a certain amount of courage from both management and programmers to embrace the change of XP.

XP Practices

There are a dozen main XP practices.

The Planning Game   This is the XP planning process. The customer plays an important role in the XP process. The customer first writes user stories, short descriptions of the behavior of the product, and ranks them by importance. Developers then estimate the development effort required. Together, the customer and developer rank the stories and select what should be implemented next and what should be deferred.

Short Releases   XP teams get a system working as early as possible, and follow up with frequent updates with added functionality, on very short cycles.

Metaphor   Communication is important, so XP teams use a common terminology and system of names to guide the development.

Simple Design   A major principle of XP is to always design as simply as possible. Thus, an XP program should be the simplest program that meets the current requirements. It should avoid adding features for the future that may never be needed. The focus is always on providing business value. To keep the incremental changes inherent to this design philosophy, XP relies on refactoring.

Testing   XP requires writing tests based on the requirements *first*, and *then* the software that meets the tests. These tend to be unit tests for specific objects that are part of the design. The customer helps to develop the overall acceptance tests for the full product.

Refactoring   Refactoring is an integral part of the XP process. All code is subject to constant refactoring to keep the design clean, simple, and complete.

Pair Programming   Pair programming is one of XP's most unusual, even controversial, features. All programming is done in pairs—two programmers working together on one machine (and not necessarily the same two all the time). The idea is to maximize productivity, reduce errors, and increase communication.

Collective Ownership   All code is owned by all the programmers. This maximizes communication, minimizes the importance of single programmers, and gives great flexibility in terms of those able to change any part of the code.

Continuous Integration   XP code is constantly integrated, perhaps several times per day. This keeps all the code synchronized and enables rapid progress with continuous feedback about the state of the software.

40-Hour Week   XP recognizes that fresh, healthy, and happy programmers are effective and productive. Tired programmers make more mistakes and are less productive. Thus, it is a core principle of XP to avoid excessive working hours.

On-Site Customer   XP requires a dedicated, on-site representative of the customer. The representative is able to determine and clarify requirements, set priorities, and answer questions as the programmers think of them. This enhanced communication can reduce the need for expensive documentation and eliminate costly delays caused by waiting for clarifications.

Coding Standards   Pair programming and shared code ownership requires that all programmers write code following a common standard. Thus, XP requires a clearly specified coding standard.

The Rise of XP

Many XP practices are indeed quite different from more-traditional approaches. XP is almost more a philosophy about how to develop code than it is a set of design rules. For example, XP does not specify the use of one design notation over another, or even any design notation at all. Some XP projects use virtually no formal design techniques. CRC cards are one of the more commonly used design tools for XP projects, partly because they are so easy to learn to use and are well suited for informal group design sessions. On the other hand, UML can and does have a place with XP projects. It all depends on the specific project and on the personalities of the programmers involved.

In many ways, XP is a programmer-first process. The pair programming, the 40-hour workweek, and the need for constant communication and feedback are all programmer-friendly practices. This alone may be responsible for the rapid rise of interest in XP in the OO programming community. XP principles are even being applied to other methodologies, such as efforts to build a variant of RUP that uses XP practices.

DSDM

The Dynamic Systems Development Method, or DSDM, is an open standard for a development process originally based on rapid application development, or RAD, principles. It is targeted at developing business systems on tight time schedules.

The DSDM Consortium met for the first time in 1994 and had 16 originating founders. The goal of the DSDM Consortium was the development of a public-domain RAD methodology. Currently, most active DSDM support is based in Europe.

The main source for information about DSDM is its Web site, www.dsdm.org. The method is independent of any particular set of software tools or techniques and can be adapted to common object-oriented or structured analysis and design practices.

Somewhat like RUP, the DSDM life cycle is iterative and incremental. It has a core five-phase process that can be adapted to the particular project.

1. Feasibility study

2. Business study

3. Functional model iteration

4. Design and build iteration

5. Implementation

DSDM also has a set of principles that sound very much like those of XP.

1. Active user involvement is imperative.

2. DSDM teams, made up of both users and developers, must be empowered to make decisions.

3. The focus is on frequent delivery of products.

4. Fitness for business purposes is the essential criterion for acceptance of deliverables.

5. Iterative and incremental development is necessary to converge on an accurate business solution.

6. All changes during development are reversible.

7. Requirements are baselined at a high level.

8. Testing is integrated throughout the life cycle.

9. A collaborative and cooperative approach among all stakeholders is essential.

Note that this is only a brief outline of DSDM. The Web site has much more information.

Crystal/Adaptive Software Development

The developers of two lightweight methodologies, Jim Highsmith, with Adaptive Software Development, and Alistair Cockburn, with Crystal, have recently joined forces to unify their work on lightweight and self-adaptive methodologies. Highsmith and Cockburn are well-known names in object-oriented software development circles.

While the combined methodology is still in development, it is likely to be an important alternative. Both Highsmith and Cockburn were signatories of the Agile Alliance manifesto. The new, combined effort will no doubt reflect its values.

Open Source Development

The methodologies we've talked about so far all have one thing in common: They are all commercial products, and other than DSDM, are proprietary to one degree or another. Someone has an interest in each, usually with the goal of financial gain. Rational Software sells support tools for the RUP. Developers of the other methodologies all profit from books, consulting, and training. There is nothing wrong with that, but it is a fact.

The open source movement provides a contrast. The main tenet of open source is that the source code of any program is available for anyone to see, use, and adapt. Open source software is usually released under one of several licenses (see the open source Web site, www.opensource.org, for details of specific licenses). Even though the source code is open, people can still gain financially by adding value to the software through support and training.

The best-known example of a successful open source project is the Linux operating system. What is commonly called Linux is really a combination of an operating system kernel, originally written by Linus Torvalds, combined with a large collection of software utilities developed by the GNU project (www.gnu.org). All are open source software licensed under the GNU Public License (GPL).

While open source is one way to release and license software, it can also be considered a development methodology. A definite set of conventions and customs describing how to develop open source software has evolved since the beginning of the movement.

Although some commercial companies are releasing code that once was proprietary under various open source licenses, most open source programs were developed by individuals all over the world. For most open source programs, the development process is really a distributed development model.

Open Source Is Distributed Development

A typical open source program usually originates with a single, dedicated programmer who sees a need for a specific program and writes it. Sometimes, a small group of programmers bands together to build a program. If the program is useful, it usually attracts a user community when it is released. These users become the customers who beta test the program and suggest changes. Sometimes, they even contribute changes directly to the source code. The original author incorporates the changes and releases new versions.

As the size and popularity of a program grows, it may attract other developers. The original author often then becomes the program's coordinator and serves mostly to coordinate and incorporate changes contributed by other developers, as well as to sanction official releases.

Most of this effort is undertaken by self-selected volunteer programmers. Linux is a prefect example of this. Originally, the Linux kernel was pretty much the result of Linus Torvalds' individual effort. Eventually, tens of thousands of programmers contributed to the whole that makes up Linux. Many years after the first versions of the Linux kernel were released, Linus Torvalds still serves as the main coordinator.

The Web has made the open source distributed development model possible. First, the Web provides a potentially huge base of users and developers for any program. Web sites, e-mail, and user groups provide a worldwide network needed for this base of users and developers to communicate.

Once an open source program reaches the point at which it has many users and developers, it requires some management. In the open source development model, program management can almost be considered as an inverted organization when compared with traditional management.

First, it is the programmers who have the most control of a project. They are mostly self-selected volunteers, who work on a program for the experience and fun of it. The programmers listen to user feedback, then decide where to take the program based on a combination of the feedback and their own personal interests. The many developers involved with a program ultimately decide on the final features through consensus, reached in group discussions carried out on the Web or by e-mail. The source code is usually held in a central repository (such as www.sourceforge.org), and changes are most commonly submitted using Concurrent Versions System, or CVS.

One of the main principles of open source development is to release early and release often. It is common practice to have stable releases at infrequent intervals and separate development snapshots that are updated frequently.

It is usually up to the development coordinator to take care of the details of building a release version of a program, and then provide for its distribution. The coordinator is just that, a coordinator and not a manager. This is the opposite of traditional management, in which programmers are guided by the manager. With open source, programmers have most of the control.

Another feature of open source development is the many-eyes method of testing and quality control. Because the source code is open for all to see, the theory is that someone will spot most bugs. Also, since programmers know their code can be viewed by many others, peer pressure encourages them to write their best code.

For the most part, open source really does deliver relatively bug-free code. Linux, for example, is well known for its rock-solid stability. It is nearly impossible to crash.

But there are some problems. Since open source depends heavily on volunteer programmers, it is difficult or impossible to have fixed feature sets or specific release deadlines. Even so, open source development tends to respond to change and produce new code quickly. Some contributor to a project might have a personal stake in adding a feature, and the release-often philosophy makes sure that such enhancements are available almost immediately.

One of the main problems with open source development is quality code. Although the peer review tends to bring out the best in programmers, many open source developers are relatively new and inexperienced. And while open source code generally works and is modified, it is not always that readable or maintainable, compared with code developed under a good common coding standard.

Open source development is not necessarily object-oriented. If the original developer was an experienced object-oriented designer, it is possible for an open source program to be a well-designed object-oriented system. However, much open source software is designed on a more-or-less ad hoc basis and isn't necessarily object-oriented.

Some large software companies thrive on the open source model, but it remains to be seen if the approach will be viable over the long term. But the open source development model has merit, and some of its principles apply to any development methodology. And open source programs need not die since their source will remain available for others to take over if necessary.

Chapter Summary

- Object-oriented development methodologies have replaced earlier structured methodologies.

- The Rational Unified Process (RUP) is the most important methodology for large-scale projects.

- Extreme Programming (XP) is the most well-known agile methodology for small-scale projects.

- Open source is an alternative development process that differs from traditional approaches.

Resources

Methodologies

Extreme Programming Explained: Embrace Change, Kent Beck, Addison-Wesley, 2000, ISBN 0-201-61641-6.

Object-Oriented Analysis and Design with Applications, Second Edition, Grady Booch, Addison-Wesley, 1994, ISBN 0-805-35340-2.

Object-Oriented Analysis, Peter Coad and Edward Yourdon, Yourdon Press, 1991, ISBN 0-13-629981-4.

Object-Oriented Software Engineering: A Use-Case Driven Approach, Ivar Jacobson et al., Addison-Wesley, 1992, ISBN 0-201-54435-0.

The Rational Unified Process, An Introduction, Second Edition, Philippe Kruchten, Addison-Wesley, 2000, ISBN 0-201-70710-1.

The Cathedral and the Bazaar, Eric S. Raymond, `tuxedo.org/~esr/writings/cathedral-bazaar/index.html`

Object-Oriented Modeling and Design, James Rumbaugh et al., Prentice Hall, 1991, ISBN 0-136-29841-9.

Object-Oriented Systems Design, An Integrated Approach, Edward Yourdon, 1994, Yourdon Press, ISBN 0-13-636325-3.

Web Sites

Adaptive Software Development: www.adaptivesd.com

Crystal: www.crystalmethodologies.org

DSDM: www.dsdm.org

Extreme Programming: www.xprogramming.com

GNU: www.gnu.org

Open source: www.opensource.org

SCRUM: www.controlchaos.com

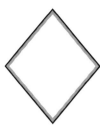

CHAPTER 10

Software Tools for Object-Oriented Development

Just as a carpenter needs a good set of tools, so does a programmer. The question is: Which tools should you use to develop your Java programs? In this chapter, we will look at some software tools that can make your programming task easier. Your final selection of tools will probably be a combination of personal choice and the tools used at your workplace. But it is good to know not only about specific choices, but of the broad categories of software tools that are available.

Discussing specific software products is a somewhat risky proposition for a book that will likely outlast some of the products. In today's volatile software industry, products come and go as companies go out of business or merge with other companies. Some of the tools covered here are likely to be around for a long time to come,[1] while some may no longer be available. However, if some tool is no longer available, there will certainly be a descendent or a similar product. What is most important is to be familiar with the range of software tools you have available to you. The book's Web site (www.objectcentral.com/oobook/ news.html) will try to keep up with the latest status of the tools discussed here.

---

[1] Specifically, open source tools such as Emacs are likely to be around for as long as programmers need an editor. This long lifetime is an often underappreciated advantage of open source software.

GUIs Versus Consoles

Today, most new software tools use a full graphical user interface, either on MS-Windows or in a graphical environment on a UNIX-like system (for example, Gnome on Linux or Motif on Solaris). And some of the best Java tools are written in Java and run the same on any Java platform.

It hasn't been that long, however, since most programming was done using 24-by-80-character terminals, and then in console windows on a graphical system. Many tools were available to run in a console-based environment.

Lots of long-time programmers consider UNIX and its descendents, such as Linux, to be the ultimate development platform. The programmer's tools include a choice of editors, a compiler system, and a set of powerful tools, such as grep, diff, make, lex, and yacc, that work together[2] to help the development process. One of the most powerful tools found on UNIX-like systems is the command shell, which allows the programmer to write scripts to automate much of the development process.

The following is a list of just a *few* of the standard software tools found on UNIX-like systems.

- **grep** This utility searches files for occurrences of regular expressions.

- **diff** This utility shows the difference between versions of code and documentation.

- **rcs, sccs, cvs** These are version-control systems that manage changes in source code. Currently, cvs is widely used by the open source software community.

- **sort** This utility sorts a file based on various criteria.

- **merge** This merges two files.

- **tr** This transforms specified characters of a file.

- **tar** This tool makes an archive of files.

- **make** This utility controls building software from various source files.

- **lex, yacc** These are tools for building lexical analyzers and parsers.

Today, Linux is the best-known UNIX-like system, and includes all the well-known software tools. These tools are also available as free open source software

---

2. The output of one tool can be fed to the input of another tool to build powerful chains of commands.

under the GNU Public License. A ready-to-run version, Cygwin (`www.cygwin.com`) runs on MS-Windows platforms. While these tools were developed before Java, they still are useful for many aspects of developing a program, including a Java program.

Editors and IDEs

The editor you use is a personal choice. Programmers are known to get into long and passionate debates about which editor is best. This section will discuss some of the characteristics of programming editors as well as integrated development environments (IDEs), which are GUI-based development tools that integrate the editor with various other tools, such as the compiler.

Characteristics of a Good Editor

Even though an editor is a personal choice, there are characteristics that every editor should have.

Easy-to-Use Command Set

First and foremost, an editor should have an easy-to-use command set. If you touch-type and like to keep your hands on the keyboard, any editor that requires you to use the mouse extensively is less than ideal.

The command set should be easy to learn and to use. Once you know the command set, your fingers will automatically do the right thing, and you will barely have to think about what you are doing. Ideally, the most common commands require you to press only a single key (or perhaps a single key combination). Less commonly used commands can use two or three key sequences. There should be some logic to the keys used for the various commands (for example, *s* for *search* or *f* for *find*).

The command set must be comprehensive. All editors let you move around the code and perform basic edits, but a programmer's editor should have other features. Some examples include easily splitting lines, changing case, matching parens, automatic indentation, and code formatting.

Powerful Finds

Being able to search for what you want in your code is important. Good editors include some kind of extended pattern matching in their find commands. The ability to search for regular expressions is considered essential by many programmers.

Another search that is useful to programmers is looking for the definition of some symbol or for all the references to a symbol, an essential feature for any good editor.

Macros

Programmers commonly need to carry out some repetitious task when editing. A simple example is renaming all instances of a variable. But a programmer should be able to repeat any sequence of commands. Thus, an editor should have the ability to define arbitrary sequences of commands and execute them. These are often called macros.

Language Awareness

Any good editor is programming-language aware. At the very least, this means the editor does syntax highlighting of the source code. Other common language-aware features include automatic completion of keywords, availability of code templates for common language constructs, and context-sensitive help for a given language.

Integration with Other Tools

More and more, it is becoming important for an editor to provide some integration with other programming tools. While it is still possible to be extremely productive using multiple command shells in a UNIX-like environment, some features are becoming a standard part of the editor. These features include the ability to work directly with the compiler and to go directly to code lines with syntax errors. Other integrations can include interfaces to file-search utilities, interface designers, class browsers, and the like.

Three Types of Editors

Currently, there are three flavors of editors: modeless and moded programmer's editors, which have evolved from console-based systems, as well as editors that are entirely GUI based. Which editor is best is up to you.

Standard Modeless Editing

Most editors can be classified as modeless editors. That is, normal character keystrokes are entered as text into the file, whereas commands require special keys or multi-key combinations to distinguish them from regular characters. The command keys are often not on the main home keyboard (for example, arrow keys), or they use a second key (for example, Alt) that borders the main keyboard. This means you have to slow down your editing while you move your hand, or use awkward finger movements that may generate sore pinkies, to press the Alt key. The best-known modeless programmer's editor is *Emacs*.

Moded Editing

In a moded editor, there are generally two modes: command mode and insert mode. When the editor is in command mode, pressing any key is interpreted as a command and will be carried out. In order to insert text, you have to enter insert mode by entering the insert command. There is then a single special key used to escape from insert mode back to command mode. One advantage to moded editors is that the regular keys can represent commands, and you don't need to press special keys or special key combinations to enter a command. Thus, the *f* key could represent the find command directly. All your fingers can stay firmly planted on the home row of the keyboard. The best-known moded programmer's editor is *vi*.

This two-moded editing can seem strange and frustrating to someone new to a moded editor, especially because almost everyone has done at least some editing on a PC, where any text you type appears on the screen. Nothing happens in a moded editor until you go into insert mode. But some informal studies have shown that expert users can edit faster with a moded editor, because their fingers don't need to leave the keyboard to fumble for special command keys as they must in a standard editor.

GUI-Based Editing

A GUI-based editor works only on a GUI-based platform, such as MS-Windows or X Windows. They are heavily oriented to using the mouse and arrow keys. GUI-based editors are almost always modeless. Most GUI-based IDEs have an editor with a default GUI-oriented command set. There are keystroke equivalents for most commands. The problem with many of these editors is that they are too generic and are often missing the more specialized commands a programmer needs and expects. Although an IDE may have many useful features, the default editor is often underpowered, compared to the more specialized programming editors such as vi and Emacs. Ideally, you should be able to substitute your own editor or your own editing command set.

Emacs

One of the most widely known and popular programming editors is Emacs, which was originally written in the mid-1970s by Richard Stallman, founder of the Free Software Foundation and the person responsible for much of the core GNU software package. The current version is known as GNU Emacs.

At its simplest, Emacs is a modeless editor. However, it really is much more. It contains its own LISP language engine, which is used to write extensions and macros for the editor. The GNU Emacs system is very large and can be made to carry out almost any task a programmer will likely want or need to do. It is possible to control the entire programming process without leaving the Emacs environment, so people claim Emacs is the ultimate IDE.

All this power is not without a cost, however. While basic editing with Emacs is not difficult, the vast power of Emacs takes significant effort to learn. Most users say that taking the time to learn the full power of Emacs is well worth it in long-term dividends.

One of the best things about the system is that there is only one main version in use for virtually every programming platform today. It is free under the GPL. Emacs is a standard part of every Linux distribution. The full distribution of GNU Emacs, including full source code and the MS-Windows executable binary, is on the CD accompanying this book. The GNU Emacs Web site is www.gnu.org/software/emacs/emacs.html.

Vi

Vi is another editor that is popular today. It was originally developed by Bill Joy, co-founder of Sun Microsystems, back in the mid-1970s while he was a student at Berkeley. It became the standard visual editor for UNIX.

Vi is a moded editor; it has command mode and insert mode. The commands are typically single-character commands, such as *x* for delete a character and *h* to move the cursor one character to the left. Others are two-letter commands, such as *dd* to delete a line and *dh* to delete a character to the left (there is a whole set of *d* delete commands). Although the command set seems a bit obscure, it is efficient once you know it.

Vi and Emacs share one important legacy. They were both developed when programmers were just starting to use terminals connected to time-sharing systems. These terminals were connected to the computer at only 300 or 1,200 baud.[3] The terminals were also very primitive compared to the GUI systems now available. Both Emacs and vi were designed when it was a challenge even to get the text on the screen, and the commands needed to be simple one- or two-character sequences.

One interesting bit of trivia about the vi command set concerns the choice of the letters *hjkl* for the left, up, down, and right cursor movements. In the mid-1970s at Berkeley, the most common terminal around campus was an ADM-3a. The terminal was not very versatile, but it was cheap. There was no separate keypad for arrow keys. Instead, the ADM-3a had arrows printed on the *hjkl* keys, which were usually used in combination with the Control key. Vi simply uses *hjkl*.

[3.] Just consider how slow even a 28,000-baud connection to the Internet seems today.

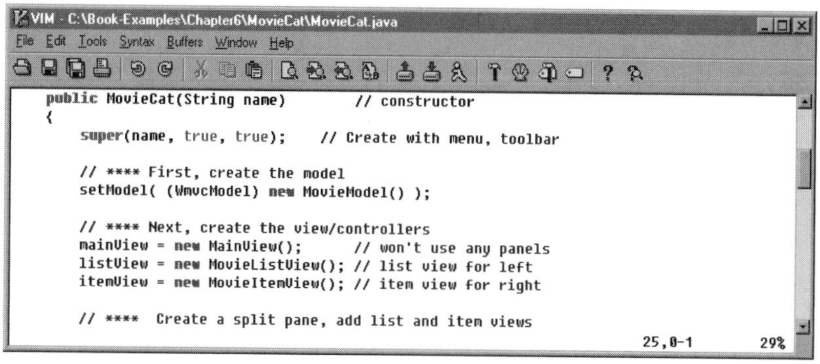
VIM - C:\Book-Examples\Chapter6\MovieCat\MovieCat.java
File Edit Tools Syntax Buffers Window Help
public MovieCat(String name)   // constructor
{
    super(name, true, true);   // Create with menu, toolbar
    // **** First, create the model
    setModel((WmvcModel) new MovieModel());
    // **** Next, create the view/controllers
    mainView = new MainView();   // won't use any panels
    listView = new MovieListView(); // list view for left
    itemView = new MovieItemView(); // item view for right
    // **** Create a split pane, add list and item views
25,0-1
29%

Figure 10.1 VIM editor

Unlike GNU Emacs, there is no standard version of vi. The original was a part of the commercial UNIX system and is not free for general distribution. There are, however, several free clones available. The most popular is VIM, or vi improved (`www.vim.org`). It is totally freeware, and the source code and an executable version for MS-Windows are included on the accompanying CD (see Figure 10.1).

Integrated Development Environments

Integrated development environments are designed to support the most common programming tasks in a single program. Some IDEs work with multiple languages, but many are designed for a specific language such as Java.

While the feature set of IDEs varies among products, most IDEs have the following features.

- Programming editor
- Integration with the compiler; supporting an easy way to go directly to syntax errors for editing
- Build control; grouping all source files required by a project and allowing the project to be compiled and built in one step
- Integration with debugger
- Advanced search facilities; including the ability to search for specific symbols within a program and to search multiple files
- Version control; integration with a version-control system
- Help; extended help facilities for both the IDE and the programming language

- Integration with other tools; the ability to work with external tools

- Other language-specific features; class browsers for object-oriented languages, user interface builders for specific GUIs (for example, Swing)

The following sections discuss some IDEs for Java.

VIDE

VIDE is a small, free IDE written by the author of this book (see Figure 10.2). It uses the author's open source V C++ GUI framework. Compared with some of the large commercial IDEs, VIDE is small and fast.

It supports both C++ and Java. C++ support includes the GNU g++ compiler and the free Borland C++ command-line compiler. VIDE also supports Sun's Java development environment, which is available for free download at java.sun.com.

The default VIDE editor supports a standard GUI modeless command set. It includes other important editing features, such as macros, code indentation, syntax highlighting, and symbol browsing. It also supports two moded command sets—a subset of vi and the See command set developed by the author.

The fact that VIDE is small and simple is both its strength and its weakness. It is quite simple to learn and supports almost all the basic tasks a programmer needs. However, it lacks some of the language-specific features found in full-blown C++ or Java IDEs, and the comprehensiveness of Emacs.

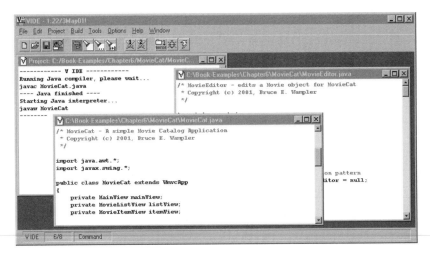

Figure 10.2   VIDE

Even so, because VIDE is free, small, and so simple, it has been adopted as a recommended choice by several introductory computer programming courses at universities and colleges around the world. An executable version of VIDE is included on the accompanying CD, and there are VIDE project files for all the Java code examples found in this book.

Borland JBuilder

Borland JBuilder 5[4] may be the best Java IDE available (see Figure 10.3). It consistently shows up as a programmer's favorite in Internet discussion groups, and it gets favorable reviews in magazines.

Like most Java IDEs, JBuilder is written in Java for Java programming. This means it is available for all Java platforms, and it is designed to support Java and associated Java packages, such as Swing.

Borland distributes JBuilder 5 in three versions: Personal, Professional, and Enterprise. Each version supports different features, the Personal Edition being the most limited.

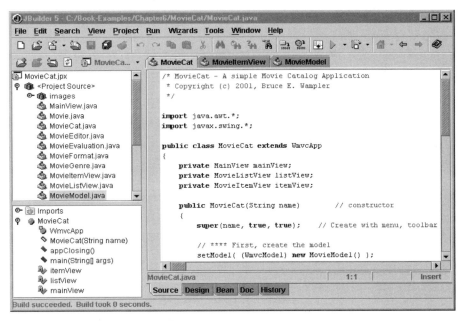

Figure 10.3   Borland's JBuilder 5

---

4. Version 5 was the latest as of this writing. New versions are available approximately annually.

The Personal Edition of JBuilder is available for download from Borland at no cost (www.borland.com). Even better, there is a copy of JBuilder 5 Personal on the book's CD. It is really an amazing piece of free software.[5]

All versions of JBuilder have the following features.

- Java language support, including syntax highlighting, class browsing, full language help support, code templates, and more

- Swing support; can interactively build user interfaces from Swing components and automatically generate Java source code

- XML support

- JavaBean support

- Full project support for compiling and debugging

- Version control

- Wizards to help create projects, build applets, and so on

The features included in the Personal Edition are really complete and can be used to build almost any Java application. However, the Professional and Enterprise editions have significant features that make it easier to develop more-advanced Java applications. It is important to remember that a programmer's time is very expensive, and providing the appropriate tools is almost always cost-effective.

The Professional Edition has the following extra features.

- JDBC; including full support for JDBC as well as extra Borland tools for building database applications

- Servlets

- Support for multiple Java development kits

- More wizards to simplify development, including building JavaBeans

- More editing features, such as customizable command set and editable templates

- Supports more Swing user interface components

- Deployment tools, including a JAR file builder

[5.] There is a real difference between open source software and software that is free. Open source software is freely available. Anyone can use and modify the source code, and it can be redistributed under the open source license. JBuilder is not open source software, even though the Personal Edition is free. Borland has not released the source code and controls distribution.

JBuilder Enterprise adds even more, including support for Enterprise Java-Beans, distributed computing applications, CORBA support, and JSP support. Any company building Java applications at this level understands the capabilities needed to support their development.

Borland also has some interactive training CDs that can help you learn JBuilder quickly. These training tools are likely to be cost-effective at getting new programmers up to speed.

A feature list is only the first step in evaluating how good a program really is. Reading reviews and what other users have to say about a product is another important step, and JBuilder really stands out. Finally, the only real way to know whether a software tool is right for you is to use it and evaluate it. The very best programs have all the features you need, yet are easy to learn and to use. JBuilder seems to meet this last test better than some of the other IDEs, such as Forte.

While JBuilder is very good, it has some faults. Programmers used to all the editing features of Emacs, vi, or even VIDE might be disappointed in JBuilder's editor. There are a few quirks in setting and using directories, but that is just a matter of learning the tool's conventions. And JBuilder suffers the same problem as do many Java-based applications—it is slow to load and sometimes a bit slow in its response. This is especially noticeable on slower machines.

There is another issue when using JBuilder or any of the other Java IDEs, and that is the automatic application-generation tools. These tools let you build simple GUI applications rather easily, but you build them the way the tools decide to build them. For example, when you use the JBuilder application wizard to build an application from scratch, it starts by creating the top-level class that extends JFrame. Although this is a standard way of building Java applications, it is not necessarily what you want to do. Be sure you use the tool to build the programs you want, using good object-oriented design, and don't get trapped into using a design structure provided by the IDE by default.

As noted earlier, a full version of the free Personal Edition is on the book's CD. You have to register this version at Borland's Web site. If you are a student or associated with an educational institution, Borland provides highly discounted prices for the Professional and Enterprise editions. You can check Borland's Web site for details. There are JBuilder project files on the CD for all the Java code examples found in this book as well.

Sun Forte

Sun Microsystems distributes a Java IDE called Forte. Forte is very similar to JBuilder in many ways. Although JBuilder seems to do better in reviews than Forte, there is a rapidly growing Forte community.

Sun provides two editions of Forte, a free community edition and an enterprise edition. The community edition has more features than JBuilder Personal. For example, there is support for JDBC. As expected, the enterprise edition has support for enterprise-wide networked applications and other advanced features.

Forte's editor is in some ways more advanced that JBuilder's. It has macros and is customizable even in the free version. However, the JBuilder editor has more total commands, and it comes with several predefined command sets. Also, the code generated by JBuilder's user interface designer seems cleaner and easier to modify than Forte's.

In the end, the decision about which IDE, if any, to use is very personal. In a large enough project, it is possible that a whole team has to use the same IDE because of the support they give for version control and project coordination, but the important issue is to use the tool that maximizes your productivity.

Since both Borland and Sun have free versions of their IDEs, it is probably worth some effort to try both if you haven't yet settled on one tool. JBuilder and Forte aren't the only Java IDEs.

Another IDE

Perhaps the most significant alternative IDE is IBM's VisualAge for Java (www-4.ibm.com/software/ad/vajava/). It has several editions, including a free version for download (although the download size is huge). The design philosophy and work model supported by VisualAge is significantly different from most other IDEs and has quite a learning curve. However, many VisualAge users claim that its approach is better than other IDEs once you get accustomed to it.

Source-Code Control

A version control system keeps track of all the changes made to a set of files. For an individual developer, that means being able to keep track of all the changes made to a program during the entire time it has been in development.

Version control systems are not only valuable, they are essential for development teams. They track changes as well as allow programmers to check out individual files, make changes, and then have those changes merged back into the main source-code repository.

CVS is the Concurrent Versions System and is currently the most widely used version control system. It is open source, and works on individual computers or over any computer network, thus making it useful for both the individual and the team.

There are other version control systems, such as rcs and sccs, but CVS is the most popular. Most IDEs either have their own version control features or integrate with CVS or another system.

Complete information about getting and using CVS is available at www.cvshome.org. It is open source and freely available. Using a version control system is an essential programming practice, and CVS is as good as any.

CASE, Modeling, and UML Tools

CASE stands for computer-aided software engineering. When CASE tools were first conceived, many hoped they would revolutionize software development. So far, this has not been the reality. While CASE tools can be useful and help keep a project on track, practices such as object orientation have proven to be more useful.

There are several kinds of CASE tools. IDEs can be considered the most basic CASE tool. Usually, however, CASE tools are tied to some software development philosophy or management practice. One such common category is the software modeling tool. There are many tools used to design and implement software using the UML. Some are methodology independent; others are tied to a specific one.

Other CASE tools are more comprehensive and contain tools for developing software using one methodology. They can include features that build certain kinds of management charts and time lines, track code, track bugs, provide process management, and more.

While a few free and open source CASE tools are available, so far none yet match the functionality and quality of commercial tools. Unfortunately for the small company or development team, most commercial CASE tools typically cost several thousand dollars per seat. A few are available for a few hundred dollars, and even they can help the productivity of a small development team (and be suitable for large teams, as well).

ArgoUML

If you want to try a basic UML design tool, check out ArgoUML, an open source project to develop a full UML design tool. As this book is written, the ArgoUML project has been under development for several years and shows real promise of becoming an excellent open source UML tool. Best of all, you can try working with UML using a free tool.

Although not as capable as commercial products, it can generate basic UML diagrams and has some interesting design critique features. Because it is an evolving program, it is not included on the book's CD. The download of the latest version is available at www.argouml.org.

MagicDraw

MagicDraw (www.magicdraw.com) is one of the more affordable UML modeling tools (see Figure 10.4). It supports the entire UML standard, and is easy to learn and to use. It is almost in a class of its own, given its features and price. Magic-Draw was used to produce all the UML diagrams for this book, and a demo version is available at their Web site.

MagicDraw facilitates analysis and design of object-oriented systems and databases. It supports the latest standards of Java, UML, and XMI and provides the comprehensive code engineering mechanism, with full round-trip support for Java, C++, and CORBA IDL programming languages. MagicDraw also provides database schema modeling, DDL generation, and reverse engineering facilities.

Rational Software

Rational Software (www.rational.com) has a full suite of software development tools. Rational Rose is their full-featured UML-based modeling tool. It is *the*

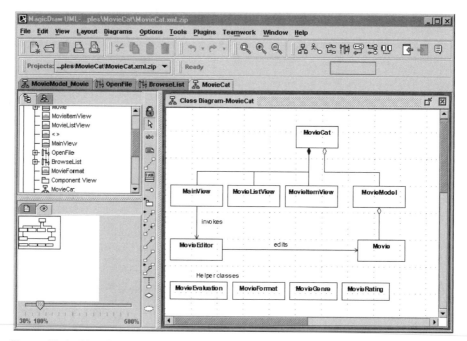

Figure 10.4   MagicDraw UML design tool

standard by which all other modeling tools are judged. The company also has tools to manage the Rational Unified Process.

Committing to Rational is essentially committing to an entire development philosophy. The decision to use Rational products is usually made at a company or project level. Once the commitment has been made, however, Rational is likely to give stable, long-term support for the system and tools.

TogetherSoft

TogetherSoft was founded by Peter Coad, who helped develop the Coad-Yourdon object-oriented analysis and design methodology. The main product of TogetherSoft is ControlCenter, which is not methodology-specific, but is more than a modeling tool.

TogetherSoft calls ControlCenter a Model-Build-Deploy Platform. Their Web site says, "With it, you can: model - EJB - pattern - edit - compile - debug - version - doc - metric/audit - provision - assemble - deploy - run." It has a UML tool, a programming editor, round-trip code engineering, software matrix tools, and more. It is a total CASE tool.

ControlCenter is an alternative to Rational Software products well worth considering. It, too, is likely to take an organization-wide commitment. See www.togethersoft.com.

Other UML Tools

There are several other UML modeling tools available.

mUML

mUML is a very low cost UML tool worth checking out. It is supported by a small company, Mount Field Computers, and supports all UML diagrams, generates Java code, and can perform reverse engineering. Although not as full featured as MagicDraw, it is quite capable, and was available for less than $50 as of press time. See www.mfcomputers.com.

ObjectDomain

ObjectDomain is a UML modeling tool that supports C++ and Python, as well as Java. See www.objectdomain.com.

SoftModeler

SoftModeler is another full-featured UML modeling tool. There are three versions, starting at a reasonably priced Standard Edition. The Professional Edition adds support for modeling JavaBeans, and the Enterprise Edition has support for shared projects. See softera.com.

Other Java Tools

JUnit

JUnit is an open source regression-testing framework written by Erich Gamma and Kent Beck. It is used to implement unit tests for Java programs. JUnit is an important tool to use when refactoring code and with XP. JUnit is in active development and can be downloaded at `junit.org`, and is also included on the book's CD. It can be integrated into JBuilder.

Jikes

Jikes is an open source Java compiler from IBM. It is an alternative to the compiler that comes with Sun's JDK. While Jikes is often mentioned in discussions of Java compilers, the future of Jikes is not clear. For the latest information about Jikes, see `oss.software.ibm.com/developerworks/opensource/jikes/`.

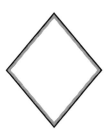

CHAPTER 11

Programming: A Personal Perspective

This chapter is a bit different from the rest of the book. I've tried to give an objective presentation of the material up to now, but this chapter represents my own subjective view of programming.

Even after programming in one form or another for 30 years, I still find programming a fun thing to do. I'm still doing active development on my own open source projects, the V C++ GUI Framework and VIDE. I'd like to extend the Wmvc framework I used for this book.

Over the years, I've programmed in many languages, including some you've probably never heard of. The main languages I've used include Fortran, Ratfor, Pascal, C, PDP-11 assembler, Intel 8080/8086 assembler, C++, and Java. Of all the languages I've used, I like C++ and Java the best, mostly because they are object-oriented. There have been many new programming ideas developed over my career, but object orientation has been the most significant. Besides the real benefits of ease of maintenance, I just find it more fun to design and program with objects.

I've been involved with programming at many levels. When I was at Sandia National Labs, I worked on a very large project with many programmers and layers of management. When I started my first personal computer software company, I learned how important it is to write software that works on different computers (Microsoft was just one of many small companies back then), and that works correctly for paying customers. My years at the University of New Mexico taught me how to teach others about programming. My favorite time was spent with my company, Reference Software, working to build a great team of programmers to develop our grammar checker and other reference software works. And during the past few years, I've tried to give something back to the software community, first by developing open source software, and now by writing this book.

In this chapter, I will cover some of the things I've found important for developing great software. Some of these are important programming principles, some simple tips or guidelines, and some a matter of philosophy.

I've divided this chapter into several sections. The first section, Programming, is about day-to-day programming—how to write code. The second is about using tools to make your programming efforts easier and more productive. The third section is about the programming work environment, and how a good work environment is critical for developing good software. And finally, I'll cover ways to use some of the many available resources to enhance your programming skills.

Programming

This section covers some practical aspects of programming. Some of these topics are really about programming; others are more philosophical. All are principles I have found important for writing better programs. Some issues apply both to a personal productivity level and to a workplace level.

Your Code Never Dies

I have found the simple realization that *your code never dies* has a profound effect on just how I program, perhaps more than any other factor. It is true. No matter how small, how trivial, or how temporary you think a piece of code might be, almost without fail, you or someone else will see that code again sooner or later. Depending on how you use this revelation, that can mean the code can come back to help you or to haunt you.

One of the best examples I can think of is an editor I originally wrote in 1980. Partly because I didn't like the editors available on the VAX computer I was working with at the time, and partly to really learn how to program for that VAX, I decided to write an editor. I wrote the first version of the editor in a language called Ratfor, which allowed you to use C syntax to write Fortran programs.

The editor worked well, and I've used it as my editor of choice ever since. Well, before long, I moved to a different computer and operating system. The first thing I had to do was move my editor to that machine. Before long, we switched to C instead of Ratfor, so I translated the program to C. Then I changed jobs and took the editor with me.

Over the past 20 years, this editor has followed me everywhere. It has undergone many transitions. First, from Ratfor to C. Then modifications to make it work on different systems with different terminals. Then to support a graphical user interface. Then to C++. And so on. Today, you can still see remnants of the original Ratfor code in the source for my free VIDE. And I'm still using it, still modifying the code, and still finding bugs. Back in 1980, I could not have imagined that I would still be using and modifying descendents of that code in 2001.

The same can be said about the millions and millions of lines of code that had to be reviewed and fixed for the millennium. If all those programmers who originally wrote this code 30, 20, or even just 5 years ago had believed their code would never die, perhaps many of the problems associated with Y2K could have been avoided.

Remember, someone (and it might be you) eventually will have to modify the code, which means that person will have to understand it. Write clear, logical code. Choose good names. Comment thoroughly and appropriately. If you had to look something up to use a library, for example, then a comment will help.

Write the best code you can. Take pride in it. You will get a great feeling when people later tell you that they were impressed with your code quality.

Don't write quick and dirty code. You might think you'll remember what you've done, but you won't. Even after a few months, let alone years, your own code might as well have been written by someone else. So when you write code, remember you will have to see it again, and you won't remember what you were doing the first time. Give yourself a break.

Although you can use refactoring later, it is easier to get it right as you create the code the first time. This doesn't necessarily mean you have to write perfect code while you are still working on it, and figuring out how to make it function, but you should refactor and fix code before you consider it finished.

Program with Style

If you know you are writing code that others will read, it becomes important that you write your code with style. Writing with style is more than having good data structures or using good algorithms. It is making code that is both easy and inviting to read.

If you read a good textbook, for example, you find it is more than just a collection of words and sentences. It has a definite style to it. The first page of each chapter has a clear and consistent design. The chapters are broken down into parts or sections that also follow a design. There is a consistency to how the pages look, how the figures are arranged. There is conscious use of white space to make the book easier to read. A significant degree of artistry has gone into the design of the book.

The same should be true for computer code. Many programmers try to cram as much code into as small a space as possible. This is not good programming. Use design principles when laying out your code, just as is done when a book is designed. Many programmers don't seem to realize that liberal, but deliberate, use of white space can make a program much easier to read.[1] The following are some of the layout principles I find important.

- Use a fixed format for each class definition and each method definition. Use white space to make them stand out. Comments with a consistent style often help.

- Indentation should indicate code structure. It should make the code easy to read. I like to indent my code using multiples of four spaces. I line up *ifs* and *elses*. I put braces on lines by themselves because that has a real visual impact on making the code easier to read. While the most common Java standard puts the leading brace on the same line as its associated control statement, I find this makes the code more difficult to read. I find the bit of extra white space accompanied by the quick visual matching of braces makes each brace on its own line much more pleasant to read.

- Take as much care laying out comments as you do laying out code. Remember white space. Group comments together. I like to use trailing comments when appropriate, keeping plenty of white space when possible, and to line them up in columns.

- Good names for classes, methods, and variables are important, too. I find the Java capitalization standard leads to the most readable names. It now seems so obviously better to me than other naming conventions that I wonder why it took so long to develop.

Know What You Are Doing

It really does help to understand what you are doing. Take the time you need to understand the problem, the computer, the programming language. For example, it really does help you program better if you understand shallow versus deep copy or how the Java runtime works. It does help to look at Swing with object-oriented eyes.

[1.] Unfortunately, because of the limits of the page size of this printed book, I haven't always been able to format the code examples the way I'd like to. I have tried my best to make the examples look good and have kept my braces on lines by themselves.

Write Practice Programs

Whenever I move to new system (a new operating system, a new programming language, a new GUI, and so forth), I spend a week or two learning about it by writing a few practice programs, or by getting some program I've worked with before to run. I can't count the number of times that getting my editor working on the new system was the first thing I did.

When moving my editor doesn't work, I try to get a few other simple programs working instead. It is important to get a reasonable understanding of the tools (editors, compilers, and so forth) available with the new system, as well as how it works. Once I have the basics down, I can move on to something real.

Practice Incremental Programming

Whenever I create new code, I practice what I call incremental programming. I add the very least I possibly can, test it to be sure it works, and move on to the next step.

For example, when I add a new class to a system, I just create the bare outline of the class, perhaps with a few stubs for methods, and get that basic outline to compile and link. Only then do I add functionality. I do that one feature at a time, and in as small an increment as possible. After I add each feature, I test to see that it works as it should and that I haven't broken anything else.

By adding one small feature at a time, you can minimize the time you spend debugging. Because you know just what part of the code you are changing, you usually know just what part of the whole program you are affecting. Then you find out what went wrong without needing to resort to your debugger.

The Tools Matter

It is important to find just the right set of tools to fit your own style. I still find I'm most productive using a UNIX-style development environment. This means a good set of separate tools—an editor, a compiler, a debugger, and some other software tools, such as CVS and grep. Other programmers thrive with a full-featured IDE in which all those tools are available from one interface.

Which tools you use is a matter of personal style. I like to do things my own way, for example, and I find the flexibility of separate tools makes this easiest. I find that using a big, full-featured IDE takes a great deal of overhead to learn to use effectively, and then it is likely to thwart the way I do things anyway. Others find just the opposite.

The important thing to realize, however, is that the tools really can make a difference. Take the time to use different tools and discover the ones that work best for you. Just because someone else thinks a big Java development tool is the way to program Java doesn't mean it is best for you. Investigate the alternatives.

Objects Really Help

Object-oriented programming really is more productive. If you have well-designed objects, you can confine changes to one object and the objects that use it. This is ideal for the incremental programming I discussed earlier.

Testing

Most of the testing I do is unit testing associated with the kind of incremental programming I practice. When I'm developing a new class, I usually write a driver program first, which really is just a test for the new class. As I add functionality to the class, I can use that driver to test the new features. With the cycle of add one thing, test that thing, I find I can produce lots of working code quickly. This is not much different from the test/code cycle of Extreme Programming.

Debugging

Since I've been doing object-oriented programming in C++ and Java, I've found I very rarely use a debugger. Every so often, especially when using a library or framework, I find I need to resort to a debugger, but that isn't often. Debuggers can also be useful when you are integrating different components of a bigger project.

When I'm working on a specific section of code, I find that incremental programming makes debugging trivial. I know what I've just changed, so I know where to look when something breaks.

When I can't find a bug, however, a debugger isn't necessarily the best first step. One of the best ways I've found to track down a bug is to try to explain the code to another programmer. Just going over the code with someone else uncovers the bug with surprising regularity. Try that first.

The nature of objects means that it can also be very informative to put trace print statements in object constructors. With Java, you can run your programs from a console and print useful information whenever an object is constructed. This often exposes what you are looking for.

When you do need to resort to a debugger, it is important to understand how the program is supposed to work. It is difficult to know where to set breakpoints, or what variables to watch unless you know what the program should be doing.

I also have one critical rule when debugging. As you debug, and try things to fix the bug change only one thing at a time. As you go over the code, it is often tempting to change another thing or two before you recompile and test again.

Resist. If you change more than one thing in the code at a time, you will not know for sure which change fixed the problem, or even if you've introduced yet another bug in the process.

Don't Reinvent the Wheel

A lot of programming problems have already been solved; avoid reinventing solutions. There are textbooks with algorithms. There are design patterns you can use. There are libraries and frameworks that can solve particular problems with minimal work on your part. The goal is to minimize the work you need to do reinventing what someone else has already done.

Sometimes It Is Better to Do It Yourself

Even though you want to avoid duplicating existing work, sometimes you have to. The existing solution you find may not do just what you need, or it may even be more difficult to use than starting from scratch. Sometimes, it is important to know when to give up and do it yourself.

One trend in software development still makes me a bit uneasy—the development of tools for automatically generating GUI interfaces, especially for Java. This is a feature of both Forte and JBuilder, for example. Although these tools can be great for exploring various user interfaces, I worry about two aspects of them.

First, you are locked into the structure of the code they generate. This means that if you want your code to have a particular organization or design, you may have to bend it a bit to fit the GUI code generated by the tool. And while the code generated by such tools isn't necessarily bad, it will always be generalized to fit the requirements of the tool, and not necessarily easy to modify or understand.

Another problem is long-term support. For example, while Sun is currently supporting Forte, there is no guarantee that in a year or two market conditions won't force Sun to drop Forte and switch to a new product. If that were to happen, then anyone who had relied on Forte to build their user interfaces might be out of luck.

So while rapid GUI designers might be great for prototypes, it is probably better and safer to build your own GUI code, or at the very least to use only open source tools. This applies to almost any kind of automatic code-generation tool.

You Can Get Ideas Any Time

Over the years, I've discovered I have some of my best programming ideas while I'm in the shower or when I first wake up in the morning. While you are intensely involved with a programming project, you are likely to find that good ideas pop into your head at almost any time. I find it valuable to be prepared for such occasions by having a small spiral notebook nearby. I can write down my ideas right away, before they get away, and then review them later when I get back to programming. I still haven't figured out how to read my own scrawling, however.

Keeping such a notebook can be useful for other aspects of programming, as well. You can keep meeting notes in it. You can write down trivial details of the installation process of some software product. While handheld organizers are great for many things, a plain old notebook is still best for writing down rapid notes.

Get a Life

I really like programming. When I'm on a roll, I become totally oblivious to what is going on with the rest of the world. But only up to a point; then I have to do something else.

I know programmers who get so wrapped up in their job that they miss out on the rest of life. Although some employers like this kind of programmer, it is very important for employees to have a life away from the computer. I find that programmers who have a life outside their jobs remain great and productive programmers for years, while those whose world is programming burn out.

Sometimes, however, you do get on a roll. You turn out code at an amazing rate, and it all works. These times can happen infrequently. If possible, take advantage of the ride. But don't overdo to the point of ignoring friends and family. These rolls usually last only a week or so, so beware if you let them go on too long.

A Plan Matters

Master programmers can sometimes program by feel. Their experience tells them just what approach to take to solve a problem and how to write the code. Unfortunately, there just aren't that many programmers with that ability. For the rest of the time, it really does matter to have a plan.

Taking the time to understand the problem, analyze the requirements, and do a proper design pays off. Using the talents of a master programmer to help make the plan can be especially productive. Once a plan is ready, then all the programmers involved are more productive and the resulting product is better. While the up-front planning may not be as much fun as building a product, the effort pays off.

The Tools

As I said in the last section, your software tools do matter. They can make you a more productive programmer and make the programming task more enjoyable. In this section, I will discuss a bit of what I believe about software tools.

Your Editor Really Matters

While you are programming, you spend a lot of your time in your code editor. Hardly any other programming tool can invoke more ardent feelings and discussions than an editor. Which editor you use really does matter. You should know about the alternatives and be able to use the one that best suits your work style.

Know About the Time-Tested Tools

Many experienced programmers find that a UNIX-like programming environment is still the best. Today, Linux is probably the best place to experience the UNIX-like environment, although there are versions that work on Microsoft Windows.

Know About the Latest Tools

While many of the standard software tools have been around for years, new ones are being developed all the time. This has been especially true with the rise in Java's popularity. Many tools have been developed for object-oriented development and for Java development. Some of the newer ones are available in free open source versions, but most are commercial products. I already covered some in the last chapter. Here is a list of the latest software tools.

- **UML** Many software tools are available for working with UML, from simply generating UML diagrams to reading and generating Java and C++ code.

- **CASE** Computer-aided software engineering tools are used to design software. Many are associated directly with development methodologies.

- **Project management** Project management tools help to manage software projects of various sizes.

- **Testing** Testing tools, such as JUnit, help to automate testing.

- **RAD** Rapid application development tools help to quickly generate code based on simple specifications or interactive input.

- **IDEs** Integrated development environments bring together many formerly separate tools into one package.

- **Code profilers** Code profilers are tools to analyze runtime characteristics and static code properties.

Tools Go Away

Software tools can enhance a programmer's productivity. There is one significant problem with many tools, however, especially commercially developed and marketed tools. Market forces change, and companies go out of business.

Remember, your programs will never die. Unfortunately, companies, methodologies, and even programming languages do. There will always be a certain amount of risk when using the latest software development technology. This risk shouldn't stop you from using the latest and greatest, but your plans should include contingencies for such unfortunate events.

The Work Environment

Even though the Internet has given many programmers the opportunity to do at least some of their work at home or on the road, most programmers still work at some kind of office, usually with a group of other programmers. The work environment can radically affect the productivity of programmers. In this section, I'll touch on a few things I learned about just how important the work environment is.

Most of the time, I talk from the perspective of management. Some of the policies I've followed as a manager seem to be common sense to me, although they aren't practiced by many companies or managers. However, I've found these concepts and practices to be true, and they help keep programmers productive.

If you, as a programmer, work at a place that is not pleasant or follows policies that don't take into consideration the special abilities and needs of programmers, you should try to convince your boss that some of my policies really work and will result in more productive programmers.

A Happy Programmer Is a Productive Programmer

The most important thing I've found is that happy programmers are productive. Thus, whenever I've worked with a team of programmers, I've tried to create a work environment that is not just pleasant, but fun.

Physical Environment

The physical environment is important. This includes not only the building, but the computers and software tools needed for programming.

I find that a private office with a door that is usually open, but can be closed, is important. The usual policy it to keep your door open to invite spontaneous and casual conversation, but to be able to close it when you need to concentrate.

I think open cubicles are too public and too noisy for programmers. They can work for support people, such as a testing group, but don't allow the quiet concentration programmers sometimes need. If the physical space or company finances don't allow for individual offices, then the cubical space must allow for as much privacy as possible.

Extreme Programming is an exception to this. XP calls for pair programming in a shared common space. However, XP also calls for quiet, private space that programmers can retreat to when necessary.

Programmers should also have up-to-date equipment and software. Spending a few hundred or even a few thousand extra dollars for programming tools for someone to whom you are paying a salary of many thousands of dollars makes sense. Keeping the software and equipment up to date helps to maximize productivity.

Flexibility

Once you give your programmers a good work environment, you then have to give them as much flexibility as possible in how they do their job. I've found that if you give your programmers the respect they deserve and flexibility in how they work, they reward you by giving back their best work.

- **Vacation** People should be able to take their vacations when they want. Vacations should coincide with family needs, not company needs. However, because vacation is very important to revitalize programmers, they should be required to use the time, not carry it over from year to year. And two weeks really isn't enough. If the company isn't able to give more than two weeks of paid vacation, then programmers should be allowed extra time off without pay.

- **Deadline time** Deadline time is special. Every project reaches important deadlines. These critical deadlines should be scheduled as far in advance as possible. To meet them, programmers should be expected to put in some extra hours and perhaps adjust their vacation schedule. However, these deadlines must not be abused. The critical time can't stretch out for more than two or three weeks, and it can't be used more than two, maybe three, times a year. Of course, programmers should be compensated for the extra hours.

- **Mostly regular hours** Most projects involving many programmers need to have all of them available for each other at the same time, which means keeping a regular work schedule. But an individual's schedule can have some flexibility and still meet the needs of the team. I found that letting the programmers set their own schedule, as long as there was always five or six hours of programmer overlap on most work days, worked very well. This policy also allows some people to work from home at least part of the workweek. Having all the programmers together for at least part of the time not only allows for required communication, it is needed to keep the people working as a team.

- **Job sharing** I've found that part-time programmers, or programmers who split one position, can be very productive. However, it is not always possible for programmers working on critical sections of a program.

40 Hours

Programming is a creative and mentally intensive task. Expecting programmers to work more than 40 hours a week on a regular basis does not work. Eventually they burn out and become much less productive. I find it significant that a 40-hour workweek is a major principle of Extreme Programming.

The Team

The importance of teamwork has long been known in the realm of sports. Having a great team of programmers who work together well is also important for software development. Not only does a great team produce great software, the team members come to count on each other, often both professionally and personally.

The work environment should encourage teams to become close. This includes putting team members physically close together in the workplace. It can also include less tangible things, such as making things fun, which may include encouraging team members to have lunch together and providing social get-togethers. If the company is small enough, these activities can extend to the entire company.

Marketing Matters

When a company produces a product for a large customer base, it no doubt has a marketing department. Conflicts between the marketing and development departments are legendary. The fact is that the efforts of the marketing team are just as important to the company's health as are the efforts of the programming team. Both sides must learn that they really need each other.

Marketers must accept realistic time estimates from the developers. Developers must listen to members of the marketing team, who often know what the ultimate customer wants, or what will make the software product most valuable in the marketplace. Developers must also give realistic estimates of time frames, without padding the estimates. And if marketing has a date fixed for a release, the developers should inform marketing what they can reasonably deliver. And marketing should listen. With mutual respect, the whole company profits.

Keep Up-to-Date

A company needs to do everything it can to keep its programmers up-to-date. This means providing access to training, sponsoring trips to relevant conferences, and providing the latest in proven hardware and software technology.

Share the Struggle

While I firmly believe that all the practices I give in this section result in increased productivity, I also know that sometimes reality intrudes onto these ideals. Companies, especially start-ups, have financial constraints. It can be a real struggle to come up with the financial resources to pay a competitive salary, hire all the programmers a project needs, and have a great physical facility. Sometimes, you just have to struggle through.

I've found it is important to avoid secrecy and to share with employees the struggles the company is going through. All the employees, including programmers, will understand, and work even harder to help keep the company going. If you respect your employees and compensate them for tough financial times by giving them extra flexibility or extra incentives, such as stock options, they will come through for you.

Let Programmers Help Make Policy

Management needs to respect the programming team. One way to show respect is to let the programmers help to make policy. This includes policy on things like the development environment. It means that if team members say they would be more productive by switching to XP, for example, management should respect this view. Give the programmers a voice, and trust them to come up with the best way to develop code.

Let Your Boss Know What You Need

Just as management needs to let the programmers help make policy decisions, programmers need to let management know when things aren't working or when they could be better. Tell management that 50- and 60-hour workweeks are counterproductive. Tell management about object-oriented programming. Tell them how to let you be more productive.

The Reference Software Story

All this happy programmer stuff works. One of my favorite stories is about the Reference Software development team I built. Reference was a bit unusual in that sales, marketing, and tech support were located in San Francisco, while the main software development team was in Albuquerque. Both locations shared the company policy of keeping the workplace fun and flexible. We did almost everything I've mentioned here—flexible hours, part-time work, a quality workplace, good equipment and software, and team building.

We established a tradition of a monthly Friday lunch for everyone who wanted to come. We would get a big table at a local restaurant, and everyone would have a good time. This simple monthly activity served to renew contacts and rejuvenate everyone's spirit. It became a great team builder.

But this is not the end of the story. WordPerfect bought Reference Software in 1992, and for some time kept the team mostly intact in Albuquerque. Business being what it is, most of the employees were given the chance to move to Word-Perfect's home office in Utah, and the Albuquerque office was closed. Most of the people found new jobs and stayed in Albuquerque. However, closing the office did not end the lunches. For several years after the office closed, the tradition continued, and many team members continued to have the monthly lunch. I hear that some still get together to this day.

There is a lesson to learn from this story. If you create a comfortable work environment in which everyone respects each other, and where everyone is happy and likes their job, you end up with a group of truly productive software developers who are part of a real team. That team can become so strong that even closing down the office won't break the social bonds that were created.

Programming Resources

Finally, I'm going to discuss some resources that are available to help improve your programming skills. It is important to keep up with the state of the art. Not only does this keep you productive, it keeps your job interesting and gives you opportunities to use your skills in new circumstances.

Use the Web

The World Wide Web is one of the most important resources available to programmers. If you need the latest information about a programming challenge, or if you want to keep up with the very latest trends and discussions, the Web is the place.

Watch Out for the Web

The Web can be too good. There is so much information, it can be overwhelming. It is too easy to follow an interesting path on some topic that is not relevant to whatever you were looking for to begin with. And there is plenty of junk on the Web, too. So be careful. If you can't find the information you need quickly, don't waste more of your valuable time following dead ends.

Use Open Source if You Can

There is some high-quality free software available, some of which can probably help you on your current project. But once again, there is a lot of junk. Don't waste time and effort tracking down free or open source software when it would be more productive to use a commercial product or develop the code yourself.

Other Programmers

One of the most important assets for programmers is other programmers. There is nothing like experience to improve a programmer's skills, and a good way to improve your own skills is to work with a more experienced programmer. This spread of knowledge is also why code reviews and team programming work so well.

Web Sites

An amazing number of Web sites have valuable resources. But besides the poor information also available on the Web, there is also the problem of longevity. If you make a bookmark list of useful resources, chances are that within a few months or a year, a large percentage of the bookmarks will no longer be valuable.

I've set up a list of useful links on my own Web site (www.object-central.com). I hope my links will be around for a long time and will continue to be resources for my readers. There is a special link for information related to this book.

CHAPTER 12

What Next?

We've covered a lot of material in this book, but there is still much more to know about object-oriented software and Java. Knowing the essentials of objects and how to use Java with objects, you should be able to handle almost any related topic.

In this final chapter, we will *briefly* list some other good books on object-oriented programming, as well as list some major Java topics we have not covered. We will also give definitions of some terms and abbreviations you are likely to encounter as you read about objects and Java.

Object Orientation

Many books have "object-oriented" in their titles, but a few stand out as important classics. Consider the following three books.

Object-Oriented Analysis and Design with Applications, Second Edition, Grady Booch, Addison-Wesley, 1994, ISBN 0-805-35340-2. Still the classic OOAD reference. Booch's notation has been replaced with UML, but is still easy to understand.

Fundamentals of Object-Oriented Design in UML, Meilir Page-Jones, Addison-Wesley, 2000, ISBN 0-201-69946-X. Very readable. Not just a UML book.

Object-Oriented Systems Design: An Integrated Approach, Edward Yourdon, Yourdon Press, 1994, ISBN 0-13-636325-3. One of my favorites. Includes some history of software design, and helps put object orientation into context. Topics covered are relevant to any methodology.

Java

In this book, we've concentrated on how to use Java to build objects. There are many important aspects of Java we've intentionally ignored. For example, we've not used exception-handling code in places where it might be appropriate for production-quality code. This helps to keep the code short and focused on the example at hand. The following is a list of some important Java topics you need to know if you want to become a competent Java programmer.

- Applets

- Exceptions

- JavaBeans

- Javadoc

- Java libraries and frameworks

- Threads

- Packages

- Deployment

You probably now know enough Java to take advantage of almost any good Java reference. There is good material included with Sun's JDK distribution, for example. Here are some good Java books to consider.

Java in a Nutshell, David Flanagan, O'Reilly, 1999, ISBN 1-56592-487-8. Comprehensive and brief. Be sure to get the latest version.

Object-Oriented Software Development Using Java, Xiaoping Jia, Addison-Wesley, 2000, ISBN 0-201-35084-X. A textbook. Covers Java and keeps the focus on objects.

Java: An Introduction to Computer Science and Programming, Walter Savitch, Prentice Hall, 1999, ISBN 0-13-287426-1. A very readable introductory textbook; great for getting started with Java and programming.

More Terms You Need to Know

As you continue to read and learn about programming, and Java in particular, you will encounter many new terms and acronyms. This final section presents some terms that you will find relevant to your understanding of Java and object-oriented computing.

Distributed Computing Terms

Distributed computing software is meant to run in an environment of different computers connected by a network. These applications can run on an internal company network, or increasingly, on computers connected by the World Wide Web. Java plays a major role in developing distributed computing applications.

Although programming distributed applications is beyond the scope of this book, you will not be able to avoid encountering a vast number of terms and abbreviations related to distributed computing when you read a computer-oriented magazine or article. The following terms should help you.

Because Sun has so many Java-related products and terms, many related to distributed computing, Sun-specific terms are given in their own section.

application server A server program that allows the installation of application-specific software components in a manner such that they can be remotely invoked, usually by some form of remote object method call.

COM COM refers to a standard developed by Microsoft Corp., which provides a framework for integrating components. DCOM is the distributed computing version.

CORBA Distributed computing standard maintained by the Object Management Group (OMG), called the common object request broker architecture.

COS naming CORBA standard for object directories.

DAP Directory access protocol, a protocol for directory services derived from X.500.

DCE Distributed computing environment is a distributed computing standard developed by the Open Software Foundation (OSF) with input from industry.

DCOM Microsoft's distributed component object model.

distributed computing A computing environment in which applications are composed of various parts and objects that can be located on different computers connected to a network. Distributed computing requires a set of standards that specify how the parts running on different computers communicate with each other. Currently, the two main standards are CORBA and DCOM.

IDL   Interface description language, CORBA's syntax for defining object-remote interfaces. (Another meaning of IDL is interactive data language, a programming tool for the interactive reduction, analysis, and visualization of scientific data and images.)

IIOP   Internet Inter-ORB Protocol, CORBA's wire protocol for transmitting remote object method invocations.

messaging middleware   Middleware that supports a publish-and-subscribe or broadcast metaphor.

middleware   Middleware is a software interface between the network and the applications. It provides services such as identification, authentication, authorization, directories, and security. The most widespread middleware standards are the Open Software Foundation's DCE, OMG's CORBA, and Microsoft's COM/DCOM.

MOM   Message-oriented middleware.

NSAPI   Netscape's C language API for adding application extensions to its Web servers.

ORB   Object request broker, a middleware technology that manages communication and data exchange among distributed objects. It is the primary message routing component in a CORBA product.

POA   Portable object adapter, a CORBA standard for defining object life cycle and activation.

servlet   Servlets are modules of Java code that run in a server application to answer client requests. Servlets don't use a specific client-server protocol but are usually used with HTTP.

Java-Related Terms from Sun

Sun Microsystems is the originator of Java and remains one of the principal vendors of Java software products. Sun's developers and marketing teams have produced a large number of products, most of them known by their acronyms.

You can find advertisements for other products, such as IDEs and developments tools that promote that they are compliant with this or that product from Sun. This section may help you wade through Sun's alphabet soup.

EJB Enterprise JavaBeans, a server component standard developed by Sun Microsystems.

J2EE Java 2 Platform, Enterprise Edition, Sun's standard for developing enterprise applications, especially targeted for distributed computing.

Java naming and directory interface The Java standard API for accessing directory services, such as LDAP, COS naming, and others.

Java transaction API Java API for coding client-demarcated transactions, and for building transactional data source drivers.

JDBC Java database connectivity technology is the Sun API that implements the X/Open SQL call-level interface specifications to provide cross-DBMS connectivity to a wide range of SQL databases. This is the main Java standard access to databases.

JNDI Java naming and directory interface.

JNI Java native interface is a standard programming interface for writing Java native methods and embedding the Java virtual machine into native applications.

JSP JavaServer pages, a technology from Sun for building dynamic Web pages using Java and XML-like tags to generate page content.

JTA Java transaction API.

JTS Java transaction service, the Java binding for the CORBA transaction service.

JVM Java virtual machine.

RMI Remote method invocation, the Java standard technology for building distributed objects whose methods can be invoked remotely across a network.

SQLJ An extended Java syntax for embedding SQL-like commands in a Java program.

Other Terms

The following are some other terms you are likely to encounter when reading about Java or Web programming.

HTTP   Hypertext Transfer Protocol, one of the main protocols for transferring Web pages.

object database   An object-oriented database system. See ODBMS and ODMG.

ODBC   Open database connectivity is Microsoft's standard based on the X/Open SQL call-level interface specifications. It does not work well with Java.

ODBMS   Object database management system, the result of integrating database capabilities with object-oriented programming language capabilities.

ODMG   Object Data Management Group, responsible for setting standards for object databases.

OMG   Object Management Group, an organization that defines and promotes object-oriented programming standards.

OODB   Object-oriented database.

OODBMS   Object-oriented database management system.

RUP   Rational Unified Process, an object-oriented development methodology from Rational Software.

SQL   Structured query language, the most widely used standardized query language for requesting information from a database.

XMI   XML metadata interchange. A new OMG standard combining UML and XML.

XML   XML is an open standard of the World Wide Web Consortium (W3C), designed as a data format for structured document interchange on the Web. For example, it allows the definition of new operations when standard HTML is not a good fit.

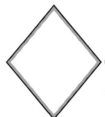

Glossary

abstract class A class that has no instances. It is usually defined with the assumption that concrete subclasses will be derived from it and extend its basic attributes and behavior. In Java, an abstract class is one that includes an abstract method.

abstraction A model of a real-world object or concept.

accessor A method that can access the state of an object.

actor An actor is an object that can operate on other objects, but is never operated on by other objects itself.

agent An agent can operate on other objects and provide services to other objects. As the name implies, it often serves as an agent or intermediary between other objects.

aggregation A whole/part hierarchy. An aggregate object includes (*has-a*) other objects, each of which is considered to be a part of (*part-of*) the aggregate object.

API Application programming interface. The specification of the way a programmer writing an application accesses the behavior and state of classes and objects.

application server A server program that allows the installation of application-specific software components in a manner such that they can be remotely invoked, usually by some form of remote object method call.

association An association is a relationship between two classes. The association will indicate how objects of the classes relate to each other.

attribute Used to hold state information of an object. An attribute might be as simple as an on and off boolean variable, or it might be a complex structure such as another object. A class definition describes the attributes and operations (methods) of a class.

base class The most generalized class in an inheritance hierarchy. Most applications have many hierarchies, with different base classes.

behavior The activity of an object that is visible to the outside world. It includes how an object responds to messages by changing its internal state or by returning state information to other objects.

callback A method that is called when an event has taken place. Usually used in association with a listener. When a listener detects an event, it invokes the callback of objects that need to know that the event has occurred.

CASE Computer-aided software engineering. Software tools used to help automate the development process. CASE tools are most often associated with a specific software development methodology (such as RUP or XP) or design notation (UML).

class A class is a description of a set of objects. The set of objects share common attributes and common behaviors. Class is similar in concept to abstract data types found in non-OO programming languages, but is more comprehensive in that it includes both structure and behavior. A class definition describes all the attributes of member objects of that class, as well as the class methods that implement the behavior of member objects.

For Java, a class definition defines instance and class variables and methods, as well as specifies the interfaces the class implements and the immediate superclass of the class. If the superclass is not explicitly specified, the superclass will implicitly be Object.

class attribute Attributes of a class that are shared by all instances of the class. There will be only one copy of each class attribute, and it is possible to access these class attributes without creating any instances of the class. These are sometimes called `static` attributes in Java.

class method   A method defined by a class, which operates only on class attributes. Class methods can be used without creating any instances of the class. These are sometimes called `static` methods in Java.

cohesion   The connection or similarity (or similarity of purpose) of the components of a class. All elements of a class should work on achieving a common purpose.

COM   COM refers to standards developed by Microsoft Corp., which provides a framework for integrating components. DCOM is the distributed computing version.

composition   A composition is a form of aggregation in which the whole cannot exist without having the parts.

concrete class   A class that is completely specified and can have instances. A Java class derived from an abstract class defines all the abstract methods from the abstract class.

constructor   An operation that creates an object and defines its initial state. For complex objects, construction can be a significant activity and cause the constructors of other objects to be invoked as well. In Java, constructors are instance methods with the same name as their class. Constructors are invoked using the new keyword.

container   A class whose instances are collections of other objects. These collections may be objects of the same type or of mixed types, although they usually have a common superclass. Containers include lists, stacks, queues, and bags. They usually provide a method to iterate over each object in the container.

CORBA   Distributed computing standard maintained by the Object Management Group (OMG), called the common object request broker architecture.

core class   A public class (or interface) that is a standard member of the Java platform.

COS naming   CORBA standard for object directories.

coupling   The interdependence of various components of the system. Independent objects should have no coupling with each other. Relying on the internal implementation of a class, or using friend access, couples two classes.

customer   The organization that needs a software system and is paying for the development. The customer should have a clear idea of what the software system needs to do, and how it can best help the customer's organization.

DAP Directory access protocol, a protocol for directory services derived from X.500.

DCE Distributed computing environment is a distributed computing standard developed by the Open Software Foundation (OSF) with input from industry.

DCOM Microsoft's distributed component object model.

deep copy Making a copy of an object that duplicates everything, including allocating space to build new copies of anything pointed to by pointers.

default behaviors In an inheritance hierarchy, the class behaviors that are defined by superclasses and that will be used by default unless they are overridden by some subclass.

derived In an inheritance hierarchy, a subclass is derived from a superclass. The derived subclass inherits the attributes and methods of the parent superclass.

destructor A destructor is an operation that destroys an object and frees whatever resources the object used. It is invoked when an object ceases to exist, such as when it goes out of scope.

developer An organization that develops software for a customer. The developer works with the customer to design a software system to best meet the customer's needs given the time and financial constraints imposed by the customer.

distributed computing A computing environment in which applications are composed of various parts and objects that are located on different computers connected to a network. Distributed computing requires a set of standards that specify how the parts running on different computers communicate with each other. Currently, the two main standards are CORBA and DCOM.

dynamic binding Definition bound at runtime.

EJB Enterprise JavaBeans, a server component standard developed by Sun Microsystems.

encapsulation The process of hiding all the internal details of an object from the outside world. In Java, encapsulation is enforced by having the definitions of attributes and methods inside a class definition.

event An occurrence that can alter the state of the system.

feasibility Given an initial specification, the developer works with the customer to decide if it is feasible to continue with the development of a software project, given the technical, time, and financial constraints. This is also known as risk assessment: Is it within acceptable risks to proceed with the project?

finalization   A finalizer method is called by the Java garbage collector when it finally frees the storage space used by an object. It is not possible to know when an object will be finalized.

framework   A collection of classes that provide services for a problem area. The designers of a framework should be experts in a problem domain and provide a design that makes it easier for an application using the framework to build software for that problem.

friend   A friend class is one that has access to protected data even though it is not a direct subclass of a given class. Friend access is provided by package access in Java.

garbage collection   The automatic detection and freeing of memory that is no longer in use. An object becomes available for garbage collection when it is no longer referred to by any other object. Java uses garbage collection rather than explicit destructors found in other OO languages, such as C++.

generalization/specialization   An inheritance hierarchy. Each subclass is a specialization of a more generalized superclass.

generic/parameterized classes   A class whose final definition is determined by parameters. One typical use is to define container classes for arbitrary types of objects. The type of the object is specified in the parameter. Parameterized classes are not supported by Java.

getter   A method that returns the value of a class attribute. Getters are also known as accessors or selectors. By convention, getter methods have names such as `getLimit` or `getWidth`.

has-a   A way to state a whole/part relationship. The whole object *has-a* part.

hierarchy   An ordering of classes. The most common OO hierarchies are inheritance and aggregation.

HTTP   Hypertext Transfer Protocol, one of the main protocols for transferring Web pages.

identity   The characteristics, or state, of an object that allows it to be distinguished from other objects.

IDL   Interface description language, CORBA's syntax for defining object-remote interfaces. (Another meaning of IDL is interactive data language, a programming tool for the interactive reduction, analysis, and visualization of scientific data and images.)

IIOP   Internet Inter-ORB Protocol, CORBA's wire protocol for transmitting remote-object method invocations.

implements   In Java, a specification that the class will implement the code required by an interface.

inheritance   A mechanism that allows one class (subclass) to share the attributes and behaviors of another class (superclass). Inheritance defines an *is-a* relationship among classes. The subclass, or derived class, inherits the attributes and behaviors of the superclass, and will usually extend or modify those attributes and behaviors.

inheritance, multiple   When a subclass is derived from multiple superclasses, it is said to have multiple inheritance. Java does not allow multiple inheritance; it provides interfaces as an alternative.

inheritance, single   When a subclass is derived from a single superclass, it is said to have single inheritance.

initial specification   An early description of what a software system needs to do. Depending on the overall size of the project, the initial specification can be simple, or it can consist of extensive documentation.

instance   A specific object that is an instantiation of a class. An instance has specific attributes and behaviors and a unique identity. *Instance* and *object* are often used interchangeably.

instance attribute   An attribute of a class that is associated with a particular instance of the class. Each instance has its own copies of instance attributes.

instance method   Methods defined by a class that operate on instance attributes. This is the most common type of method defined by a class, and an instance method can be used only with the associated instance of the class.

instantiation   Creating an instance of an object of a given class. Instantiating an instance brings it into existence.

interface   In Java, an interface is a specification of methods that must be implemented by a class using the interface. An interface is a specification and does not define any code. It provides an alternative to multiple inheritance.

is-a   A term used in inheritance hierarchies. In general, a subclass *is-a* specialized kind of a more general superclass.

is-a test   A simple test to check for proper inheritance design. If you cannot say a subclass *is-a* kind of the superclass, then inheritance is probably not appropriate.

iterator   An iterator is a method (or methods) used to access or visit each part of an object. This allows the outside world controlled access to all important parts of an object, without the need to know its internal implementation details. Iterators are often used with container classes. They typically work by accessing the first item in a container, then each subsequent object, until all objects have been accessed.

J2EE   Java 2 Platform, Enterprise Edition, Sun's standard for developing enterprise applications, especially targeted for distributed computing.

Java naming and directory interface   The Java standard API for accessing directory services, such as LDAP, COS naming, and others.

Java transaction API   Java API for coding client-demarcated transactions, and for building transactional data source drivers.

JDBC   Java database connectivity technology is the Sun API that implements the X/Open SQL call-level interface specifications to provide cross-DBMS connectivity to a wide range of SQL databases. This is the main Java standard access to databases.

JNDI   Java naming and directory interface.

JNI   Java native interface is a standard programming interface for writing Java native methods and for embedding the Java virtual machine into native applications.

JSP   JavaServer pages, a technology from Sun used to build dynamic Web pages using Java and XML-like tags to generate page content.

JTA   Java transaction API.

JTS   Java transaction service, the Java binding for the CORBA transaction service.

JVM   Java virtual machine.

link   A reference to another class. Used to build associations among classes.

listener   A method that responds to events. These are usually system events, such as mouse clicks and timer events. The listener typically invokes callbacks of objects that need to respond to the event.

member   An attribute or method that belongs to a class.

message   A message is an operation one object performs on another. Messages are usually sent by invoking a specific method or operation provided by another object.

messaging middleware   Middleware that supports a publish-and-subscribe or broadcast metaphor.

method   An operation or service performed upon an object, defined as part of the declaration of a class. Methods are used to implement object behavior. Synonyms for method include member function, operation, and service.

middleware   Middleware is a software interface between the network and the applications. It provides services such as identification, authentication, authorization, directories, and security. The most widespread middleware standards are the Open Software Foundation's DCE, OMG's CORBA, and Microsoft's COM/DCOM.

mix-in   A class (or usually an interface in Java) that is used to define a single behavior. Mix-ins are usually not stand-alone classes, but they are used to provide a standard for implementing the designed behavior.

modifier   This is an operation that alters the state of an object.

module   A module is a basic technique of organizing a program. It is usually thought of as containing all the code and declarations needed to implement one part of a design. The module is the basic unit of encapsulation. In an OO design, each class is usually implemented as a separate module and encapsulates all the data structures and methods and controls access by the outside world.

MOM   Message-oriented middleware.

multiplicity   An attribute that quantifies an association among objects. The multiplicity is specified as a range of the number of objects that can participate in the association, usually in the form $n..m$, where n is the lower limit and m the upper limit. A * means an unlimited number, although a single value can also be used. Common multiplicities include *1, 0..*, 1..*,* and *.

NSAPI   Netscape's C language API for adding application extensions to its Web servers.

object   The basic unit of object orientation. An object is an entity that has attributes, behavior, and identity. Objects are members of a class, and the attributes and behavior of an object are defined by the class definition. An object and an instance are the same thing.

object database An object-oriented database system. See ODBMS and ODMG.

object lifetime The time an object exists, from its instantiation in its constructor until the object no longer exists and has been finalized by the Java garbage collector. The creation point of an object is under program control, but the exact moment when an object ceases to exist cannot be determined because of the way the Java garbage collector works.

object orientation A method of developing software that uses abstraction with objects, encapsulated classes, communication via messages, object lifetime, class hierarchies, and polymorphism.

ODBC Open database connectivity is Microsoft's standard based on the X/Open SQL call-level interface specifications. It does not work well with Java.

ODBMS Object database management system, the result of integrating database capabilities with object-oriented programming language capabilities.

ODMG Object Data Management Group, responsible for setting standards for object databases.

OMG Object Management Group, an organization that defines and promotes object-oriented programming standards.

OODB Object-oriented database.

OODBMS Object-oriented database management system.

operation A class definition describing the attributes and operations of a class. Attributes are implemented as variables; operations are implemented as methods.

ORB Object request broker, a middleware technology that manages communication and data exchange among distributed objects. It is the primary message routing component in a CORBA product.

overriding When a subclass specifies an alternative definition for an attribute or method of its superclass, it overrides the definition in the superclass. Also called overloading. Java can only overload methods.

part-of The opposite of *has-a*. The component is a *part-of* the whole.

persistence Objects can be thought of as persistent when their existence transcends time. Persistent objects usually provide methods that save and restore their own state (to disk, for example).

POA   Portable object adapter, a CORBA standard for defining object life cycle and activation.

polymorphism   Polymorphism allows the appropriate method for any object to be used automatically. Polymorphism goes hand in hand with inheritance and classes derived from a common superclass. It is supported by dynamic binding of an object to the appropriate method.

private, protected, public   Private, protected, and public are access concepts within a class. Private data and methods are available only to instances of the immediate class. Protected items are available to other classes directly derived from the immediate class. Public items are available to the world. It is usually best to keep all data items and structures private or protected, and allow public access to a class only through public methods.

problem domain   The field or area for which a software system is developed. An accounting system would fall into a financial problem domain and require input from financial experts for its design, for example.

problem statement   A plain-language description of what a program must do. A problem statement does not include details of how a program is going to do something. The statement must be written in the vocabulary of the problem domain. For example, the problem statement for an accounts payable system should be written in the vocabulary of an accountant, not that of a computer programmer.

reference   A data element whose value is an address. In Java, all objects are accessed by reference. Any object variable is a reference to an actual object, not the object itself.

RMI   Remote method invocation, the Java standard technology for building distributed objects whose methods can be invoked remotely across a network.

root class   The top-most or most-generalized user class of an inheritance hierarchy. In Java, all classes are at least implicitly derived from the Java `Object` class, which makes it the most primitive root class. Most applications have many hierarchies with different non-`Object` root classes.

RUP   Rational Unified Process, an object-oriented development methodology from Rational Software.

selector   This is an operation that gets information about the state of an object without altering the state of the object.

servlet Servlets are modules of Java code that run in a server application to answer client requests. Servlets don't use a specific client-server protocol, but they are usually used with HTTP.

setter A method that allows the outside world to modify an attribute of a class. Setter methods are also known as mutators or modifiers. Setter methods by convention have names such as `setLimit` or `setWidth`.

SQL Structured query language, the most widely used standardized query language for requesting information from a database.

SQLJ An extended Java syntax for embedding SQL-like commands in a Java program.

state State reflects the current values of all the attributes of an object and is the result of the behavior of an object over time.

subclass In an inheritance hierarchy, a subclass is derived from an associated superclass. A subclass is a specialization of the generalized superclass.

superclass In an inheritance hierarchy, a superclass is a more generalized class. A subclass is derived from a superclass. (A superclass is also known as a parent class or a base class)

this Also called *self*. A reference to the current object. Within a class definition, references to the attributes and methods of the class are implicit. The *this* reference can be used for clarity to make a reference explicit. Most commonly, however, *this* is used to pass a reference to the current instance on to another object.

visibility The ability of one class to see and use the resources of another class. Visibility is controlled by various programming language features, such as Java's public, protected, and private specifiers.

whole/part A relationship among classes in which one class is made up of or contains objects of another class.

XMI XML metadata interchange. A new OMG standard combining UML and XML.

XML XML is an open standard of the World Wide Web Consortium (W3C), which is designed as a data format for structured document interchange on the Web. For example, it allows the definition of new operations when standard HTML is not a good fit.

INDEX

A

abstract classes
  defined, 267
  overview of, 29–30
Abstract Windowing Toolkit (AWT), 109,
    110
abstraction
  defined, 11, 267
  with objects, 13, 29
accessor, 267. *See also* getter
action events, Swing, 112
activity diagrams, UML, 102
actors, defined, 267
Ada, 3
Adaptive Software Development, 227
agents, defined, 267
aggregation
  defined, 21, 267
  in Java, 54–57
  in OO relationships, 27–29
  in UML, 18
Agile Alliance
  methodologies, small projects, 217–219

software development manifesto, 218–219
  Web site resources, 217–219
anonymous listener, Swing, 118
application servers, 268
ArgoUML
  software tools, 241–242
  Web site resources, 242
association
  defined, 19, 268
  in Java, 54–57
  in OO relationships, 27–29
  in UML, 17
attributes
  class, 33
  defined, 268
  encapsulated classes, 14
  instances, 33
  of objects, 8
AWT (Abstract Windowing Toolkit), 109

B

base classes, defined, 268
Beck, Kent, 104, 219

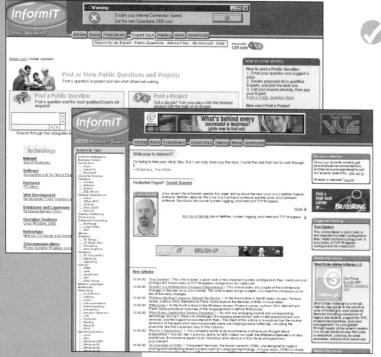

CD-ROM Warranty

Bruce E. Wampler and Addison-Wesley warrant the enclosed disc to be free of defects in materials and faulty workmanship under normal use for a period of ninety days after purchase. If a defect is discovered in the disc during this warranty period, a replacement disc can be obtained at no charge by sending the defective disc, postage prepaid, with proof of purchase to:

Editorial Department
Addison-Wesley Professional
Pearson Technology Group
75 Arlington Street, Suite 300
Boston, MA 02116
Email: AWPro@awl.com

System Requirements

Book Source Code:
  Any system with Sun JDK 1.3 or later
  (Sun JDK 1.3 included with JBuilder 5)

Borland JBuilder 5:
  128 MB RAM, 500 MB disk space
  Windows 98/Me/2000/XP
  -or- Redhat Linux 6.2 (manual install for other Linux systems)
  -or- Solaris 7/Solaris 8

Other software:
  128 MB RAM, 10 MB free disk space
  Windows 9x/Me/2000/XP

ABOUT THE CD

The CD that accompanies this book includes the source code of the book's examples and several software tools useful for programming in Java. All the software included on the CD is discussed in the text of the book; experiment with it and discover what helps to improve your own programming.

This CD includes:

- The complete Java source code for the book's examples.
- The complete Personal edition of Borland's JBuilder 5 for Windows, Linux, or Solaris, including the Sun Java 2 SDK (JDK 1.3).
- VIDE—the author's free IDE for C++ and Java.
- Emacs for Windows—a complete version of the Emacs editor for Windows, including the source code.
- VIM for Windows—the Vim version of the vi editor for Windows.
- JUnit 3.7—the JUnit Java testing framework.

To install the software included on this CD, follow the instructions in the index.html file of the root directory of the CD. If you insert the CD into a Windows-based computer, that file will automatically be displayed in your browser.

Note that errata for this book and other related news can be found at www.objectcentral.com/oobook/news.html.